MUSICAL MEANING AND INTERPRETATION
Robert S. Hatten, editor

Intertextuality in Western Art Music

MICHAEL L. KLEIN

Intertextuality in Western Art Music

INDIANA UNIVERSITY PRESS
Bloomington and Indianapolis

This book is a publication of

Indiana University Press
601 North Morton Street
Bloomington, IN 47404-3797 USA

http://iupress.indiana.edu

Telephone orders   800-842-6796
Fax orders   812-855-7931
Orders by e-mail   iuporder@indiana.edu

Library of Congress Cataloging-in-Publication Data

Klein, Michael Leslie.
   Intertextuality in western art music / Michael L. Klein.
      p. cm. — (Musical meaning and interpretation)
   Includes bibliographical references (p.) and index.
   ISBN 0-253-34468-9 (cloth : alk. paper)
   1. Music—Philosophy and aesthetics. 2. Intertextuality. 3.
Music—Semiotics. I. Title. II. Series.
   ML3877.K58 2005
   781'.1—dc22
                                                2004007880
1 2 3 4 5   10 09 08 07 06 05

For Michelle,

who cannot read it

and

For Tamae,

who will not read it

Contents

Preface

One can hardly write a book on intertextuality without acknowledging that the opening pages will feel in advance the weight of a convention to say what other prefaces have already said. It is too late to dodge the cliché that is the preface: that necessary supplement, that announcement of an authorial act long complete, that bit of text written last but appearing first, that set of directions for use.

Even Umberto Eco's strategy to introduce commonplaces with the phrase "in the words of" seems too weak a transformation to avoid the irony or sentimentality that inevitably accrues to the embarrassed quotation. Still, I have no other rhetorical gesture to convince that I say what I mean, and I mean what I say without irony. In the words of Kofi Agawu, analyzing comes more easily to me than theorizing. In the words of Robert Hatten, there is always more to meaning than can be theorized. In the words of Raymond Monelle, let us hope that this book makes sense. In the words of Daniel Chua, prefaces speak of anxiety. In the words of the anonymous preface, this book's strengths belong to others, while its weaknesses belong to me alone.

This book is about that cultural net of musical texts that we bring to music as we struggle to make sense of it. That constellation of texts speaking both with us and among themselves is what literary critics call *intertextuality*. Despite the opening paragraphs of this preface, this book is not about quotation. You will find no calculus within these pages to measure the differences between quotation, allusion, and the happy coincidence. Though this book often brings Harold Bloom's anxiety of influence within its purview, it makes few claims about influence as a specific form of intertextuality. Instead, this book aspires to bring together a counterpoint of texts and wonder how the voices of Mikhail Bakhtin, Umberto Eco, Hans Robert Jauss, Julia Kristeva, Paul Ricoeur, and many others might be brought together as an intertext granting us a meaningful perspective on music as a signifying text. These voices bring this book in contact with semiotics, hermeneutics, aesthetics, and narrativity, though I make no claim to speak as an authority in any of these areas. This book is an intertextuality.

The writing of this book would not have been possible without the help and support of more people than I can list fully. Among these, Robert Hatten deserves my deepest thanks. It was while reading Hatten's work that I first realized that the questions I had about music needed an approach different from any I then knew. This is not to say that Hatten was the first to ask those vexing questions about music and meaning, but only that his book came to me at just the right time, having a profound effect on how I thought about music. Later, when I began delivering papers on intertextuality at national conferences, Professor Hatten was among the first to encourage the direction my work was taking. His suggestions upon reading an earlier draft of this book have proven invaluable.

In addition, an anonymous reader of that same early draft lent keen insight to some of the problems I was trying to address. Reader, whoever you are, you have my thanks.

Jane Lyle, Gayle Sherwood, and Donna Wilson are among those at Indiana University Press who have my appreciation for their calm and confident expertise in bringing this book to publication. Thanks as well go to David Anderson for his careful editing. I am confident that any errors in the text are traceable to me alone.

In the years that I have struggled with the ideas in this book, I have had remarkable correspondence with Sumanth Gopinath, now finishing a dissertation at Yale University. I am indebted to him for his many penetrating questions about my research. Yayoi Everett read a late version of part of this book, and I thank her for some wise advice.

My dear colleague and friend David B. Cannata has lent a sympathetic ear during the many times I have wanted to give up this project. I cannot thank him enough for his gentlemanly prodding to finish my work.

A study leave in spring 2003 and a summer research grant in 2001 from Temple University lent me valuable time to research, think, and write.

Finally, from friends, colleagues, and institutions, I turn to my family and offer my wife, Yu-Hui Tamae Lee, and my daughter, Michelle Lee Klein, my love, strength, honor, and devotion. I have tried to write this book during Michelle's hours asleep, so that she would never need to look at it and wonder how much more she would have seen her father if he had never written it.

My thanks to the following publishers for their kind permission to reprint portions of the following:

Sonata for Piano
By Charles T. Griffes
Copyright © 1921 (Renewed) by G. Schirmer, Inc. (ASCAP).
International Copyright Secured. All Rights Reserved.
Reprinted by Permission.

Study No. 1 from Two Studies for Piano (2 Etiudy na Fortepian)
By Witold Lutosławski
Copyright © 1946 by PWM Edition, Kraków
Copyright renewed 1974 by Dr. W. Lutosławski.
Transferred to Chester Music Limited.
Copyright © Chester Music Limited for the World except Poland, Albania, Bulgaria, China, the territories of former Czechoslovakia, the territories of former Yugoslavia, Cuba, North Korea, Vietnam, Romania, Hungary, and the whole territory of the former USSR. International Copyright Secured. All Rights Reserved.
Reprinted by Permission.
Measures 1–7, 12–13, and 32

Intertextuality in Western Art Music

1 Eco, Chopin, and the Limits of Intertextuality

> Until then I had thought each book spoke of things, human or divine, that lie outside books. Now I realized that not infrequently books speak of books: it is as if they spoke among themselves.
>
> —Umberto Eco (*The Name of the Rose*, 286)

1

As a reader of Eco's *The Name of the Rose* comes to the passage quoted above, she may interpret these words of the character Adso as consistent with his earlier utterances. Adso is a monk living in the fourteenth century, accompanied by an older, wiser man, who instructs on matters worldly and religious. Because Adso is young, with a poetic frame of mind, the reader may hear his metaphor of books speaking among themselves to be a natural turn of phrase for a man of his character. "Yes," the reader thinks, "I imagine that this is how a monk of the fourteenth century might have described books." A tiny miracle of textual complicity allows the reader to make this leap with no real knowledge of monks or the fourteenth century. The text is harmonious, unified, closed.

Theories of intertextuality, however, claim that a reader always brings other texts to an understanding of the single text, so that all writing is filled with allusions, quotations, and references to other writing. Coming to the same passage from *Rose*, the reader may be reminded of Harold Bloom's familiar aphorism:

The meaning of a poem can only be another poem. (Bloom 1973, 94)

Because books speak like humans in Adso's description, his metaphor is a trope of *prosopopoeia* on Bloom's claim about poetry.[1] Eco weakens this trope with the qualifying phrase *as if*. Stronger the imagery would be had Eco written "books speak among themselves." The reference to Bloom, though, does not close interpretation of Eco's *Rose*. Contemplating Bloom and Eco, the reader may recall a portion of Günter Grass's *The Tin Drum*:

Funerals always make you think of other funerals. (Grass 1990, 402)

Drum interprets *Rose*. When Adso tells us that books speak among themselves, he means that books make us think of other books, much like funerals remind us of other funerals. Should the reader be familiar with Bloom and Grass, she could tell herself that because books remind us of other books, the meaning of one book is echoed in another. A book speaks; another responds. Should the reader become a writer, she might add her voice to this dialogue:

> The dead speak among themselves.

Another reader, struck by the strangeness of this sentence, might recognize its resemblance to Eco, or Bloom, or Grass, and settle upon a meaning. The dead remind us of other dead. One silent mind speaks, and another responds; it is *as if* they spoke among themselves.

The references to Bloom and Grass fail to close the web of allusions that reach out from Eco's text. A portion of Michel Foucault's *Archaeology of Knowledge* also forms the intertext around Adso's metaphor:

> The frontiers of a book are never clear-cut: beyond the title, the first lines, and the last full stop, beyond its internal configuration and its autonomous form, it is caught up in a system of references to other books, other texts, other sentences: it is a node within a network. . . . [I]ts unity is variable and relative. (Foucault 1972, 23)

Like the passages from Bloom and Grass, this one underscores how Eco animates the metaphor that describes one book's dialogue with another. Foucault's writing here is direct, with phrases whose pseudo-scientific echoes ("internal configuration," "system of references," "node within a network") lend a detached and clinical aura to his argument, as if it should be apparent to anyone rational that texts are open. Perhaps unsatisfied in regard to the completeness of this intertext, we might turn to a passage from Roland Barthes's *S/Z*:

> To interpret a text is not to give it a (more or less justified, more or less free) meaning, but on the contrary to appreciate what plural constitutes it. Let us first posit the image of a triumphant plural, unimpoverished by any constraint of representation (of imitation). In this ideal text, the networks are many and interact without any one of them being able to surpass the rest. (Barthes 1974, 5)

Like Foucault in *Archaeology of Knowledge*, Barthes uses the metaphor of a network to explore the relationships between texts (books in *Archaeology*). And where Foucault weakens a metaphor of the book as territory by claiming that its frontiers are never clear-cut, Barthes shatters notions of unity altogether with his description of the text as plural. Eco avoids notions of unity and plurality, making Adso's statement terse while leaving to the reader the work of deducing its implications.

We have not finished our intertextual detective work. Those who know Barthes know that he both influences and is influenced by the writings of Julia Kristeva. In what is one of the most quoted passages in intertextual studies, we can see how Kristeva anticipates all of the previous passages:

> The text is therefore a . . . permutation of texts, an intertextuality: in the space of a given text, several utterances, taken from other texts, intersect and neutralize one another. (Kristeva 1980a, 36)

In many ways Kristeva's ideas are the most radical of those quoted so far, because the text is not engaged in a conversation with other texts (Eco), nor is it caught up in a network of references (Foucault and Barthes), but it is already the site of many utterances taken from other texts. Using the binary opposition inside/outside as a metaphor for these various passages, we come to understand that Kristeva inverts the placement of speech that is central to Adso's utterance. According to Adso, books speak among themselves, implying that a conversation is taking place outside of the frontier of each book. According to Kristeva, such a dialogue is already inside the frontier of the text, by definition the site of several intersecting utterances.

But even here our intertextual journey is unfinished. Students of Kristeva know that her work is influenced strongly by Mikhail Bakhtin, and her definition of the (inter)text bears resemblance to his definition of the novel:

> The novel can be defined as a diversity of social speech types (sometimes even diversity of languages) and a diversity of individual voices, artistically organized. (Bakhtin 1981, 262)

One of Kristeva's tropes on Bakhtin's definition is that she expands his notion of the novel to embrace the more general term *text*.[2] This substitution reminds us that there is no consistent term used in all of the passages above. More striking for an interpretation of Adso's passage is that Eco uses the word *book* where *manuscript* might have been more appropriate for a fourteenth-century monk.[3] This detail may give the reader a sense that it is not really Adso but Eco himself who addresses us. When Eco allows his mask, Adso, to slip, he gives the reader a clue to a writerly anxiety.[4] By allowing a fourteenth-century character to speak about intertextuality, Eco performs a narrative slight of hand in which Adso's words become the precursor text to twentieth-century writings by Bakhtin, Foucault, Kristeva, and Barthes.

Continuing this search outward from Eco's text sends us on a potentially unlimited journey through other texts. Even in its present condition, though, this intertextual collection may strike some readers as problematic, because I have sidestepped some questions about intent. Conceding that, as a professor of semiotics, Eco is likely familiar with all of the texts I have quoted, how do we know that he was referring to these particular passages when he wrote *Rose*? Did Eco intend the reader to recognize these intertextual relationships? What proof shall we accept to support our answers to those two questions? These types of problems were once an important part of literary criticism, especially early in the twentieth century, and they still have a place in musicology today.[5] Oddly though, as studies of intertextuality intensified during the latter part of the twentieth century, many literary critics ceased to concern themselves with proving influence. Bloom, for example, claims disinterest in tracing sources, an odd assertion for a critic whose writings have made such an impact on how we study influence.[6] We even hear a note of disdain in Foucault's description of those who hunt down a writer's sources:

> [T]o seek in the great accumulation of the already-said the text that resembles "in advance" a later text, to ransack history in order to rediscover the play of anticipations or echoes, to go right back to the first seeds or to go forward to the last traces, to reveal in a work its fidelity to tradition or its irreducible uniqueness, to raise or lower its stock of originality, to say that the Port-Royal grammarians invented nothing, or to discover

that Cuvier had more predecessors than one thought, these are harmless enough amusements for historians who refuse to grow up. (Foucault 1972, 144)

Though the re-creation of the contexts for each point in a chain of influence remains an important goal of much historical research, pace Foucault's sneer at such pursuits, these contexts are nearly irrevocable because each of the texts involved is already tainted by our readings of other texts. The reader who comes to Eco first already brings *Rose* to her understanding of Bakhtin, despite the inversion of history that such a reading entails. The reader who comes to Vladimir Nabokov's *Invitation to a Beheading* before Franz Kafka's *The Trial*, or who knows something about the horrors of the Nazi death camps before reading Kafka's "The Penal Colony" brings to those older works new contexts difficult to repress. Rather than view texts as links in a chain of influence, we can use the metaphor of a web to show that texts are interlinked in multiple directions. As I have tried to show with a relatively small sampling, ideas about the ways that books (texts, manuscripts) refer to (speak with) other books are particularly numerous, so that any single text referring to these ideas is caught up in a dense web of intertextual relationships.

As we shall see, a distinction needs to be made between influence and intertextuality, where the former implies intent or a historical placement of the work in its time or origin, and the latter implies a more general notion of crossing texts that may involve historical reversal. Also useful is a distinction between our conceptions of the work and the text, especially in evaluating critics' claims and in uncovering their agendas. Before theorizing these terms, however, I would like to turn to a musical intertext that can match the multiple references that we saw in Eco's *The Name of the Rose*.

2

The frontiers of music are never clear-cut: beyond its framing silence, beyond its inner form, it is caught up in a web of references to other music: its unity is variable and relative. Musical texts speak among themselves.

Example 1.1 shows the opening of Witold Lutosławski's Study No. 1 for piano, which always reminds me of Chopin's monumental Etude in C Major, Op. 10, No. 1, shown in Example 1.2. Though each composer penned other etudes, I shall call these works "Lutosławski's study" and "Chopin's etude" for ease of reference. I make no claims that Lutosławski modeled his study on Chopin's etude, though as a Polish pianist and composer he undoubtedly knew Chopin's music before he composed his study. Since Lutosławski's training was somewhat conservative, involving the use of nineteenth-century works as models, it is also likely that he would turn to the music of Chopin before embarking on what was planned to be a larger set of studies. Finally, Lutosławski composed his study soon after escaping from a Nazi work camp; therefore, it is easy to imagine that he might make a patriotic gesture through an allusion to Chopin's music.[7] Many points of contact support an intertext between these works. The opening octave C in the left hand of Lutosławski's study, followed by the ascending pattern of sixteenth notes, in addition to the return of these gestures to commence the second phrase in m. 7 all point to the opening of Chopin's etude. The strength of these connections seems too good to be true, making us wonder why Lutosławski made the intertext so obvious. He may have wanted his Polish listeners to recognize a patriotic allusion to Chopin; but one wonders, in this case, why the reference is not to one of Chopin's more openly Polish works, like a polonaise or mazurka. A Bloomian argument suggests that Lutosławski, the anxious ephebe, is too flooded with his predecessor's music to make a break, and so he allows another voice to possess him. Alternatively Lutosławski, the intrepid young artist, boldly borrows from his predecessor, both possessing and transforming the music of his compatriot.

Another possibility, which I prefer, requires a second intertextual link. Already in m. 2 of the study Lutosławski breaks from Chopin's pattern of keeping the moving part in the right hand. As the left hand enters with its own melody in m. 2, the right hand remains frozen in the upper register, breaking the symmetrical arches that characterize Chopin's etude. That left-hand melody has the unmistakable imprint of the voice of Bartók. The stepwise pattern with unordered pitch intervals of one and two semitones that reverse upon themselves to fill gaps in the chromatic collection is a melodic figure found in countless works by the Hungarian composer. Example 1.1 highlights the pattern in Lutosławski's study. Now the more obvious reference to Chopin takes on a new meaning. We are meant to notice the reference to Chopin so that we might miss the allusion to Bartók. The ploy has at least three effects. First, Chopin's music is updated by what Martha Hyde calls *heuristic imitation;* that is, Lutosławski digs into the roots of his musical past and renews them with a fresher musical language from his own time.[8] Second, the sudden swerve from Chopin's model shows us that Lutosławski is not the mere reverential ephebe, lending his voice to a precursor. Third, the reference to Bartók obscures the appeal to Polish patriotism, but only for listeners later in the twentieth century, for whom Bartók's music has become canonical.[9]

We might expand this intertext by claiming that Chopin's etude refers to the first prelude from J. S. Bach's *Well-Tempered Clavier,* whose opening is reproduced in Example 1.3. Although other writers have noted this same connection, it is difficult to assess whether Chopin's contemporaries would have heard this intertext.[10] Chopin published his Op. 10 in 1833, four years after the landmark revival of Bach's *St. Matthew's Passion,* but well before the German composer would come to the center of musical imagination. A nineteenth-century Parisian musician, who would have had the earliest access to Chopin's first set of etudes, would more likely have drawn comparisons between Chopin's etude and a number of others by I. Moscheles, J. C. Kessler, J. N. Hummel, and L. Berger.[11] The point I wish to make here is that the intertext around Chopin's etude changes with time. A text (Bach) that lay dormant during the 1830s may dominate our hearing today, while some texts (Moscheles et al.) with resonance to listeners of an earlier time may now be irretrievably lost. As listeners we too suffer the weight of history, so that, putting aside any intractable question of quality, Bach's omnipresent prelude gives an etude by Berger little chance for intertextual survival, despite the recovery efforts of scholars.

Example 1.1. Lutosławski, Study No. 1 (1940–41)

Like the prelude, Chopin's etude arpeggiates a harmonic progression in C, whose first chord spans an interval of a tenth. On this pattern the composer performs what Bloom calls a *tessera,* or completion of a fragment, by repeating each chord of the progression in multiple octaves, exploiting the entire register of the keyboard. To the perfect symmetry of this registral expansion, Chopin adds those imposing octaves in the left hand, which not only anchor the harmonic content of the virtuosic arpeggios but also highlight the prolonged stasis of each pattern in relation to those of Bach's prelude. We remember now that Lutosławski performs a

Example 1.2. Chopin, Etude in C Major, Op. 10, No. 1 (1833)

similar trope in his study when he adds to these left-hand octaves the melodies that
allude to Bartók. Seen from this perspective, Lutosławski's study is a *tessera* of a
tessera, and as such it leads our hearing backward through Chopin to Bach.

So far I have tried to document each intertextual connection, making this a
study of influence. But an intertextual account need not confine itself to influence.
From Bach's prelude we can move forward in time, because the syncopations suggested by pattern repetitions in the arpeggiations of the prelude produce a 2 + 2 +
3 rhythm, reminding us of a similar pattern in Chopin's Etude in C Minor, Op. 25,
No. 12. The syncopations in the two texts are highlighted in Examples 1.3 and 1.4.
The intertext here is ahistoric: Bach's prelude summons Chopin's C-minor etude
as a precursor. The prelude tropes the C-minor etude by shattering the registral
arches played by both hands. In order to fill the same four beats per harmony, the
Bach prelude features a repetition of each pattern within the measure, solving an
analytical puzzle that involves just those repetitions of each harmony. From most
analytic angles (melodic, harmonic, rhythmic, and hypermetric) there is simply no
structural reason that compels the twofold appearance of each harmony. Through
the intertext with Chopin's C-minor etude, I assert outrageously that these repeti-

Example 1.3. Bach, Prelude in C Major, *WTC* I (1722)

Example 1.4. Chopin, Etude in C Minor, Op. 25, No. 12 (1837)

tions exist to make clear just that connection between the two texts. Thus Chopin is the precursor to Bach because he asks us to hear the earlier composer's prelude in a new way. The prelude as newly heard has no existence prior to Chopin's etude.

We can move forward again in time. Those intertext-forming syncopations may be salient to us only because we fail to sublimate our hearings of ragtime music, in which such rhythmic patterns are a stylistic feature.[12] Example 1.5 highlights syncopations in a Scott Joplin rag. When we attend to these rhythms and use them to associate texts by Bach, Chopin, and Joplin, we cease to concern ourselves with matters of influence and cross into a realm that is purely intertextual. Syncopations now recontextualize the entire set of texts in this intertextual web. Chopin's etude (C major), for example, lacks these additive rhythms, and from this perspective we might describe the C-minor etude as a correction of the rhythmic flatness in the earlier text. Listening again to Lutosławski's study, we hear a pattern repetition in the opening measure that forms this type of additive rhythm in a revolving 4 + 3 pattern (shown in Example 1.1), troping such patterns in the other texts by spilling

Example 1.5. Joplin, "Original Rag" (1899)

Example 1.6. Lutosławski, Study No. 1, m. 32

over the first measure. These additive rhythms become an issue throughout the study, with a striking instance appearing in m. 32 (Example 1.6), forming instantly an intertext back to Chopin's C-minor etude. This allusion to a second Chopin etude within Lutosławski's study prompts a reassessment of an earlier interpretive stance. Finding both the first and last etudes from Chopin's set of twenty-four (Opp. 10 and 25) embedded in Lutosławski's study suggests that Lutosławski boldly hopes to embrace the entire breadth of Chopin's virtuosic style within the boundaries of a single, short study.

The same C-minor etude bears a striking resemblance to the piano accompaniment in the opening of "St. Veronica Wipes His Face" from Peter Maxwell Davies's *Vesalii Icones,* shown in Example 1.7. Quite different from the other works in this intertext, *Vesalii Icones* makes explicit the intertextual sweep of western music by quoting liberally and openly from a variety of precursors. This excerpt contains a number of simple modifications of Chopin's C-minor etude, including changes in key, mode, and tempo, in addition to a gradual flattening out of the syncopated rhythm. Here the piano part plays an accompanimental role to a cello line, marking this excerpt as a *tessera* of different type, because the implication is that Chopin's etude lacks a melody, marking the work as incomplete. The implication spreads throughout this intertext, reminding us that Bach's prelude was once the object of completion by Gounod's *Ave Maria.* The melody/accompaniment opposition becomes a problem in each of these texts and seems especially ambiguous in both Chopin's etude and Lutosławski's study. Are those whole notes in the left hand of

Example 1.7. Davies, "St. Veronica Wipes His Face" from *Vesalli Icones* (1969)

Example 1.8. Shostakovich, Prelude in C Major, *Preludes and Fugues* I (1951)

Chopin's etude the missing melody of the piece, and is the incredible speed of the right hand meant to ensure that the lower voice moves quickly enough to be perceived as a melody? Is the allusion to Bartók in m. 2 of Lutosławski's study the real melody of this music after all, and should the pianist herald it? Of course, any theorist will argue that there is a melody in Bach's prelude, and by implication in the other works as well. But those who trust composers more than theorists can look to Dmitry Shostakovich's Prelude No. 1 from volume I of his *Preludes and Fugues*, shown in Example 1.8. Here Shostakovich makes plain the melody of Bach's prelude by removing the arpeggiated rhythmic pattern in a trope whose textual simplicity attempts to make his prelude the precursor to this entire intertext.[13]

I have moved fairly quickly through some music that I think forms an intertext around Chopin's etude, and I shall form a second intertext around this work in Chapter 2 in order to suggest ways in which intertextuality problematizes structural analysis. First, it seems wise to compare this musical intertext with the literary one presented earlier. In both cases I have tried to illustrate that the references of books to other books and music to other music are potentially unlimited. I am also arguing that the relationship between the texts in these intertexts is dynamically bilateral. Not only do Grass and Chopin help us interpret Eco and Lutosławski, but Eco and Lutosławski help us interpret Grass and Chopin as well. If, as Peter Burkholder argues, the historicist mainstream in music has created a collection of museum pieces, that museum contains galleries unlike any in the real world, because the pictures are constantly at play, adjusting, moving, and even painting over the artworks that are hung around them (Burkholder 1983; 1984; 1991). For the most part musicology has engaged in an archaeology that seeks to undo the ludic moves that have brought the museum to its present state. This pursuit continues at the expense of a strategy that abolishes historical contradiction, allowing us the pleasure of reading Brahms as if he were the father of Beethoven, or Chopin as if he inspired Bach. Yet it may seem mere postmodern posturing to recognize an aleatoric and ahistoric intertextuality while losing studies of influence that seek to be precise in determining exactly which works a composer has brought to her music. How we proceed to deal with the implications of intertextuality will depend both upon how we structure that concept and upon how we distinguish the musical work from the musical text. As such, I now turn to theorizing intertextuality.

3

Although intertextuality has received enormous attention in literary criticism since the term *intertextualité* was coined by Kristeva, critics have shown little agreement on a precise definition.[14] As we have seen, for Kristeva intertextuality *is* the text, within whose boundaries many types of writing interact. For others, like Bloom, intertextuality is a critical space outside of a text's boundaries, from which the critic compares two or more literary works. Because intertextuality is often taken to be synonymous with influence, Jay Clayton and Eric Rothstein have made a useful distinction between the two:

> Since both terms have too many operative definitions for us to fix on one for each, we will start with the generalization that influence has to do with agency, whereas intertextuality has to do with a much more impersonal field of crossing texts. (Clayton and Rothstein 1991, 4)

Following the implication of this distinction, any crossing of texts is an instance of intertextuality, while within the potentially unlimited range of a particular intertext, any form of agency in which an author borrows from or alludes to another text is a more narrow instance of intertextuality called influence. Broadly conceived, intertextuality has the potential to disrupt our notions of history and the unidirectional timeline that runs from an earlier text to a latter one. As part of his definition of the intertext, for example, Barthes describes how all literature, for him, is a remembrance of the work of Marcel Proust:

> I savor the sway of formulas, the reversal of origins, the ease which brings the anterior text out of the subsequent one. I recognize that Proust's work, for myself at least, is *the* reference work, the general *mathesis,* the *mandala* of the entire literary cosmogony. . . . Proust is what comes to me, not what I summon up; not an "authority," simply a *circular memory.* (Barthes 1975, 36)

Barthes is making no claims about the historical importance of Proust, perhaps as measured by his range of influence, nor is he arguing that Proust is at the center of the literary canon, as determined by some intersubjective standard. Instead, Barthes indulges in the pleasure of a readerly solipsism that thrusts Proust to the center of a personal literary intertext.

Restating the words of Clayton and Rothstein, there are simply too many operative definitions of intertextuality to fix upon one, and there is no small irony in the fact that a radical intertextuality prevents us from defining precisely that term.[15] Various types of intertextuality suggest themselves. We may concern ourselves with just those texts that an author brought to her writing and study a *poietic* intertextuality. We may concern ourselves with the texts that a society brings to its reading and study an *esthesic* intertextuality.[16] We may confine the text to its own time and study a *historical* intertextuality, or we may open the text to all time and study a *transhistorical* intertextuality. The intertexts we make may be within a *style* or within a *canon.* We may make efforts to deafen ourselves to the multiple references of a text to others across styles and histories, or we may remain attentive to an *aleatoric* intertextuality that roams freely across time. From the perspective of an author to that of a reader, from the boundaries of the historical to the boundlessness of the transhistorical, from the competencies of understanding a style to those of understanding a canon, the ways that we define and confine intertextuality hold court over our perspectives on the text and how we make sense of it. Since as readers we bring texts to our understanding of the single text, some notion of intertextuality, however defined, must underpin explicitly or implicitly our struggle to make meaning of a text.

These suggested forms of intertextuality are neither exhaustive nor mutually exclusive. In addition, multiple forms of intertextuality may interact in the writings of any critic. For example, when Bloom claims of his theory of influence that it is a study of "the life-cycle of the poet-as-poet," he appears to engage in a poietic form of intertextuality (Bloom 1973, 7). In poietic readings the critic often is concerned with influence and its implications for the history of a work and its author. In musicology such studies follow the familiar path of proving connections between works. Composer A must have borrowed material from Composer B, because she studied the older master's music as a student, she kept copies of Composer B's scores on her piano, and by some luck of documentary evidence we can prove that she attended a concert of Composer B's music on the very night preceding the composition of work X, which so obviously testifies to Composer B's influence. But because we may find it difficult to ignore Márquez when we encounter Faulkner, or disregard Chopin in our hearings of Bach, intertextual criticism may roam beyond the territory of documented influence and wander toward the ahistoric. Though Bloom is certainly alert to this tendency, he allows his literary readings to enter an intertextual space beyond a narrowly poietic one in order to show how language and meaning, syntax and semantics, are redistributed and recontextualized from text to text. When Bloom claims, for example, that a precursor can be "the poem we write as our reading," he is engaging in an open intertextuality that recognizes the role of the reader in text production; further, when he offers the anachronism that a later poem can influence an earlier one, he surrenders to a solipsism that is the mark of the intertext as Barthes describes it (Bloom 1973, 15–16, 139–55). Bloom's vision of the poet is a canonical one, and so the life cycle that he describes is not of a historical figure but of a deeply personal and imagined author, conjured from texts in confrontation with other texts.

Whether intertextuality is limited or unlimited, critics studying the crossing of texts often concern themselves both with the linguistic (musical) codes that bind texts together and with the tropes that transform these codes from text to text. Chapter 3 discusses semiotic codes in more detail, but for now it suffices to note that codes may be syntactic or semantic. As for the term *trope*, it has a wide range of meanings in the study of rhetoric, but a broad definition brings it in contact with the term *figure*: a striking configuration of words or phrases that often involves the use of nonliteral language (see Lanham 1991, 78–80, 154–57). Finding a correspondence between a trope in language and one in music would appear to center on the difficulty of defining what it means for music to be nonliteral. Robert Hatten, however, recognizes that troping involves style expansion, and he defines the trope in music as a figurative play in which established types (codes) come in contact with one another to "spark an interpretation based on their interaction" (Hatten 1994, 295; see also 166–72). According to Hatten's conception, the musical trope is involved with metaphor. His definition of troping is precise and soundly supported within his theory of markedness and correlation. However, at the risk of offering a broader definition for the term, I view a trope within a theory of intertextuality as any sign or configuration of signs in one text that is a transformation of such signs in another text.

Music theory's study of tropes has focused primarily on the syntactic level. In addition, appeals to Platonic forms, models, and types have often hidden the intertextual nature of these transformations as music theory seeks to align itself with certain structuralist tendencies to reduce the number of musical configurations to a relatively small number of basic patterns. In order to understand what I mean by this last statement, it will be instructive to consider Barthes's characterization of the structuralist project:

> There are said to be certain Buddhists whose ascetic practices enable them to see a whole landscape in a bean. Precisely what the first analysts of narrative were attempt-

ing: to see all the world's stories (and there have been ever so many) within a single structure: we shall, they thought, extract from each tale its model, then out of these models we shall make a great narrative structure, which we shall reapply (for verification) to any one narrative. (Barthes 1974, 3)

Barthes's tone is ironic, and his description is inadequate to the range of methodologies necessary for any project that would consider itself structuralist. I return to this problem in Chapter 2. But Barthes does not exaggerate in his account of approaches in which the analyst searches for deep patterns and their replication across repertoires.

If we are uncomfortable with Barthes's tone, however, we can find a more straightforward description of one type of structuralist analysis in Claude Lévi-Strauss's *Look, Listen, Read,* where we find an astonishing perspective on Rameau's theory of chords:

In his theory of chords, Rameau stands as a forerunner of structural analysis. . . . He demonstrated that all chords can be generated from their counterparts in the major key by a series of inversions. Structural analysis proceeds in the same way when reducing the number of rules concerning marriage or myth: it reduces several rules to a common type of matrimonial exchange, or several myths to the same mythic armature, subject to different transformations. (Lévi-Strauss 1997, 41)

Particularly striking here is the term *transformation,* which is something of a shibboleth for contemporary music theory. One wonders if Lévi-Strauss knows that it is with modern music theory that the search for basic patterns and their transformations has one of its greatest successes. Literary criticism rarely accounts for every word of a text in the same way that music theory can account for every pitch in a tonal work and show its level of significance within the voice-leading paradigm of the Schenkerian *Ursatz.*[17] It is the *Ursatz,* in fact, that comes closest to fitting Barthes's notion of the quest to see all the world's stories (music) within a single structure. This success, however, comes as the result of an intertextual pursuit of tropes across a repertoire. When we propose structures and their transformations, we verify them through a vast sampling of the literature for which they are intended as models. Confirmation of a model simultaneously creates an intertextual link across the repertoire, and this link is an agent of dispersion that threatens the unity of the single text. Counter to claims of the unity of a work, the only totally unified text is precisely the one whose hermetic form is impervious to both analysis and comprehension, because it forms no intertext.

Music theory's efforts at analysis, with the concomitant implications of unity, have marginalized the dispersion inherent in recognition of an intertext. We may hear many voices while listening to music, but when contemplating music we narrow our focus to one voice, one piece, one structure. Bakhtin famously called the emphasis on a single voice in a writer's work *monologism,* and he located its opposite, *dialogism,* within the rise of the novel (Bakhtin 1981). Once literary theory became sensitive to the multiple voices that appear within the novel, it was not long before critics found dialogism wherever they cast their glance. By the time that Kristeva refocuses Bakhtin's ideas, she finds that all texts contain varying degrees of monologism and dialogism. Texts have tensions between an impulse to unity (*phenotext*) and dispersion (*genotext*).[18] The appeal to unity, perhaps the central metaphor for twentieth-century music theory, has already been the subject of scrutiny by those steeped in postmodern writings.[19] Worth further investigation, though, is how unity and organicism align themselves with theory's appeal to science, an appeal at least as old as Rameau, though renewed in Fétis, and reawakened in Milton Babbitt and his followers.[20] I can imagine that the sociological story of music theory's desire to be seen as scientific will include an account of a rationalist rhetoric that sees as antiscience any notions that pieces have multiple and conflicting structures. Science offers single answers to puzzles. Even when many hypotheses suggest themselves, it is always a matter of choosing only one. Truth claims must be monolithic, not multivalent. When a theory of music's structure fails to produce analyses that are both singular and reproducible, the response has been to shore up loopholes in the theory. Schenkerian analysis has been a particular target for this type of response, eliciting as late as 1997 an attempt to make at least part of Schenker's theory scientific (Brown, Dempster, and Headlam 1997). Oddly, hopes for a scientific musical analysis continue during a time when some in the philosophy of science have questioned whether even scientific thought can claim to have escaped a poststructuralist threat to break down disciplines into different kinds of writing with no special claim to truth.[21]

We may call upon intertextuality to refocus our thinking about current analytical theory. Rather than view contradiction and ambiguity as weaknesses that threaten theory's claim to science, we can argue that the structure of a piece of music, however secure, rests upon a particular intertext. As new pieces enter that intertext, their structures and transformations of structures impact the very theory called upon to elucidate them. From this perspective, for example, we might reread Schenker's work as a theory of tropes culled from an intertextual study primarily of German nineteenth-century music. In a thesis that parallels one by Leslie Blasius (1996), we could argue that Schenker makes two important moves to insulate his work from the implications of open intertextuality.[22] First, Schenker separates pieces from their composers, so that music lives in a Platonic realm far from the effects of both biography and influence: thus, the problems of poietic intertextuality are forestalled. Second, Schenker closes the canon of tonal masterpieces so that no new work can redistribute musical language and affect the list of tropes. In this reading of his project, the events of the first-level middleground are the master tropes that stabilize analyses. Much writing has concentrated on a critique of Schenker's work on the grounds that it ignores history and focuses on a closed body of compositions; but theories of intertextuality show us that his moves were essential to the creation of his analytical system. Opening up Schenker's theory to history would mean opening up the text to a multiplicity of structures. I shall revisit and expand the impact of intertextuality on structural analysis in Chapter 2.

Efforts to limit intertextuality also leave their mark on musicology. One among countless examples appears with reference to Chopin's so-called *Funeral March* Sonata, Op. 35. Borrowing from Bloom (1973) via Kevin Korsyn (1991), Wayne Petty (1999) situates Chopin's sonata as a response to the ghost of Beethoven. Petty hears an intertext in the opening of Chopin's sonata that points to the first measures of Beethoven's Op. 111; further, he draws a connection between Chopin's funeral march and that in Beethoven's Op. 26. Petty supports this intertext with structural analysis; in addition, he takes some pains to prove intent on the part of Chopin (influence), reminding us that the Polish composer played and taught Beethoven's Op. 26. Jeffrey Kallberg takes Petty to task for just this attempt to place the allusion to Beethoven on a historical level, arguing that these connections rest "on a problematic chain of musical and circumstantial evidence" and that the similarity between the works "falters on the very generality of the musical resemblances" (Kallberg 2001, 19, n50). Kallberg is certainly in his element when he questions the level of documentation that might support a claim of influence in Chopin's music. Kallberg is also on point when he argues that a Bloomian analysis pitting Beethoven against Chopin tells us more about our own anxieties than about those of a Polish pianist/composer looking to make his way in the salons of nineteenth-century Paris. But should analyses like Petty's be ruled entirely out of court?

In order to answer this question, it will be useful to examine briefly a postmodern distinction between work and text. For Barthes the text and the work are not interchangeable, and where common usage views the text as another signifier for a physical document, Barthes reserves the term *work* for that concept:

> A work is a finished object, something computable, which can occupy a physical space (take its place, for example, on the shelves of a library); the text is a methodological field. . . . The work is held in the hand, the text in language. (Barthes 1981, 39)

Tied up with the work are conceptions of stable meaning and authorial intent, though this connection does nothing to deny that an author may have multiple meanings in mind when producing a work (Allen 2000, 66). Tied up with the text are conceptions of multiplicity, openness, and the ways that language deftly slips away from our efforts to pin down meaning. Arguing against the possibility of stable meaning for the text, Jacques Derrida will write the oft-quoted "There is no outside-of-the-text."[23] Borrowing these ideas for music, Raymond Monelle claims that "the text is *whatever criticism observes,* whatever analysis expounds" (Monelle 2000, 153).

Viewing analysis as a concern with the text as opposed to the work, theorists of intertextuality from Foucault and Bakhtin to Kristeva and Barthes maintain that they have no interest in tracing sources or proving influence. Texts simply cross other texts without regard to the limits of history. Even in Bloom's *The Anxiety of Influence* there is rarely convincing documentation of sources. Bloom simply hears Milton's voice at every turn and renders compelling readings of literary texts regardless of even a standard of proof that could support real influence. Thus his theory strains under the tensions between different types of intertextuality as he transfers to his imaginings of poets' psyches his own dread of the uncanny resemblance between poems. Though I shall return to these issues in Chapter 4, it may suffice to say here that as an analysis of a work on the poietic level, Petty's claims are vulnerable to the types of questions that Kallberg raises. But we can refocus Petty's analysis by aligning it with a broader vision of intertextuality and maintaining that it involves a text, not a work. Such a strategy would alter the nature of his claims and make explicit that we are the ones who must face down Beethoven's ghost in the music of Chopin. To limit intertextuality by rejecting that ghost denies us our own compelling readings of Chopin's music.

4

The references to Bloom remind us that it is his work on influence that has made the most successful move from literary theory to music theory. Bloom argues that great poets make space in the canon for their works by appropriating and willfully misreading the works of their precursors. Borrowing is not only the unavoidable process by which the poet learns to be a poet, but also the source of an anxiety that all writing is a repetition compulsion circling the already read, the already thought, the already written. Because the great poet fears writing poetry that merely reflects uncritically the poems of her precursors, her poetry aspires to transform earlier texts as a psychic defense against the anxiety of influence. Bloom's theory thus develops six revisionary ratios, rhetorical tropes that detail the ways in which poets transform their precursors. In the analysis of Chopin's etude, for example, I have made reference to a revisionary ratio that Bloom calls *tessera*, which describes any transformation that curtails poetic excess in the work of a precursor. In this trope the later poet aspires to an economy of means that will point back to the precursor as if to say that the earlier poet might have been more succinct.

Two significant efforts to appropriate Bloom's work for the study of music are Joseph Straus's *Remaking the Past* (1990) and Korsyn's "Towards a New Poetics of Musical Influence" (1991) (see also Hussey 1996, Korsyn 1996, and Petty 1999). Straus's work did not enjoy sympathetic readings among musicologists and theorists despite a fairly comprehensive attempt to develop a theory of tropes for the study of early-twentieth-century music (Krims 1994; Taruskin 1993).[24] Straus's concern with the music of this period parallels similar prejudices on the part of Kristeva and Barthes, who tend to focus on modernist literature for its foregrounding of intertextual references. For Straus the atonal works of Schoenberg, Stravinsky, Webern, and Berg testify to a place in history where the weight of the past becomes too much to bear, and where the old procedures of tonal music become the site of a dismantling of syntax that makes space in the canon for new music. Beyond this master narrative for atonal music, Straus is interested neither in mapping Bloom's six revisionary ratios onto six musical ones nor in matching those ratios with the Freudian psychology that richly informs Bloom's analytical practice. Straus's work thus remains largely on a syntactic level as he offers eight well-defined musical tropes that describe the ways that a small group of composers transform their tonal heritage. Despite some criticism, *Remaking the Past* does point a way to the study of twentieth-century music from an intertextual perspective. One can envision, for example, a new angle on David Lewin's transformational theory that sees those transformations as enlarging Straus's list of musical tropes, forming intertextual links across the literature.

In contrast to Straus, Korsyn makes every effort to match Bloom's six literary ratios with six musical ones, keeping as well the Freudian implications of those ratios as psychic defense mechanisms. In virtuosic displays of Schenkerian, motivic, formal, rhythmic, and harmonic analytic techniques, Korsyn's analyses nimbly dissect the interrelationships between a work and its precursor. Both the strength and weakness of his approach is that he refuses to define exactly the correlation between Bloom's ratios and their musical counterparts. As such he follows Bloom's notorious refusal to give criteria for the application of these ratios. Korsyn also has written about Bakhtin, arguing that his contribution to intertextuality points to new analytical paradigms that can help us rethink our notions that musical works are closed and unified (Korsyn 2001). Curiously, though, I find that, for all their richly detailed comparisons of two works, Korsyn's analyses à la Bloom only underscore our idea of the great artwork as univocal utterance of the great composer. Though Korsyn admits that a composer may be responding to many precursors in a work (Korsyn 1991, 21), his emphasis on a single precursor, coupled with his desire to prove that precursor as precursor, and his focus on the effect of the resulting intertext on our view of the composer's life cycle as composer testify to analysis of the work (as opposed to the text) on a level that is relatively closed to the echoes of intertextual relationships. Korsyn will have us believe, for example, that the middle section of Brahms's Romanze, Op. 118, No. 5, finds its precursor in Chopin's Berceuse, Op. 57. He offers structural and historical evidence to support this mark of influence, and it may well be true that the Romanze *is* Brahms's response to the Berceuse. In a discussion of the coda to the middle section of the Romanze, Korsyn observes that a move to the subdominant via V^7/IV over a tonic pedal points to a similar progression in the coda of the Berceuse. He admits that this harmonic procedure is also common to works of the Baroque period, but nowhere does he explore the ways that the intertext might open up if we were to consider fully those other precursors. The intertext remains confined to two pieces in an analytical practice that bears little resemblance to the radical opening of texts that we see in the writings of Bakhtin, Barthes, Kristeva, Derrida, and others.

This discussion is no criticism of Korsyn's work, which certainly repays study. Had Korsyn decided to pursue some of the intertextual connections to which he hints, his application of Bloom's theory might have become too unwieldy for a publication that was already enormously detailed. The larger issue, I think, is to what purpose we use a theory like Bloom's, with its unabashed emphasis on greatness. Korsyn's appropriation retains the idea that a critical analysis of a composer's struggle with the anxiety of influence lays a foundation for determinations about which great work wins the agon in a contest to enter the canon. Thus we read that Brahms "breaks with Chopin's text, resisting influence," and that "he achieves a deeper repression of the Berceuse, making a sublime climax possible," and at last that "having wrestled successfully with Chopin, Brahms wins strength" (Korsyn 1991, 57). I must confess to having little sympathy for such determinations, and not just because I happen to like the Berceuse more than the Romanze. I have greater interest in those places in Korsyn's analysis where he leaves behind the grand narratives of the great composer in the battle for poetic strength and instead considers what these pieces can mean to us in other terms, as when he tells us that the Berceuse presents "a world in which desire and gratification coincide" (ibid.). These pieces do things to us, psychically and emotionally; and though the imagination with which they create new worlds has much to do with their composer's abilities to renew the musical language into which they find themselves, I suspect that our responses to these texts depend little upon whether we view Brahms or Chopin as victors in musical battle.

I am more interested in opening our readings of these pieces by considering the multiple texts into which they weave themselves. Korsyn rightly associates the middle section of Brahms's Romanze with the innocent and gratifying world of Chopin's Berceuse. In the Romanze our entrance into that world gains a touch of the magical in the chromatic submediant relationship between the home key, F major, and that of the middle section, D major. But Brahms does not grant us that sudden change of perspective so miraculous in music like Schumann's *Widmung,* where the turn to the chromatic submediant takes place over the barest connection between common tones. Instead, this text carefully prepares the move to D major with a double-tonic complex in its opening section, where phrases change their focus from F major to D minor. The magic accruing to the middle section of the Romanze comes not as sudden insight but rather as a carefully prepared argument: the text wants to reach the magical change, willing it in advance. In the middle section the recurring and striking G♯ adds a Lydian implication to the variations. Aligned with the modality of an earlier time, this G♯ may signify a past tense situated prior to Chopin's composition of the Berceuse. A Bloomian reading of this G♯ would contend that Brahms attempts to make himself the precursor to his own precursor by referencing a modal vocabulary used well before Chopin's time. I prefer to read the signification of the past tense here in light of the title, Romanze, as an evocation of the ancient and exotic. Mozart, for example, uses modal features in Pedrillo's *Romanze* in *Die Entführung aus dem Serail,* and Brahms's Romanze participates in a similar evocation of an otherness from the past.

But if the middle section of Brahms's Romanze signifies the past, then the outer sections surely force us to face a present tinged with the longing and regret of old age. A walking topic governs the opening measures, but the slow tempo and iambic patterning of the outer voices deny the youthful vigor and confidence that we hear in a text like the second movement of Schumann's *Fantasie,* where the walking topic takes on a swiftness of pace marking true self-possession. And here that text we call the life of the historical figure Brahms comes to play. We bring him forward as character in his own drama, brooding in his final years over an innocent past that never existed. As such, the middle section has much in common with a pastoral topic in literature, where constructions of an idyllic Arcadian past represent the longing to recover from the mists of mythology a pristine loveliness and calm (see Gifford 1999). We can hear how that pastoral longing also fills the opening measures of the Romanze, as a descending thirds sequence governs the harmonic progress. Beethoven uses this same sequence in the final movement of his *Pastoral* Sonata, Op. 28; and he problematizes that sequence as it opens his Sonata in E Major, Op. 109, where the untroubled simplicity of the first measures soon faces the doubtful qualm of the Adagio espressivo section that follows. Brahms's doubts about the pastoral come in the opening measures of the Romanze, as the descending thirds redirect the tonality away from F major and toward D minor. The musical character has some trouble re-creating the pastoral in the present, and so he or she must look to the past for renewal.

This sketch of an intertextual analysis makes no claims to being definitive, authoritative, or closed. Instead, it is an example of the multiple texts that we bring to understanding music. In order to situate the Romanze, this short analysis references other musical texts (Mozart, Schumann, Beethoven), biography as text (Brahms's life), and literary theory as text (pastoral constructions). Further, we glimpse the way that a short piece of music can reference what Bakhtin would have called multiple *speech types,* from pastoral and walking topics, to the evocation of the past through modality, to the longing and desire signified by a major tonality that veers toward its relative minor (the double-tonic complex in the opening section). This mixing of allusions, topics, citations is, I believe, what Bakhtin had in mind when he described the dialogism of the novel, and it is what I have in mind when borrowing literary theories of intertextuality.

Those writers who come closest to understanding the implications of intertextual analysis are also the ones versed in semiotic practice. Kofi Agawu (1991), Robert Hatten (1985; 1994), Raymond Monelle (2000), and Robert Samuels (1995) have all addressed the problem of intertextuality and its tendency to open up readings that threaten stable systems. Though intertextuality receives little development in Agawu's study of topics, he readily points to its dual nature as the connection between texts that makes possible both our recognition of a topic of musical discourse (Turkish music, *Sturm und Drang,* for example) and the possibility that that topic may become historically too scattered to be of much use. Thus, Agawu tells us, "it becomes necessary to restrict the domain to which the process [of intertextuality] is applicable" (Agawu 1991, 35). In accord with this view is Hatten's use of intertextuality in interpretive analyses of late Beethoven. Well aware that intertextuality threatens his very project of reconstructing listener competencies, Hatten both confines its definition to any allusion or quotation that crosses stylistic boundaries and discounts "patterns or templates that are part of the anonymous heritage of a stylistic language" (Hatten 1994, 196–97). This definition has both poietic and esthesic implications. The composer (poietic) alludes to the music of a precursor, but that allusion is only marked for the listener (esthesic) when it comes from an earlier stylistic period. If Beethoven uses an Alberti bass, that pattern is just a part of the anonymous heritage of his stylistic era, and so it fails as an example of intertextuality. But if Mozart writes counterpoint in the style of Palestrina, his allusion to an earlier stylistic period counts as an example of intertextuality. This maneuver to confine intertextuality would seem to make moot the kinds of problems that I shall discuss in later chapters. It is crucial to remember, though, that Hatten's remarkable project is directed at the "historical reconstruction of an interpretative competency adequate to the understanding of Beethoven's works *in his time*" (Hatten 1994, 3; emphasis added). Part of the argument I am developing, though, is that our place in history, from which we can hear Beethoven alongside Berio, Bartók, and Byrd, questions the stylistic integrity that allows a narrow definition of the intertext. Perhaps the writer who comes closest to describing the intertextuality that I have in mind is Monelle, who, in a description of what it is like to approach a Mahler symphony, offers a figure in the shape of a network, whose central node is just that music of Mahler we hope to understand (Monelle 2000, 155, Fig. 6.1). Around this central node Monelle includes other nodes that reference texts of all kinds, including theoretical ones ("tonal irrelevance"), biographical ones ("Mahler, the German-speaking, Christianized Czech Jew"), historical ones ("Germanic nationalism"), musical ones ("the *Volk: Wunderhorn*"), cultural ones ("Christmas angels"), etc., in an open-ended invitation to consider the full effect of intertextuality and its implication that there is nothing outside of the text.

The journey I propose, then, is one that promises no definitive, closed, unquestionable, or complete theory of intertextuality in music. I offer no new methodology for uncovering authoritative readings of works but only suggest initiatives for opening up texts. The map sketched in these pages only points directions toward the types of questions that intertextuality raises. In Chapter 2 I take up the problem of structuralism and its uneasy relationship to music theory and discuss the ways in which intertextuality both underlies and threatens music analysis. In Chapter 3 I confront the problems of music and meaning, showing how intertextuality informs semiotic codes, allowing for a reconsideration of the extent to which topics govern our understanding of music since the eighteenth century. Chapter 4 considers a theory of strangeness culled from an intertextual reading of texts by Riffaterre, Bloom, and Freud. Riffaterre, struggling to confine the effects of intertextuality, reads ungrammaticalities in texts as signals of an intertext. I hope to show how this theory intersects with Freud's well-known essay on the uncanny and Bloom's statement that strangeness is the mark of greatness, in order to illustrate how critics deal with their own anxieties about how the texts they hold dear answer to charges of influence. Finally, Chapter 5 turns to the relationship between intertextuality and narrative in music. In particular, the chapter brings together Chopin's Fourth Ballade and Lutosławski's Fourth Symphony to illustrate how we situate musical texts in order to understand musical plot.

The reader may charge that, in search of musical examples, I too readily turn to what Joseph Kerman called "the piano teacher's rabbit hutch" (Kerman 1985, 71). I plead guilty to this charge with only the explanation that, after thirty-five years of playing the piano, I hear its repertoire all too readily when contemplating music: it is a circular memory that comes to me, not what I summon up. A more adult theory of intertextuality would surely require an engagement with a repertoire both broader and deeper than the one cited in these pages, but such a theory is well beyond my limits and awaits another book open to the ways that musical texts speak among themselves.

2 The Appeal to Structure

One cannot define structuralism by examining how the word has been used; that would lead only to despair.

—Jonathan Culler (*Structuralist Poetics*, 3)

1

Nearly three decades after Jonathan Culler mapped out the range of discourse around structuralism, there is still little hope that we might decide upon a narrow definition of that term by examining its use, and this problem is no less difficult when we turn our attention to the practices of music theory over the last fifty years. Though Joseph Kerman reminds us that the distant past brought "almost any kind of disciplined thought about music" within the purview of music theory, and though recent programs for meetings of the Society for Music Theory demonstrate that this broad definition is still valid, a survey of the field over the past fifty years lends credence to Claude Palisca's claim that music theory "is now understood as principally the study of the structure of music."[1] The rise of the modern theorist in the mid–twentieth century was the rise of structural music analysis. But it is questionable whether that fact alone has the power to align music theory with the concerns of structuralism as it was practiced in everything from Jacques Lacan's reinterpretation of Freudian analysis in *Écrits* to Roland Barthes's study of fashion in *Système de la mode*.

Culler may have forecast despair at defining structuralism, but he quickly noted a connection between its diverse practices and the semiotics of Ferdinand de Saussure. Most later attempts to define structuralism begin by reestablishing this same connection (Hawthorne 1994, 200–202; Norris 1991, 1–14; Eagleton 1983, 91–126). Broadly, the model of Saussurian semiotics infused structuralism with an objective —to uncover and formalize the conditions of meaning in cultural phenomena. The distinction between what things mean and how they mean underpins the structuralist project. And it is that very term *meaning* that gives us pause to consider whether the musical structuralism of the twentieth century was ever anything more than a poetics of formalism, and whether it could claim alliance with Saussurian semiotics, concerned with the how, if not the what, of meaning. Of course, semiotics would make an impact on theory and musicology later in the century. Jean-Jacques Nattiez's semiological tripartition in *Music and Discourse* (1990b), Kofi Agawu's semiotic interpretation of topic theory in *Playing with Signs* (1991), and Robert Hatten's theory of markedness in *Musical Meaning in Beethoven* (1994), to list only three examples, clearly follow the broad concerns of structuralism viewed as an extension of semiotics. What appears to separate their work from the broader project of twentieth-century music theory is that the structures of interest to them involve a semantic level. Nattiez structures the conditions of meaning in the poietic, immanent, and esthesic levels of communication. Agawu structures the interaction between surface topics and deeper-level tonal processes, viewing them, respectively, as extroversive and introversive semioses with the power to point both outside and inside the musical work.[2] Hatten structures meaning in Beethoven as the interaction of a system of marked oppositions, and of tokens and types within a style. In addition to these writings, which openly borrow semiotic theory, the work of both Leonard B. Meyer and Edward T. Cone has strong tendencies toward examining what makes music meaningful. Their concerns with hermeneutics, criticism, and style make it easy to understand why Kerman holds up Cone and Meyer as laudable models for theory and analysis, contrasting the structure run amok that he reads in both Schenkerian and set-class approaches.

When thinking about music theory in relation to its sister disciplines, questions arise concerning the types of structures peaking theorists' interests and the ways in which those structures entwine themselves with the problem of meaning. Here it is worth returning to theory's modern canonical texts in order to remind ourselves what motivated the concern with structure. For the most part these texts direct themselves toward analysis. Though the field of music theory surely includes research on theoretical systems (speculative theory), pedagogy, perception/cognition, and the history of music theory, "the central thrust of the discipline is in fact powerfully directed toward analytical theory and its use" (McCreless 1997b, 15–16). Before proceeding, though, it is necessary to consider the entanglements around analysis, particularly in the areas of composition, performance, and aesthetics.[3]

Nicholas Cook resorts to no hyperbole in writing that analysis is "the backbone of composition teaching" (Cook 1987, 2). Even in sites outside the composition studio, the study of music analysis often directs itself toward model composition (see Cook 1996). In realms headier than the undergraduate theory curriculum, Milton Babbitt's famous dictum about the use of scientific language in the study of music entails a critique of those composers who would indulge in idle experimentation to discover musical properties more readily gleaned by formal thinking; in addition, Babbitt challenges the superstition that theory ought never precede practice (Babbitt 1972a; 1972b). Reading volumes of *Perspectives of New Music*, one concludes that analysis has been the royal road to composition for countless composers. Still, one is struck by how few of music theory's modern canonical texts treat analysis as a step toward composition. Heinrich Schenker's *Free Composition* (1979) makes claims neither about teaching composition nor about retracing its history, except by the most subconscious of routes. Allen Forte's *The Structure of Atonal Music* takes as its goal "to provide a general theoretical framework, with reference to which the processes underlying atonal music may be systematically described," where that framework is an end unto itself (Forte 1973, ix). David Lewin's *Generalized Musical Intervals and Transformations* (1987), that model for modeling musical space, makes few explicit connections between a theory of transformations and the act of composing. Even when composers are involved in writing theory, they often bracket off composition from analysis. Benjamin Boretz would later claim of his remarkable and sprawling "Meta-Variations" (1970) that he was struggling "to think about (and talk about) music in such a way as to reflect and probe, in an adequate and believable way, the thought *in* music which I perceived to be its creative content, its ontological reality" (Boretz 1989, 111). Clear thinking, not composing, seems to have been the goal of Boretz's meta-analysis of music theory. Following the practices of Chomskian linguistics, Fred Lerdahl and Ray Jackendoff in *A Generative Theory of Tonal Music* write that their theory is meant to generate not tonal pieces but structural descriptions of tonal pieces (Lerdahl and Jackendoff 1983, 6). A notable counterexample to this separation of analysis from composition is Robert D. Morris's *Composition with Pitch-Classes* (1987), where one senses that exceptionally clear and formal thinking about music is constantly at play with such thinking about how to compose music.

But marking a trend among the texts of modern theory to keep analysis away from composition does not suffice for a statement that the business of musical analysis is analysis. Beginning at least with Hugo Riemann and followed by Schenker, there are appeals to performers, whose woeful ignorance of matters music-analytic belies a disregard for deep and meaningful engagements with the score. Despite some important writings intent on detailing how analysis can inform performance (Berry 1989; Schmalfeldt 1985; Cone 1968), it is still easy to agree with Wallace Berry that "music theory has, by and large, surprisingly little to say about issues of interpretation as these might reasonably derive from observations and hypotheses about musical form, structure, and process" (Berry 1989, 1). Though theorists may agree that a knowledge of key, interval, chord, phrase structure, and cadence are invaluable tools to aid the performer in finding her way through a score, theorists confront difficulties in trying to show how the finer details of analytical thought, from the events of the Schenkerian foreground to the operations of a Lewinian FLIPEND, might find articulation in a performance. Is it even desirable to imagine how a performer might bring out all of the voice-leading levels of a Schenkerian graph, the transformations of a Lewinian network, or even the motivic forms of a Schoenbergian *Grundgestalt*? One wants to conclude, however crudely drawn this sketch of performance and analysis may be, that analysis does much the same thing for the performer as for the theorist: it anaesthetizes the breathing music, making of it a sculpture that the musician can walk around in order to calculate distances. Analysis engages the performer in tasks of *Tonvorstellung* as Brian Hyer nuances that term: acts of imagining, of representing, of seeing the music (Hyer 1995, 102–104). The performer needs analysis in order to hold music still in her mind's grasp before she sets it free again. Analyses become, in Lewin's terms, "goads to musical action, ways of suggesting what *might* be done, beyond ways of regarding what *has* been done" (Lewin 1986, 377). Performances become, in those same terms, acts of perception. Analyzing, composing, performing, and perceiving collapse into one another as the faces of musical behavior.[4] In this model we find it difficult to divorce analysis from composition and performance after all. But if analysis gains status as a musical behavior entangled with performance, it is still a mystery to know how structural analysis informs those decisions regarding tempo and articulation that Berry suggests as the only domains of expressive freedom allowed the performer (Berry 1989, 2–3).

Minds less charitable might see a bid for power veiled in the claim that analysis is a musical behavior equal in status to composition and performance. Patrick McCreless argues soundly that motivations to make analysis scientific include a desire to make space in the academy for music theory as a discipline separate from musicology (McCreless 1997b). Analysis becomes ensnared in a power relation over what will count as musical knowledge and who will act as authority in governing it. In this light one reads with concern Matthew Brown and Douglas Dempster's statement that music theory "must clarify the nature of music and thereby guide our musical activities, whether they be performance, composition or historical research" (Brown and Dempster 1989, 65). Richard Taruskin's response to Brown and Dempster's scientific image of theory evidenced the understandable reaction that at least one sister discipline was in no mood to grant music theory the status of a governing musical authority (Taruskin 1989). Closely aligned with this will to academic power is the long association between structural analysis and aesthetic evaluation. Kerman writes that "analysis exists for the purpose of demonstrating organicism, and organicism exists for the purpose of validating a certain body of works."[5] That analysis as aesthetic validation has broken through the barriers that once insulated German instrumental music from other repertoires, that theory widened its scope of analytic inquiry, particularly into popular music—both will be of little comfort to those who see these broader interests as merely a means of grabbing more traces for the analytical mill and of propping up a power base that all along has depended on analysis.[6]

Analysis makes monuments (Chua 1999, 235–44). Even when analysis updates its procedures by recourse to other disciplines, it reserves for itself the right to define, to erect, and to dismantle the monumental. Analytical studies relying on intertextuality, a concept whose focus on interwoven texts threatens notions of the monumental artwork, tend to bend this critical stance toward aesthetic considerations nonetheless. Early in her study of borrowing in twentieth-century music, for example, Martha Hyde turns to the problem of canon formation and T. S. Eliot's question "What is a classic?" (Hyde 1996, 201, quoting Eliot 1968). Hyde brings her discussion of the ways that composers confront the music of the past in service of a critical evaluation of musical artworks that might rank them as worthy of the canon. Neither Kevin Korsyn's nor Joseph Straus's co-opting of Harold Bloom's *Anxiety of Influence* could remain innocent of Bloom's defense of the western canon. Korsyn embraces more openly a model that judges works on the basis of how adeptly they shatter old monuments to make room for new ones. And though Straus appears to have less concern with this application of the poetics of influence, Taruskin's unfair panning of *Remaking the Past* rests on a (mis)reading of Straus's work, in which Schoenberg and the German tradition wrongly and at the expense of Stravinsky become the sole inheritors of monumentality for twentieth-century musical culture (Taruskin 1993).

Choosing music for analysis can be read as a gesture toward monumentalizing one work at the expense of the countless others around us. Critical, however, has been the motivation to let structural analysis alone do all the work of monumentality without recourse to history, ideology, meaning, and marketplace. Here we must face what Cook calls "Hanslick's legacy" in voiding music of its meaning in pursuit of the absolute (Cook 2001, 174). Returning to Hanslick's *Vom musikalisch-Schönen* one is struck by its tensions. Hanslick quickly lays out the argument that music neither contains nor arouses feelings (Hanslick 1986, 3). Yet shortly after denying this content, the text affirms music's power to awaken intense feelings, and Hanslick expresses anxiety over minimizing this "most beautiful and redeeming" mystery (7). Mediating these two positions is the claim that feelings form no basis for aesthetical principles, and that they have no place in strictly scientific inquiry (6–7). Music does arouse feelings after all, but it would be best if we were to ignore them in aesthetics. Perhaps sensing that feelings will not be bracketed off so easily, Hanslick tells us that "love and anger occur only in our hearts," reminding us that feelings are not in the music but in our reactions to it (9). Anachronistically we might say that Hanslick has developed a semiotic system half a century before Saussure. Musical tones are signifiers that produce sensations, stimulating thought and feeling, those signifieds that dwell in us.

But if music is to be absolute, separate, independent, and beautiful, we must extricate it from our messy feelings.[7] Hanslick revisits Boyé's analysis of Gluck's "Che farò senza Euridice!" from *Orfeo* to demonstrate that without a text the aria in question might just as well point to an expression of joy rather than grief (17–18). The connection between musical signifiers and expressive signifieds is too contextual for Hanslick. No tidy links bind the semiotic system. That signs are arbitrary and unstable threatens any aesthetic project hoping for the precision of a science. Thus, in Hanslick's system, musical signifiers must point only to themselves. Having removed feelings as signifieds from music, Hanslick is free to make his claim:

The content of music is tonally moving forms. (29)[8]

The signified of music is music. Any extra-musical meaning must be spent in unfaltering analysis of music's introversive semiosis. As the by-product of analysis, monumentality exists to mark the place where meaning once stood. The analyst must empty music of meaning so that she can ossify the free-floating signifiers into something that will withstand the flow of time. Music must die and become its own monument. Music's meaning must turn inward to those empty signifiers that murmur among themselves the absolute. Music must mean nothing so that it can mean everything.[9]

But if it were true that analysis in the tradition of Hanslick had denied meaning altogether, then it would be a simple matter to conclude that music theory in the twentieth century had little to do with the structuralism practiced by literary and cultural critics, historians, and anthropologists. Music analysis under such a reading would be viewed as mere formalism, finding in the aesthetics of structure a recompense for the awful truth that we cannot know music's meaning. Such a reading, though, would deny that meaning for the music theorist *is* the analysis. Early in his *The Structure of Atonal Music* Forte writes of a novel pitch combination in

Schoenberg's George *Lieder* that "it could occur in a tonal composition only under extraordinary conditions, and even then its meaning would be determined by harmonic-contrapuntal constraints" (Forte 1973, 1). By *meaning,* Forte surely has no interest in the rhetoric of the chord in question, nor in how it might contribute to an emotional response to the music, nor in anything now called with misfortune *extra-musical.* Forte's interest is in a musical coherence earned through a taxonomy of pitch-class sets that can tame the unruly surface of music via similarity of interval-class content. Those intervals and their associations *are* the meaning of this music from a music-analytic point of view.

The reinvestment of musical meaning into the notes themselves happens earlier and more dramatically in Schenker's metaphors for music, where "we perceive our own life-impulse in the motion of the fundamental line, a full analogy to our inner life" (Schenker 1979, 4). Pitches take on psyches in Schenker's structures, swerving from obstacles and overcoming uncertainties. Pitches live and die in a purely musical narrative, and from our safe vantage point outside the music we may cheer their victory or mourn their passing. We can hear echoes of Schenker's metaphors in Lewin's work as well. Introducing the intuitions that underlie measurements of intervals, Lewin will ask us to imagine not that these measurements are "out there" separate from ourselves, but that if "I am at s, what characteristic transformation do I perform in order to arrive at t?" (Lewin 1987, xiii). For Lewin we are no longer observers of musical space, but participants in it. By placing us in the music, Lewin reinvigorates Schenker's metaphor of pitch as psyche. In the final pages of "Music Theory, Phenomenology, and Modes of Perception," the reinvestment of our psyches into the narrative of pitch completes itself as Lewin asks us to imagine that we play the dramatic role of F♯/G♭ in Beethoven's Fifth Symphony (Lewin 1986, 389–90). We become characters in the inner life of music, and as such we take on the musical meanings that are its routes through musical topography.

When musical structure *is* meaning, the relationship between analysis and modern structuralism appears closer. Especially evident is an intertext between music theory's pursuit of analysis and Claude Lévi-Strauss's study of myth in *The Raw and the Cooked* (1969), a book in which everywhere and at once, from the dedication "To Music" with its incipit of a melody by Emmanuel Chabrier, to the chapters with headings like "Fugue of the Five Senses," music's influence is plain.[10] Writing of the "surprising affinity between music and myths," Lévi-Strauss makes some extraordinary observations:

> If Wagner is accepted as the undeniable originator of the structural analysis of myths . . . it is a profoundly significant fact that the analysis was made, in the first instance, *in music* (Lévi-Strauss 1969, 15)

and later

> Because of the internal organization of the musical work, the act of listening to it immobilizes passing time; it catches and enfolds it as one catches and enfolds a cloth flapping in the wind. It follows that by listening to music, and while we are listening to it, we enter into a kind of immortality. (16)

Lévi-Strauss expresses no interest in understanding what these myths might have meant to the cultures that sustain them, because his concern is not in "how men think in myths, but in how myths think in men."[11] The immortality that we enter as we listen to music or attend to a myth is the participation of our mind in the one activity that binds us across both time and culture: the process of structuring phenomena. So much of Lévi-Strauss's approach to myth seems transferable *mutatis mutandis* to music analysis, whose claims would appear to be about how music thinks through the structuring mind. As he says of myth, it makes little difference whether those structures uncover the operations of a mind historically situated with the music at hand, or whether they illuminate the mind of the analyst situated in a different time and place (13). What matters is that those structures are the operations of the mind writ large as an immortal object.[12]

Though Lévi-Strauss largely concerns himself with structure as an operation of the mind, he cannot refrain from an aside in which he entertains the effect that music has on individuals. Even here, though, his words echo with voices from music theory:

> The musical emotion springs precisely from the fact that at each moment the composer withholds or adds more or less than the listener anticipates on the basis of a pattern that he thinks he can guess. (17)

Reading the excerpt outside of its context, we might take it for a passage by Meyer, explaining how emotion and meaning in music result from implications unrealized. In Chapter 1 we saw how Lévi-Strauss pushed the historical origin of structural analysis back to Rameau, perhaps in an effort to transplant the roots of structuralism from the foreign soil of Wagner's operas back to the familiar climes of French thought.[13] The conclusion is still the same: the aims of music analysis predate and prefigure a poetics of structuralism in its manifestation in Lévi-Strauss's study of myth. In music analysis as in myth, the structure *is* the meaning.

But facile transference of Lévi-Strauss's project to the aims of music theory must be read in light of his earlier work in structural anthropology, where his arguments reveal that a field of research must do more than exhibit a mere fascination with deep patterns and their formalization in order to engage meaningfully the methodologies of structuralism. In Lévi-Strauss's classic study of kinship, "Structural Analysis in Linguistics and in Anthropology" (1963), he makes clear his debt to the hypotheses of Saussure's semiology and its development in structural linguistics. We learn that in addition to a concern with the conscious and unconscious infrastructures of the mind, structural anthropology must treat its terms as a system of oppositions; it must grasp that system as a whole, and it must discover the general laws that transform that system.[14] Finally, lest anthropology blind itself in beholding the wonderment of these structures, it must realize that "what confers upon kinship its socio-cultural character is not what it retains from nature, but, rather, the essential way in which it diverges from nature" (Lévi-Strauss 1963, 50). The structures of kinship, and by extension the human sciences, must take into account the impact of culture.

It is at the point where culture enters the structuralist project that many of the analytical technologies of twentieth-century music theory are left behind. Though we find instances where structural music analysis defines its terms as a system of relations and of transformations (Lewin's work comes to mind), we still stumble upon the problem of culture and its impact on the structures we call forth to explain musical phenomena. Jean Piaget warns us that "the study of structure cannot be exclusive" (Piaget 1970, 137). Rather than suppress the human, and the human sciences, structuralism eagerly seeks to engage them at every turn, bringing together the methodologies of other disciplines. Piaget's human view of structuralism is at odds with any who take too seriously Foucault's pronouncement that the pursuit of structures spells the death of man (see Foucault 1970). Though the human subject must often decenter herself and the achievements of individuals in order to participate in structural analysis, she must return to herself and her culture in order to view these structures in the act of becoming (Piaget 1970, 139–40). A structure is a dynamic event.

Often content to remove its interests from the reach of culture, the structuralism of music theory, even with its involvements in composition, performance, aesthetics, and formal thinking, is a symptom of a wish fulfillment in which meaning turns upon itself and feeds the syntactic level of musical forms. Thus much music analysis occupies a strange place in the human sciences. While Lévi-Strauss openly acknowledges music as inspiration to his study of myth, music analysis only partially fulfills the methodology he demands of structuralism. Though we might hear echoes of semiotic-structural thought in music theory's preoccupation with formalization, group theory, and transformation, few of music theory's analytical models engage the same kinds of questions of culture, sign systems, and the conditions of meaning that inform the methodologies of structuralism. Music analysis appeals to structures without structuralism; it is a poetics independent of signification. There is a danger, though, in confusing the foregoing with an implicit acceptance of Kerman's well-known challenges to music theory and analysis. Acknowledgment that the music theorist's preoccupation with structure often comes at the expense of meaning and culture need not lead us to the conclusion that severe limitations on deep readings of musical structure will somehow solve the problem of music analysis. Though this chapter promises no solution to this problem, it will suggest that part of a solution may come from more open acknowledgment of the intertextual nature of analysis.

2

The conflation of structure with meaning clarifies the readiness with which music theorists have appropriated the major tenet of Bloom's theory of anxiety and influence:

The meaning of a poem can only be another poem. (Bloom 1973, 94)

Lewin is perhaps least literal in applying this aphorism to music. Concerned with broadening our thinking about perception, he includes performance, analysis, composition, and critical writing as acts of perception that create the "other poems" with which we understand a prior poem (Lewin 1986, 382). This reading resonates with theories of intertextuality that define the text widely as any cultural artifact. Here is Bloom's theory stripped of its "bleakness—a view of human nature founded on jealousy, territoriality, resentment, and of human relations founded on corrosive rivalry, contention, strife" (Taruskin 1993, 114). Instead of agon, Lewin's reading offers a more humane anxiety to understand music through acts of perception, defined as the creation of other music in forms that range from analysis to composition.

Straus and Korsyn wrestle with Bloom's theory more directly. As I have discussed in Chapter 1, Straus confines his analyses of influence to a study of tropes on the syntactic level. Though he retains Bloom's notion that texts transform other texts as a way of clearing space in an overcrowded canon, Straus spends little energy developing the psychological nuance that underpins the various tropes as Bloom envisions them. Straus's preoccupation with the syntactic transformations by which composers distance themselves from their heritage allows us to misread Bloom by replacing the word *meaning* with *structure:*

The structure of a poem is another poem.

Korsyn engages more fully the problem of that word *meaning* in Bloom's original. Turning to Bloom's self-commentary in *Kabbalah and Criticism,* Korsyn reminds us that Bloom's critical practice rarely centers on what a poem signifies but rather takes the precursor poem itself as a signifier for otherness. In the end, though, Korsyn too focuses primarily on the structure of these pieces and the ways that they deny, complete, answer, and transform the structures of other pieces. Still, his mapping of Freudian psychic tropes onto musical ones does return to music the rapacious struggle of Bloom's theory.

If these gestures toward embracing Bloom's *Anxiety* have only reinvigorated a convention among theorists to take structure as meaning, they have also shown that intertextuality is the precondition of finding structure in music. Again Lévi-Strauss uncovers a methodology common to the study of myth and the analysis of music:

[T]he context of each myth comes to consist more and more of other myths.[15]

Culler explains that lacking an interest in recovering the meaning of myth, and possessing no means of confirming meaning, Lévi-Strauss settles on a methodology that reads a first myth in light of a second one, and brings to bear upon this pair a third myth, and a fourth, etc., until each myth becomes a relational event among all of the others (Culler 1975, 43). The analyst must proceed *as if* the myths in question were similar in meaning, with the assumption, once again, that the real object of inquiry is the structure of the mind. Regarding the choice of myths to bring together into an intertext, Lévi-Strauss confines himself only to the mythologies of the New World, an area much too vast for anyone seeking to analyze the historical/cultural conditions of extroversive semiosis. As for his choice of a central myth around which this intertext is woven, he expresses little interest in finding one that is more archaic or simple or complete than the others; rather, the myth in question is one "especially likely to stimulate reflection" (Lévi-Strauss 1969, 2).

Lévi-Strauss's study of myth suggests a methodology for the intertextual analysis of musical structure. Faced with the chaotic musical surface, the theorist pursues a structure as the result of bringing a text within the context of a second, and third, text. A musical structure is a relational event among texts. A musical structure is an intertextuality. For the remainder of this chapter I illustrate the intertextual nature of structure with two analyses. In the first of these I begin with the opening of Bartók's First Violin Sonata as a central myth especially likely to stimulate reflection. From this myth I turn to others with a goal of settling upon a structure that ultimately binds these pieces together. That structure will be read not as the guarantee of organic unity, but as the relation of the sonata to two other musical texts. In the second analysis I reconsider Chopin's Etude in C, Op. 10, No. 1, in order to argue that its intertext threatens to dismantle the very structures it supports. Here I shall bring together five musical texts in a Schenkerian analysis of the etude, in order to answer questions regarding one passage where I find it difficult to settle upon a single structural meaning. I hope to show that when the other texts are brought to bear on the central myth, the etude, they only underscore the aporia of the passage in question. Thus intertextuality has centripetal and centrifugal forces that both support and threaten stable structures. Taken together, the intertextual analyses of Bartók's First Violin Sonata and Chopin's Etude in C Major may be viewed as the creation and destruction of a myth that musical meaning is a unified structure.

3

Bartók was fond of Szymanowski's *Mythes*, Op. 30 (1915), which he often programmed in his collaborative recitals with young Hungarian violinists. We can only speculate that Bartók's composerly attraction to this work had its basis in a recognition that Szymanowski too was confronting the music of contemporary French and Russian composers in an effort to break away from the hegemony of modern German music. As early as 1913 Szymanowski had studied the music of Stravinsky, Skryabin, Debussy, and Ravel in search of new musical resources, and *Mythes* would be his first mature work to integrate successfully characteristics of these composers' music into his own.[16] Malcolm Gillies takes the first movement of *Mythes*, "La fontaine d'Arethuse," to be a major influence on Bartók's development of new violin techniques (Gillies 1992), and it is the opening of this same movement that I take to be the precursor to the first theme of Bartók's Violin Sonata No. 1 (1921). Examples 2.1 and 2.2 show the opening measures of the two works. Bartók's introduction curtails the length of Szymanowski's in a trope that Bloom would likely describe as *kenosis*, a "breaking device similar to the defense mechanisms our psyches employ against repetition compulsions"; *kenosis* is a revisionary ratio in which the ephebe strives for concision in her own poetic language in order to point out excess in that of her precursor (Bloom 1973, 14). Here the breaking device concerns pattern repetitions. The two-measure introduction of Bartók's violin sonata underscores undue length in the introduction of "La fontaine," which begins with a one-measure pattern that appears four times in eight

Piano (Violin tacit till m. 3)

etc.

[E,2,5,7]
(0258)

[8,T,1,4]
(0258)

[1,2,4,5,7,8,T,E]
oct. collection

Example 2.1. Bartók, Violin Sonata No. 1 (1921), I

measures. By breaking this repetition compulsion, Bartók's text tells us that it is capable of expressing in two measures that which Szymanowski's text expresses in eight. The result of this *kenosis* is that the violin sonata is emotionally charged from the beginning, and its aggressive character is reinforced when the violin enters *forte* in a register that is nearly two octaves lower than that of the violin entrance in "La fontaine."[17]

The intertext of these two passages becomes stronger if we attend to their articulations of octatonic collections. Examples 2.1 and 2.2 illustrate prominent pitch-class sets that structure the two introductions when they are read as a pair. Common to the two texts are members of set-class (0258), subsets of the octatonic collection. We can conceptualize the opening of "La fontaine" as a layering of musical spaces, pentatonic in the left hand, and diatonic in the right hand. The pitches in the left hand travel through two pentatonic steps that come in two chromatic sizes: a large pentatonic step from E♭ to G♭, and a small pentatonic step from G♭ to A♭.[18] The right hand mirrors this route but does so in diatonic space, moving through a diatonic minor 2nd from F to E, and a diatonic major 2nd from E to D. The pentatonic motion in the left hand outlines a chromatic interval of five semitones, while the diatonic motion in the right outlines three semitones; as Example 2.3 shows, these chromatic intervals structure the violin's melody. The trope that transforms the opening of "La fontaine" into its correlative in the violin sonata is what I call a *syncretism* of musical space. Syncretism occurs whenever two or more independent lines are conceived newly as a vertical structure.[19] For example, when the independent lines of Renaissance counterpoint are conceived newly as a succession of triads, syncretism occurs. The trope has esthesic and poietic dimensions. The theorist hears the octatonic subsets in Bartók's sonata *as* harmonies in them-

Piano (Violin tacit until m. 9)

[9,0,3,5]   [4,6,9,0]   [8,9,0,2]   [5,9,0]   [9,0,2]
(0258)   (0258)   (0146)   (037)   (025)

[9,0,4]
(037)

[3,6,8]
(025)

[2,4,5]
(013)

[8,9,0,2,3,5]
(014679)
oct. subset

diatonic major 2nd and minor 2nd

pentatonic "major" 2nd and "minor" 2nd

Example 2.2. Szymanowski, "La fontaine d'Arethuse" from *Mythes* (1915)

selves rather than as the result of an interaction among independent lines. This response makes no claims about Bartók's view in the matter. We might find evidence to conclude that Bartók did attend to these harmonies in this way, that he recognized a harmonic resource resulting from the interaction of independent lines in "La fontaine," and that he used these harmonies without recourse to linear interaction in his sonata. Such evidence, if ever unequivocal, would point to syncretism on the poietic level, bringing this intertext in the service of a study of influence.

But why do we need to invoke these embedded musical spaces in order to understand Szymanowski's music? After all, in the opening of "La fontaine" we do hear two instances of tetrachord (0258), familiar from the tonal repertoire as the dominant and half-diminished-seventh chords. That these same chords are now well-known subsets of the octatonic collection allows us to make some intertextual connections between this piece and any number of works by Stravinsky, Bartók, Debussy, and, if Forte is right, Webern.[20] Further, the fact that Bartók's sonata

(melody performed 2 octaves higher)

Example 2.3. Violin melody from "La fontaine"

opens with the same seventh chords as those in "La fontaine" would seem to indicate only a weak trope on Szymanowski's music. Imagining the passage from "La
fontaine" as a layering of spaces, though, is the result of reading this work intertextually with "Brouillards" from Book II of Debussy's *Préludes* (1913). Here the connection begins to range beyond influence into a more open intertextual field; although we know that Szymanowski was studying the music of Debussy during the
period in which he wrote "La fontaine," we have no evidence that he ever studied
this particular prelude, to say nothing of the type of proof we might accept that
the prelude was active in his imagination during the time he composed *Mythes*.
The intertext in this case narrows the many possibilities for structuring Bartók's
violin sonata. From the untamed surface of one musical myth, we move to the surface of another, and reading the two against a third text, we settle upon a structure.

Example 2.4 shows the opening of "Brouillards," which articulates an octatonic
collection through a layering of diatonic space in the left hand and pentatonic
space in the right, suggestive of the layering in "La fontaine."[21] The difference in
"Brouillards" is that the right hand moves out of pentatonic space, and the layering
results in more than one octatonic collection. By comparison to "Brouillards," the
layering of spaces in "La fontaine" results in a single octatonic collection, as the left
hand remains on the black keys. Lost are the shifting collections of Debussy's prelude. Bartók's sonata, as we have seen, ignores the layering altogether, syncretizing
the spaces and articulating the tritone axis of the octatonic collection in the $C\sharp_3$
and G_3 that initiate the patterns in each hand.

Connecting "Brouillards" to Bartók's sonata and Szymanowski's "La fontaine"
allows us to reevaluate their opening material in terms of what Hatten calls the
locational function, the ordering of themes in a presentation-development-closing
paradigm (Hatten 1994, 119–26). In the light of the other two works, our perspective on "Brouillards" changes as we begin to question the locational function of its
first theme. Do the first few measures represent an accompanimental pattern for a
melody yet to come, as is the case in the sonata and "La fontaine," or are these
shifting harmonies presentational, standing as the only object of our attention?
This second possibility gains momentum when the opening figuration continues

Example 2.4. Debussy, "Brouillards" from *Préludes,* Book II (1913)

for nine measures; but when sustained pitches appear in mm. 10–15, we may consider the possibility that a rather extended introduction has just ended as a melody begins. The first eight measures of "La fontaine" play upon this same locational ambiguity, since the piano part seems to go on almost too long before the entrance of the violin. We can view the violin's melody as commenting on "Brouillards" in much the same way that Gounod's *Ave Maria* comments on Bach's Prelude in C Major, outrageously trying to complete the earlier work by adding a melodic line. The melody of "La fontaine" brings a new subjectivity into its orbit as the violin becomes a musical persona, an observer viewing the play of water before her. The fountain takes on a reality as the object of contemplation, distanced by the violin's subjectivity. In "Brouillards" the mists *are* the subjectivity; mist is both an object and a subject, appropriating reality around it and engulfing melody, engulfing us, in its expressive world.

Bartók's violin sonata avoids these locational ambiguities altogether by confining the introduction to two measures. Finding intertexts with nineteenth-century sonatas, where a brief opening statement by the piano establishes a tonal center, the first measures of Bartók's sonata approach the absolute as they invite no wonderment about their function within a locational rhetoric. Although the opening of the violin sonata may be viewed as an act of *kenosis* that points to excess in "La fontaine," the net effect of this trope simply brings the sonata back in line with the rhetoric of nineteenth-century sonatas. "La fontaine" and "Brouillards" come off as more daring in their play with the rhetoric of thematic location. In this regard we see how contingent are those analyses that try to make claims for canonic greatness with respect to an intertext. As we surround the violin sonata with other texts, we show its attributes to be relational to an intertext, making conditional our claims about the sonata.

The problem is no less precarious for the structures we make of these attributes. As the theorist applies models of analysis to the single text, she often finds the way uncertain and asks questions like How shall I segment this piece? Which harmonies warrant structural weight? Which collections govern the interaction of motivic forms? These questions bring on rules of preference and well-formedness as we hypothesize about our ways of perceiving and thinking about music. Such rules, themselves the product of intertextual inquiry, are rarely enough to establish a single, uncontestable structure for a text. In the end, as with Lévi-Strauss's study of myth, the structure of a musical text becomes more and more the structure of another musical text. Thus among the many ways that we might structure the opening of "La fontaine," we choose a layering of musical spaces because that structure has been read in the opening of "Brouillards" as well. In relation to these texts, we read Bartók's violin sonata as a syncretism of that layered musical space and view its structure as a response to a structure.

But bringing musical texts together cannot solve the problem of establishing stable structures. As we bring more texts into an intertext, we risk destabilizing the very structures we wish to affirm. In order to illustrate this effect, the next section returns to Chopin's Etude in C Major and forms a second intertext around it in an effort to establish a single voice-leading structure. I hope to show that rather than answer questions about a Schenkerian reading of the etude, these other pieces only problematize such a reading.

4

In Chapter 1 I placed Lutosławski's Study No. 1 within an intertext with unlimited potential to spread outside the historical context of that work. Here I shall revisit Lutosławski's study and Chopin's etude and surround them with a different intertext, focusing particularly on a formal feature of the study that calls into question the structure of the etude. References to published analyses by Forte and Schenker form a part of my discussion. I wish to make it clear, however, that it is not my objective to engage in a critique at the expense of these two theorists. What follows is not a matter of wishing that Schenker had been more consistent, or scientific, or clear in his theory, or of hoping to illustrate faults in Forte's application of that theory. The objective is to suggest how a reading of Lutosławski's study might point to an alternate reading of Chopin's etude. My approach may be reminiscent of deconstructive strategies, particularly as they are employed in the more pragmatic writings of American literary scholars.[22] Although my analysis parallels such strategies by highlighting marginalized elements in two readings of the etude, leading to aporia, a fuller intertextual account would include more than two readings. In addition, the analysis will make no claims about a subversive subtext in Chopin's etude—a strategy central to Derridean deconstruction. The motivation here is to show how a reading of a later text can impact the analysis of an earlier one.

In addition to the many surface features discussed in Chapter 1, Lutosławski's study and Chopin's etude share a ternary form. Forte's analysis of Chopin's etude interprets the parallel period that opens this piece as coextensive with its A section

Example 2.5. Lutosławski, Study No. 1, third phrase

(Forte and Gilbert 1982, 203, Ex. 177). Many theorists would probably agree that an authentic cadence in m. 16 completes the first formal section, and Schenker's analysis, to which I shall turn shortly, matches Forte's in this respect. Lutosławski's study also begins with a parallel period, following the structure of Chopin's etude. Example 2.5 shows that changes in texture, dynamics, and motivic content suggest a new section in m. 12, but the repetition of a three-beat pattern in mm. 15–17 marks this phrase as closing material. When another, more striking change of texture occurs in m. 20, we realize that it is only now that a new section of the study has begun. This B section is marked by a quote from Chopin's Etude in C♯ Minor, Op. 10, No. 4. We come to reinterpret the A section of Lutosławski's study as a three-phrase structure, where the first two are a parallel period, presentational in function, and the third is a closing phrase, cadential in function. This hearing is confirmed at the end of the study, where the three phrases of the A section return to conclude the work.

In a Bloomian reading of the study we might view Lutosławski's departure from the formal model of Chopin's etude as a misreading, a way of distancing his music from its model. In Bloom's terms the point where Lutosławski adds the third phrase to the opening section (Example 2.5) is an instance of a trope called *clinamen,* or swerve—that is, Lutosławski has followed the precursor up to a point and then changed direction to show how Chopin should have continued his etude. The fact that this swerve adds motivic content to the study also suggests a trope of *tessera,* or completion, which might be added to the other forms of *tessera* mentioned in Chapter 1. Turning to Straus's terminology, we find that two different tropes, *centralization* and *generalization,* characterize the material that forms the third phrase of Lutosławski's study.[23] While the rising perfect fifths that begin this phrase may be traced to material in mm. 1–2 of the study, they can also be heard as extensions of the first intervals of Chopin's etude. Though the perfect fifth (C_3 to G_3) in the first measure of Chopin's etude is unquestionably part of a compound melody that unfolds a C-major harmony (refer back to Example 1.2), Lutosławski's study offers a new hearing by shedding this interval of its harmonic status and adding a second perfect fifth to form a new melodic line. Thus Lutosławski's text *centralizes* a detail of Chopin's etude; the study then *generalizes* the resulting trichord, treating it as a member of set-class (027), which appears consistently in transposition and inversion throughout the remainder of the third phrase.

The Appeal to Structure 37

But I am more interested for the moment in how Lutosławski's study prompts us to reconceptualize Chopin's etude. More precisely, because Lutosławski's study so openly takes Chopin's etude as a model, its three-phrase opening suggests that we might learn to hear the earlier text in the same way. We might interpret the study's A section not as a Bloomian swerve that willfully departs from its model, but as a close reading that hears past the putative two-phrase opening of the etude in order to find a new formal boundary after the third phrase. Hearing Chopin's etude through the intertext of Lutosławski's study results in a second Schenkerian reading for the etude. The two readings appear in Example 2.6. At the top of the example is a rhythmic reduction of mm. 16–48, comprising both the third phrase of the etude and what Schenker and Forte take to be the entire B section. Below this reduction I have aligned Schenker's middleground sketch (Schenker 1979, Fig. 130/4b), and in the lowest staff I have resketched the same passage according to the implications of Lutosławski's study. I shall refer to the two sketches as Sketch 1 (Schenker) and Sketch 2 (Klein). Before proceeding, I wish to make clear that I have tried in every respect not only to follow Schenkerian practice in the creation of Sketch 2, but also to alter Sketch 1 as little as possible. In particular, the reader will note that the sketches are nearly identical for mm. 25–47. Important for the discussion of the two sketches is the phrase in mm. 17–24, which Sketch 1 clearly shows to be the beginning of the B section. As such, it indicates a new *Stufe* (VI) in m. 17, beneath which we find the formal marker *b*. Although the harmonic progression of the entire B section is directed toward an E-major triad in m. 47, this chord functions as V/VI in Sketch 1, so that VI (A minor) acts as the middleground *Stufe* governing this section. In Sketch 2, following the implications of Lutosławski's study, the phrase in mm. 17–24 is heard as the close of the A section instead of the opening of the B section. As such, this phrase is directed toward an E-major triad that acts as the new *Stufe* governing the B section. The III chord functions as a third divider that is prolonged until m. 48 before the entrance of a middleground dominant, supporting a neighbor note in the upper voice.

Since Sketch 2 treats the dominant (E major) of a key (A minor) at a higher structural level than the tonic, it might be well to point out that Schenker himself resorts to such a ploy in his sketch of Chopin's Etude in F Major, Op. 10, No. 8 (Schenker 1969, 47–51). In that case the B section begins unambiguously in D minor, but rather than raise that key to a middleground level, Schenker chooses the key's dominant (A major) as a middleground *Stufe* (III in the home key of F). Possibly influencing Schenker's sketch for the F-major etude is that its B section comes to rest on a dominant pedal (A) that never returns to a root-position triad in the local key (D minor). Though the situation is not entirely analogous, the C-major etude does move quickly to the dominant (E) of A minor in the B section, which also closes on that dominant in m. 48. And although the first dominant in m. 24 moves to an A-major harmony in m. 25, this putative tonic includes a seventh that marks it as a new dominant that will commence a sequence. Throughout the B section of the C-major etude, the dominant (E) never returns to a root-position A-minor triad. In any case, Schenker's sketch for the F-major etude allows room in his theory to raise a local dominant to a higher structural level than its tonic. More

Example 2.6. Two sketches of Chopin, Etude in C Major, Op. 10, No. 1, B section precisely, V/vi may gain the status of a III *Stufe* within the voice-leading structure of a tonal work. Thus Schenker's reading of the F-major etude is another text in the intertext that informs Sketch 2.

As is common with structuralist accounts, both of the sketches in Example 2.6 marginalize features of Chopin's etude. In the interest of brevity I will remark on only one of these features, namely, the status of the upper voices in the chord of m. 17, which is marked by a destabilizing dissonance between E_5 and F_5. If, as in Sketch 1, we wish to hear m. 17 as the initiation of an A-minor harmony, we must do something about that troublesome F_5, covering the more structural E_5. The solution in Sketch 1 is to leave F_5 out of m. 17 altogether and withhold it until the following measure, where it functions as a neighbor note. In many ways, marginalizing F_5 is the only logical solution to the problem of raising VI to the level of a middleground *Stufe*. To be sure, there is another A-minor chord in m. 20, which does not include the offending F_5; but if we were to raise the harmony of that measure to middleground status, its appearance in the middle of a phrase would naturally direct our hearing back to m. 17. If Sketch 1 had included F_5 in m. 17, it would have drawn attention to the fact that with this pitch the harmony of that measure is not VI (in C) but IV_5^6, in which, ironically, E_5 is a dissonance. As a dissonant seventh, E_5 must resolve down by step, and this is precisely how Chopin treats it in the etude.

Sketch 2 reintegrates F_5 into the harmony of m. 17 and shows this pitch participating in a sequential passage. Here F_5 initiates a dissonant 3-line over the interval of a diminished third, while the bass arpeggiates from B_2 down to F_2; together, upper and lower voices prolong an augmented-sixth chord, leading to the E-major harmony of mm. 23–24. This same sketch, however, fails to capture the dominant function of the III *Stufe*; in other words, the A-minor quality of the passage is largely absent because Sketch 2 has lowered the status of the chord in m. 17. The recompense for this loss comes when we realize that Chopin revisits III during the return of the A section. While the second phrase of the opening A section had a fairly straightforward descent in the bass from $\hat{1}$ to $\hat{5}$ via an upper neighbor $\hat{6}$, the second phrase of the closing A section has an expanded line in the bass, descending to $\hat{3}$ and supporting III as shown in Example 2.7. From this point Chopin closes the phrase harmonically with the chords II, V^7, and I. This return of the E-major chord may make us wish that Schenker had entertained the possibility of interruptions at III as well as V; the first-level middleground of Chopin's etude would thus be I–III ‖ I–III–V–I. Such a reading would be supported by the inverted dominant in m. 48 that connects the end of the B section to the beginning of the final A section. Notice that both Sketches 1 and 2 read this chord as a substitution for a root-position dominant, an important interpretive gambit for showing the return of opening material in m. 49. If we were to allow interruption at III, an E-major chord on the first-level middleground would mark the boundary of the B section at m. 48, making unnecessary a misreading that raises the status of the inverted dominant in m. 49 for the sake of showing a thematic return.

Sketches 1 and 2 point out what Michael Riffaterre would call an *ungrammaticality* in the structure of Chopin's etude (Riffaterre 1983, 62, 292); that is, the

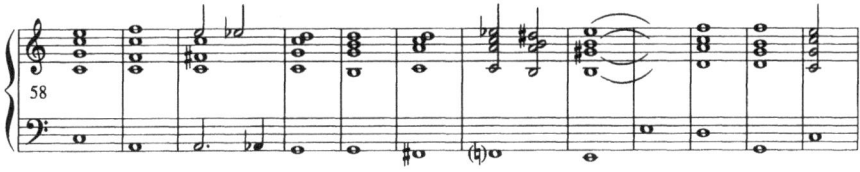

Bass Sketch

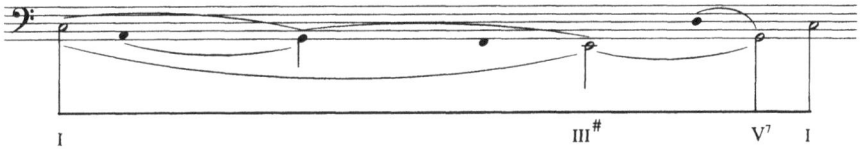

Example 2.7. Bass sketch of Chopin etude, mm. 58–69

phrase in question fails to fit squarely into the syntactic classifications of key and chordal function. Riffaterre suggests that the search for intertextual references on the part of the reader is signaled by such ungrammaticalities, and in Chapter 4 I shall apply this theory to extra-musical meaning. Facing an ungrammaticality, a strangeness, in Chopin's etude, we are prompted to move outward into other texts whose structures might help us to understand better the workings of this musical phrase. In an essay on Chopin's precursors, for example, Simon Finlow reveals that movement from I to III was a common maneuver for etudes in C major, though he does not discuss whether III (E) functions as V/vi on a local level (Finlow 1992, 64–65). A look at Hummel's Etude in C Major, Op. 125, No. 1, which Finlow considers as well, is particularly instructive, since the composer wastes no time in traversing the tonal space from C to E.[24] Example 2.8 reproduces the opening eight measures, which form the short A section of Hummel's etude. As with Chopin's etude, the move to an E-major harmony is accomplished as part of a sequence with a quicker harmonic rhythm in relation to previous material. Although the sequences in the two etudes are of different types, they both move from or through A-minor triads, so that a plausible hearing interprets the E-major triad as a V/vi, forming a half cadence at the end of the first section. The augmented-sixth chords resolving to E in m. 7 complicate this interpretation somewhat. Though the augmented sixth usually functions as a pre-dominant, research by Daniel Harrison, among others, informs us that, in the chromatic harmony of the nineteenth century, the same chord often resolves directly to the tonic (among other possibilities); and some unpublished work by Charles Smith finds the move from augmented sixth to tonic so prevalent that the chord in question is really an altered dominant, forming a musical pun with its pre-dominant cousin.[25] In the case of Hummel's etude, the multiple repetitions of the E-major chord, moving to the augmented sixth, followed by the rests in m. 8 make the same kinds of rhetorical noises that dominant-to-tonic gestures do in cadential passages. Hummel clarifies the status

The Appeal to Structure 41

Example 2.8. Hummel, Etude in C Major, Op. 125, No. 1 (1833)

of E in the next ten measures, where a second sequence moves through another E-major chord, this time with an added seventh marking it as a dominant that eventually resolves to A minor. A final sequence moves down to G, acting as the dominant of the home key that ushers in the thematic reprise.

Much later in the nineteenth century it was still practically obligatory for an etude in C major to make some move to an E-major triad. Moritz Moszkowski's Etude in C Major, Op. 72, No. 8, for example, exhibits such a harmonic structure. During the late nineteenth and early twentieth centuries, Moszkowski's music was central to the pianist's repertoire. The etude in question is an example of a fading intertext that was once vibrant.[26] Already in the first measure of Moszkowski's etude, the figuration of the right hand moves from D#5 to E5 as a harbinger not only of the harmonic moves to come later, but also of this etude's place in an intertext that plays upon a move to E. The first section ends in the dominant (G), from which it proceeds to an E-major triad via some now familiar routines. Example 2.9 is a harmonic reduction of the passage in question, showing that a

Example 2.9. Moszkowski, Etude in C Major, Op. 72, No. 8, B section

sequence moves through dominant sevenths on G, A, and then B, with each arrival marked by an augmented-sixth chord, maintaining its standard role as a pre-dominant. When the B-major triad of m. 24 lands on an E-major harmony in m. 25 with the inception of a new texture, it seems that we have found an etude that marks E unambiguously as a tonic. But in that same measure the introduction of D♮ marks E as a dominant, which then commences a new sequence. Crucial for the discussion that follows is the end of the middle section, mm. 37–40, where the etude returns to an E-major triad that moves directly to a dominant on G, thence back to the home key and the thematic reprise.

Before returning to the structure of Chopin's etude, I shall expand this intertext and move backward in time from Moszkowski to Mendelssohn, whose *Spinnerlied*, Op. 67, No. 3, traverses the harmonic space from C major to E major within a rhythmic perpetual motion that shares the virtuosic style of these etudes. The first of this piece's three sections closes in the tonic, C, and the second section moves directly to a dominant ninth on E, commencing a sequence that moves through A minor without establishing it cadentially. A second sequence reaches the material

Example 2.10. Mendelssohn, *Spinnerlied,* Op. 67, No. 3 (1845), end of B section

of Example 2.10, where E major at last appears as a tonic with its own dominant. A final sequence brings E up by step to F major, and finally to G major, which acts as a dominant that brings in the home key and the thematic reprise.

In review, a number of common procedures form an intertext around Chopin's etude. First, beginning in C major, each piece moves to an E-major triad made prominent by a repetition, a cadence, a pause, or a change in the texture. In most cases the E-major triad reappears near the end of the second formal section before a thematic return. In some cases the function of the various E-major triads fluctuates: in the Moszkowski etude, E sounds first and briefly as a tonic before a seventh marks it as a dominant; in Mendelssohn's character piece, E sounds first as a dominant and later returns as a tonic. Second, sequences characterize the sections that feature harmonic motion to the E-major triad. In Hummel's etude the sequence appears in the first phrase, which cadences on E; the second section also consists primarily of sequential material. In Moszkowski's etude the sequences are confined primarily to the second section, within which E-major triads appear a number of times. In Mendelssohn's *Spinnerlied* sequences within the second section move from and to E, but they are not confined to this section, which includes whole phrases that are transposed versions of previous material. Third, augmented-sixth chords play a role in the harmonic motion to an E-major triad, and in the case of Hummel's etude we may come to hear these chromatic chords as altered dominants. Finally, each of the etudes returns to a prominent E-major triad at the end of the B section, and most of the etudes resort to a second sequence in order to move the E-major triad up to a root-position dominant on G, which resolves to the home key, C.

It is time to take these various strands and return to the two analyses of Chopin's etude that served as a point of departure. Regarding the sequences, Sketch 1 shows a conservative approach to the interaction of design and harmony. Aligning the B section with the A-minor triad of m. 17 corrals the sequences formally, allying Chopin's etude with the staid form of Moszkowski's etude. Sketch 2 marks Chopin as a cousin to Hummel and Mendelssohn, since the sequences spill out from the B section and make their presence felt at the end of the previous section. Concerning the augmented sixth, Sketch 1 avoids the issue somewhat by swallowing that chord within a standard progression of tonic to space filler to dominant (fifth divider). As such, the answer to the status of the E-major chord in m. 23 is decisive: E is the dominant of A and remains so through the end of m. 47. This answer spreads to other etudes in the intertext. In Mendelssohn's *Spinnerlied,* for example, we begin to hear the entire second section as resting on the dominant of A, despite the fact that no cadence confirms that key. In Sketch 2 the augmented sixth comes to the fore and functions like an altered dominant that leads to E as a structural point. The same sketch shows how Chopin's etude expands this issue of the augmented sixth, since that chord unfolds over the course of mm. 17–22. A weakness in the sketch is that it shows a pre-prolongation, so that the function of mm. 17–21 becomes clarified only at m. 22. Sketch 1 has no such weakness. Sketch 2's response to the augmented-sixth question also spreads through the intertext. In Hummel's etude, for example, we may be more inclined to hear E in m. 8 as a tonic, as the augmented-sixth chords surrounding it take on a dominant function.

Finally, turning to the chords of m. 48 that complete the second section of Chopin's etude, we find that both sketches show a root-position dominant seventh, where an inverted dominant actually appears. Further, Sketch 1 interpolates a II chord that has no existence whatsoever in these measures. Contemplating first the interpolated chord, we can guess that Schenker in Sketch 1 was looking ahead to the end of the etude, where a III chord in mm. 65–66 moves to II–V–I, closing the piece harmonically before the coda (see Example 2.7). By interpolating the II chord at the end of the B section, Sketch 1 also includes a proper preparation for the F_5 in the dominant seventh of m. 48. As for the root-position dominants that appear almost unaccountably in both sketches, the intertext formed by the other etudes shows us that Chopin has troped the usual exit of E major. In all cases E moved to a root-position dominant on G, often achieved by sequence. Chopin opts out of the sequence from E to G, and perhaps finding the root-position dominant too closural, he inverts the seventh chord and saves the root-position dominant for the end of the etude. From the Schenkerian perspective, this inverted dominant changes everything: though it heads for the thematic return in the home key, the inverted chord can have no structural weight to signal an interruption or an upper-voice neighbor on the first-level middleground. Though Sketch 1 places the dominant in m. 48 in root position, it stops short of placing it on the first-level middleground. Sketch 2, however, responds to the intertext around Chopin's etude and claims outrageously that the chord in that measure not only stands in for a root-position dominant but also does so as an event on the first-level middleground.

Following poststructuralist practice, we might argue that since both readings necessarily marginalize features of the etude, neither deserves to be privileged.

Contrary to some very fine theoretical work that attempts to articulate criteria for choosing between two or more conflicting analyses, intertextual readings are reluctant to settle for either/or and more content to revel in either/nor, neither/or.[27] As I have tried to explain, in offering two Schenkerian analyses it has not been my intention to embark on the anachronism of blaming Schenker for failing to account for postmodern critiques of structuralist thought. It is only natural that, coming from a different perspective, Sketch 2 often comes out the winner in responding to an intertext that I have set up around Chopin's etude. For all efforts to follow Schenkerian practice, though, Sketch 2 is not Schenkerian, because it was forged not only in the light of the *Ursatz* but also in the heat of a small intertext, calling into question the very structures that it sustains.

There is a terrible Freudian ambivalence about the way this analysis has both embraced and rejected an appeal to structure. Refusal to give up on the music-analytic structuralist project even while embracing postmodern trends has received some thoughtful analysis by Adam Krims (1998). Although I believe theories of intertextuality offer one means of responding to what he sees as a failure in music theory to integrate adequately poststructuralist critique into analytical paradigms, much of the analysis offered here is formalist/structuralist through and through. I hope to have shown, however, that there can be no single structure of a musical text. When we read attempts at such an analysis, we have the right to wonder what ecology of pieces has formed the intertext for the analyst. When we are offered a single structure for a text, we must ask what voices in that intertext have been lost to a quest for unity.

5

I would like to awaken an intertext suggested by the ecology metaphor at the end of the previous section. Common to much music theory for nearly two decades has been a response, be it defense, concession, or counterattack, to some now canonical writing by Joseph Kerman:

> Music's autonomous structure is only one of many elements that contribute to its import. Along with preoccupation with structure goes the neglect of other vital matters—not only the whole historical complex referred to above, but also everything else that makes music affective, moving, emotional, expressive. By removing the bare score from its context in order to examine it as an autonomous organism, the analyst removes that organism from the ecology that sustains it. (Kerman 1985, 73)

One wonders how surprised Kerman might be that music theory's responses to his detailed polemic in *Contemplating Music* have been so varied and sustained. How odd, for example, to see that Matthew Brown, Douglas Dempster, and Dave Headlam feel compelled to refer to Kerman's book at the end of an article that proposes a method for confirming scientific hypotheses culled from Schenker's writings, as if shoring up Schenkerian analysis somehow addresses Kerman's objective to move musicology away from its positivist roots and toward culturally "thick" interpretations of music.[28] How strangely appropriate is Lee Blasius's decision to conclude his *Schenker's Argument* (1996) with a closely argued account of Kerman's critique in relation to Forte's equally canonical "Schenker's Conception of Musical Structure" (1959), as if these polemics were somehow bound up with the cultural, ideological, and historical contexts that underpin Schenker's thought.

If, for a number of theorists, responses to Kerman's *Contemplating Music* seem out of proportion now, the reason is not only that it is nearly two decades since publication of the book, which even Kerman had guessed would remain part of active debate for a period of only about ten years, but also that so much of his proposal for musicology seems tame today, and further that certain theorists even in the early 1980s had already begun to explore areas that resonated with the tones of his new musicological paradigm (Kerman 1985, 221). Kerman's conviction that the most interesting work will be found at the points of contact between musicology, ethnomusicology, and music theory and his exhortation to members of those fields to turn their attention to criticism, interpretation, and meaning are an accepted part of the academic musical landscape today. To pick at random among dozens of publications in music theory, for example, Patrick McCreless's "A Candidate for the Canon?" (1997a), which combines a penetrating analysis of Schubert's *Fantasie* for violin and piano with a re-creation of the historical context of the piece in service of some insightful critical evaluations, fits remarkably the new paradigm that Kerman describes. If contributions like McCreless's fail to make up the lion's share of music theory today, they are at least prevalent enough to mark a trend. And we perhaps give Kerman too much credit for such work. Can he really have been oblivious, for example, to Leonard Ratner's contribution to style, expression, and meaning in *Classic Music* (1980), which would form obvious intertexts with later work like Agawu's *Playing with Signs* (1991), Hatten's *Musical Meaning in Beethoven* (1994), and Monelle's *The Sense of Music* (2000)?[29] These books are a far cry from the philosophical base of those myopic, structure-driven theorists that Kerman finds so objectionable.

Inevitably one suspects that there is more than a claim to music criticism that drives the various responses to Kerman's work still appearing today, and it may be that another piece of first-rate work by McCreless offers clues to just what is at stake. In his "Rethinking Contemporary Music Theory" (1997b), McCreless proposes that the tensions between theory and new musicology today might be mapped onto the tensions between modernism and postmodernism. A rather lengthy portion of this argument is worth reviewing:

> Modern theory, as a product of the 1950s and 1960s, predictably bears a distinctive stamp of structuralism and formalism; it has been grounded philosophically in the same positivism that for so long guided historical musicology, except that theory has leaned toward the model of sciences, developing and extending explicit and testable theories for analysis, while musicology followed a more humanistically based program and concerned itself less with theory proper than with a positivist view of what constitutes historical data and how that data may be organized into historical "facts." The new musicology, on the other hand, as a child of the 1980s, exhibits the traits of post-

modernist thought: rejection of the structural autonomy and immanent meaning of the work of art, questioning of the received canon of works, concern with surfaces rather than deep structures, and viewing the work less as a self-contained coherent whole than as a complex product of the signifying practices and social norms of a particular culture. In their approach to the work, then, modern theory and the new musicology are respectively modernist and postmodernist. (McCreless 1997b, 42–43)

McCreless is the first to say that this opposition is ready for deconstruction, since there is research on both sides that fails to fit squarely into modern or postmodern paradigms. A growing trend in music theory to examine popular music, for example, opens the canon in ways that are in line with postmodernism, although the impulse in some of this work simply to bring the same structuralist techniques to this repertoire belies an unwillingness to adopt wholeheartedly postmodern poetics. On the side of musicology the association between Kerman's work and postmodernism is also overstated somewhat, I believe. Although McCreless is right in claiming that much of the new musicology is postmodern, Kerman never mentions postmodernism in his *Contemplating Music*. The association seems to have been pushed back to this book simply because the term *new musicology* appears with some fanfare at the end of a section devoted to musicology and criticism (Kerman 1985, 134). Nevertheless, the tension between modernism and postmodernism does appear to account for some responses to Kerman's work. Regarding Brown, Dempster, and Headlam's abrupt turn toward Kerman's *Contemplating Music* in their "♯IV (♭V) Hypothesis," for example, an intertext with McCreless's "Rethinking Contemporary Music Theory" makes the subtext of their thoughts clear: they will have nothing to do with the postmodernism conjured up by Kerman's new musicology; instead they will retrench music theory in the modernist appeal to science. The strategy may be understandable enough, since who can resist the well-trodden path of logical analysis, coupled with observations of data culled from the immanent artwork in the service of pronouncements that have the ring of truth?

Among those in academia who still wish to maintain a distinction between music theory and musicology, there are a growing number who are concerned that if the strategy of music theory is simply to stay the modernist course through the postmodern storm, then the discipline may well find itself falling outside the intellectual milieu that surrounds it, until music theory becomes a virtual anachronism. For those in music theory interested in staking their own clams to postmodern territory, some gambits seem facile enough. We can read the growing trend to include for analysis repertoires that are sensitive to popular culture, gender studies, and ethnomusicology as a response to the challenges of postmodernism. Despite this and other trends, however, the single most problematic portion of music-theoretic paradigms in relation to postmodernism is analysis. Many writers (Kevin Korsyn, Adam Krims, Richard Littlefield, Judy Lockhead, Alan Street, and Rose Subotnik, to name a few) have pondered just what postmodern analysis looks like. But if music theory takes seriously the postmodern emphasis on surfaces, then much of the hard-won achievements in the creation of music-analytic machinery, from Schenkerian graphs to Lewinian networks, must be lost in an effort to forgo unity, organicism, and the concomitant assumptions of deep structure. If these analytical techniques were to be lost, it would be difficult to see what differentiates the music theorist from the musicologist, unless theory concentrates its energies in perception and acoustics, musicianship and pedagogy.

The problem of postmodern music analysis helps situate this chapter's exploration of intertextuality. Though the analyses presented here are far from the postmodern ones that many try to envision, a broader definition of intertextuality within these analyses does point to ways in which deep structures can participate in the very critique that is their undoing. When we willfully misread Bloom's aphorism and claim that the structure of a piece of music is another structure, we do more than color structural analysis with a passing reference to literary theory in the hope of achieving the aura, if not the substance, of an interdisciplinary perspective. Instead we commence an argument whose assumptions implicate music analysis in the postmodern strategy to contextualize language, art, music, culture, and meaning. Structures are culturally situated. Structures are promiscuous. Structures are critiques of other structures. A theorist is not a modernist because she finds a deep structure for music, but because she curtails promiscuity by reducing music's multivalent structures to univocal utterances. A theorist is not a postmodernist because she denies deep structures for music, but because she allows them to proliferate and to call forth their progeny.

In the metaphors of these last sentences it must be clear that intertextuality participates in a gendered discourse. One of the metaphors that recurs in poetics from ancient Greece to the present day likens the poet's use of sources to western man's (and here the masculine gender is important) imaginings of the woman's role during sex. The poet who borrows is passive, he feminizes himself by allowing another voice to enter him. To Plato the poet is a "Bacchic maiden," to Bloom the ephebe is "flooded." This feminizing threat is sometimes veiled by a more virile, masculine metaphor: the models of the apprentice writer are territories to be conquered. These opposing metaphors are often combined into a narrative that attempts to characterize the artistic life of the great composer: the young ephebe is flooded with the voices of his older masters, but with much effort he overpowers the feminizing threat of these models and achieves his own univocal, masculine voice, which ever after threatens to drown out the voices of younger poets. From this gendered discourse of intertextuality, we might show that analyses that are intent on presenting unified, single structures collaborate with meta-narratives that marginalize the feminine characteristics of composing music. Part of such a study will surely be an examination of the ways in which analysis normalizes strangeness, marginalizes anomaly, and resolves aporia.

Where gender was, there shall power be. The will to unified structures is the wielding of a power over the untamed surface of music. It is no surprise, then, that I suggest intertextuality's place in pointing to power relations in regard not only to a metaphysics of analysis but also to a theory of canon formation. Concerning the latter, although I am not comfortable with claiming that power relations alone account for a canon that includes Chopin's etude at the expense of Hummel's, I do believe that insight can be gained from a study of those spheres (economic, political, social, sexual) that affect the intertexts available to us at any time. In areas from (post-)structuralism to gender and power, from the contexts of history to those of analysis, intertextuality offers new avenues of inquiry. Though I have tried to shed light in this chapter on those avenues that affect structural analysis, I hasten to point out that, by its very nature, a description of intertextuality and its implications must remain incomplete. But the impossibility of mastering the topic, like that of mastering analysis, must not lead us into acts that either tame or abandon it too readily. One of the tenets of intertextuality is that texts release meaning when surrounded by other texts, and this vantage point seems no less true for those who would reduce meaning to a structure.

3 On Codes, Topics, and Leaps of Interpretation

Every sign *by itself* seems dead. *What* gives it life?—In use it is *alive*. Is life breathed into it there?—Or is the *use* its life?

—Ludwig Wittgenstein (*Philosophical Investigations*, §432)

The wheelbarrow, the lawnmower, the sound of poplar trees, leaves whitening before rain, rooks cawing, brooms knocking, dresses rustling—all these were so coloured and distinguished in his mind that he had already his private code, his secret language.

—Virginia Woolf (*To the Lighthouse*, 9-10)

1

A code is a convention of communication that organizes signs into a system correlating signifiers to signifieds within a particular cultural domain. The term *code* is oppositional to *message* and aligns itself with other semiotic oppositions: *langue* versus *parole, type* versus *token, style* versus *strategy, synchronic* versus *diachronic.* A code is a synchronic sign system within a language, a type within a style. The *Encyclopedic Dictionary of Semiotics* invites us first to understand codes in terms of elementary set theory, where one set contains elements called signifiers while another contains elements called signifieds (Krampen 1994, 125–27). Under this conception a code is a conventional way of mapping the signifiers from one set onto the signifieds in the other. Early theories of semiotic codes barely ranged beyond this simple conception, which implies that meaning is nothing more than a decoding exercise, as if one looks up the signified for a signifier in a dictionary of codes.[1] Viewed as such, codes are authoritarian objects that limit interpretive freedom and imply hypostasized meaning.

Umberto Eco's *A Theory of Semiotics* (1976) develops a more nuanced theory of codes, in which both the producer and the receiver of a text bring to it their own conventions of interpretation. Codes not only organize signs but also "provide the rules which *generate* signs as concrete occurrences in communicative intercourse" (Eco 1976, 49). It is by a code that we recognize a sign as a sign, and it is within a code that we situate the sign by an act of semiosis. Following Peircean semiotics, Eco's theory empties the sign of its content, making it a node in a network of signs that interpret one another.[2] The meaning of a sign is another sign and another sign within that network, of which a code is a provisional picture. Signs seem dead by themselves. Signs come to life with their use in an ecology of signs.

Even Eco's more fluid theory has been the target of critique, however, in musicology most notably by Jean-Jacques Nattiez, who finds Eco's gathering of codes with their limitless expansion of signs as interpretants too unwieldy to be efficacious in modeling communication (Nattiez 1990b, 19–28). What is the point of a code that limits interpretation, if that code itself is potentially limitless? Read cynically, Nattiez's critique of Eco's theory is a Bloomian misreading, in which space is made in a crowded field for the semiological tripartition as a model of communication. Nattiez admits, for example, that Eco's theory accounts for the possibility that a code may be different for addresser and receiver, pointing to implicit poietic and esthesic levels in that theory (21). Striking too is Nattiez's definition of denotation as a *"constellation of interpretants that are common to the poietic and the esthesic"* (24). But what is that constellation of interpretants in Nattiez's definition, if not a code? A code is a constellation, a configuration of signs around a sign.[3] A message is a text of empty signs to which the reader brings her codes. As the reader and her codes produce both the text and her sense of the text, those codes are open to the possibility of redistribution by that very text. Eco is cautious in describing these codes, avoiding implications of crystalline structures that guarantee meaning.[4] Alert to Eco's unwillingness to pin down codes, Nattiez attributes to the theory an epistemological blind spot that forces Eco's semiology to consider only the immanent level of communication while at the same time finding that level inadequate to the task.

Nattiez overstates the case against Eco's theory, but his point is clear: any attempt to situate codes on the immanent level alone risks sustaining an illusion that meaning and communication can ever be unquestioned. David Lidov rather harshly characterizes Nattiez's work as a "pathological semiotics" that refuses to acknowledge how often we do seem to share strategies of interpretation, making us feel as if we have common experiences even with intractable artworks (Lidov 1999, 64–65). A code is a desire for community. Though we may revel in our freedom to interpret artworks by a personal code, in the end our readings reach out to that imagined other who might understand the artwork as we have.[5] Imagination shudders at the prospect of explaining the semiosis of the text without some recourse to codes, even if conditional, hypothetical, and open to limitless expansion into subcodes.

Robert Samuels is more sympathetic to Eco's theory and recognizes the freedom that it grants the reader in her ways of making sense of the text (Samuels 1995, 6–8). Samuels's work allows for the intertextual nature of codes, a topic I shall revisit shortly. Of interest here, though, is his acknowledgment that Eco allows culture and ideology to play a role in semiotic codes. In Eco's theory not even the traffic light affords opportunity for simple assignments between signifieds and signifiers. Figure 3.1 is adapted from Eco's provisional picture of a code for the traffic light (Eco 1976, 128). The figure is a diagram only and ought not be taken as a formal model or graph of a code (see Lidov 1999, 196–98). Words within nodes are signs, and lines connect those signs to other signs as interpretants. Distance between nodes only roughly pictures how closely the signs within them are associated.[6] The figure shows *green* versus *red* as an oppositional node within a network

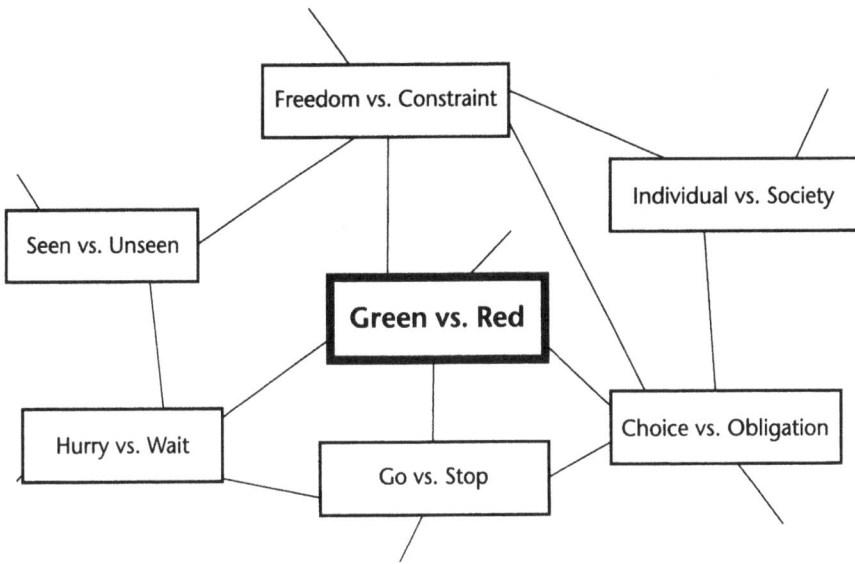

Figure 3.1. Code for the Traffic Light

of signs. Among the other nodes we find *go* versus *stop* in what Eco describes as an "international code" (Eco 1976, 127). But this opposition brings in other signs. Shall we *hurry* through the traffic light, or shall we *wait*? Do we feel an *obligation* to stop, or do we have a *choice*? Does that obligation, if so felt, depend upon whether we feel *seen* or *unseen*? Is the traffic light an affront to our personal *freedom,* or does it reestablish a necessary *constraint* upon society? Each of the nodes in this network participates in its own code. For example, *individual* versus *society* brings with it other signs in a web of interpretants that are only suggested by lines leading outward in the figure. Thus the code for the traffic light has potential to commence unlimited semiosis by which the web of signs branching out of *stop* versus *go* reach ever outward to more signs. Traffic lights, it seems, are complex animals.

The code as pictured in Figure 3.1 is necessarily provisional and incomplete as it situates the traffic light within a perspective, an ideology. We might well argue that, within any private code for the traffic light, the irreducible remainder will always be *go* versus *stop*, pointing to a conclusion that the code ought encompass no more than those signs. But such a purely immanent code, the only probable signs common to the limitless personal codes for the traffic light, misses utterly the sense of this sign from a point of view within a culture. Even for a child, the traffic light is more than a simple sign for *go* versus *stop*. The traffic light is also the site of danger or safety, where the impersonal affront of a monstrous steely object on wheels has the potential to rend life and limb.

When Eco pictured a code for the traffic light, he made no effort toward intersubjective analysis, no recourse to documents or eyewitnesses in order to confirm a conventional organization for that sign. As a member of the culture within which traffic lights are active, Eco knew well the signs that form a network around them. Even from his perspective he could imagine other stances within his culture that might bring different codes to the traffic light. People working with implicit or explicit theories of codes would say that Eco is competent with the traffic light within his culture. That word *competent* will be its own nexus for the problems of codes, particularly with regard to artistic texts. Michael Riffaterre, alluding to Roman Jakobson's well-known schema of communication, reminds us that artistic texts often reduce the elements of that schema to two: the message and the reader.[7] We are left to reconstruct the author, the codes of a culture, and the context of a text. Every serious effort at understanding interpretation, though, recognizes, as does Riffaterre, that "we cannot hope to reconstruct the code they [the text's first readers] used, at least not well enough for our purposes, and evidence of their re-actions is also fragmentary."[8] If we wish to invoke a code as a convention, we need to posit a reader whose competency includes that code.[9] But the exact constitution of this competent reader is often vague, becoming a mask for the interpreting critic: the competent reader is exactly that person within a culture who attended to this text in just the way that I have attended to it.

Who hears these codes? The creation of a hypothetical and competent listener who is the answer to this question involves a historical stance whose problematics are familiar to hermeneutics. Realizing that a code is a convention would seem to make imperative a hermeneutics of recovery, a rediscovery of how people once un-derstood an artwork by reconstructing its original context and its conventions of interpretation. Robert Hatten, for example, writes of his hermeneutic-semiotic project:

> I am developing a modern theory of meaning compatible with Peircean semiotic theory, and applying that theory to the historical reconstruction of an interpretive competency adequate to the understanding of Beethoven's works in his time. (Hatten 1994, 3)

In the first chapter, though, Hatten makes a gambit that exposes the difficulties involved in reconstructing that interpretive competency. The chapter is an inter-pretation of the third movement of Beethoven's *Hammerklavier*, in which he writes:

> If the interpretive journey has been convincing to this point, one reason is that all the outstanding or salient structural events have been related to an overarching hypothe-sis. (28)

To which we might ask, Convincing to whom? Surely Hatten means convincing to us, his readers. And his interpretation is convincing, even brilliant. But we his read-ers are in no historical position to judge this interpretive journey. Of course, docu-ments give us an idea, refracted through another interpretation, of how listeners understood Beethoven's music in his time. Hatten could be asking if we find his interpretive journey to have convincing resonance with an understanding culled from these documents. I suspect, though, that this text wishes the interpretation to be convincing both to us and to our notions of how Beethoven's contemporaries heard his music. We can hear the music this way, and we can believe that Beethoven's contemporaries also heard it this way.

But one wonders, in that case, how many in Beethoven's time cared to listen in the way that we do, to grasp the fullness of meanings in the unfolding of musical time. Daniel Chua's work on absolute music reminds us how often the topical interplay of the classical style was apprehended as a riot, an unintelligible mess. Thus, for example, "Fontenelle confronted the sonata not because it signified nothing, but because it signified too much" (Chua 1999, 63). Our Derridian visions of the unfixed sign pointing everywhere at once become the measure of how fragile musical meaning can be, even to those listeners born within the time and place of the historical work. Jonathan Culler's critique of Norman Holland's *Five Readers Reading* shows how precarious is a project to uncover competency even in our own time. And Culler's pragmatic suggestion that the semiotician ought study her own competency, since "one's notions of how to read and of what is involved in interpretation are acquired in commerce with others," suggests that all along what we hope to reconstruct is not the responses of the anonymous and unknown dead, but our own responses as they might be if we could cast ourselves back through time (Culler 1981, 52–53).

Even if the only competency we can ever know is our own, though, we ought not delude ourselves into believing that we can turn our backs on the past. Understanding of a text's original historical-cultural context is both an end to itself and a means of determining where we are in relation to where we have been. In addition, Roger Scruton, reflecting on how willingly we divest our interpretive energies into reviving the past, compares artistic contemplation to religious ritual and reasons that changes in either disturb us because they deny a connection between the living and the dead, implying that one day we too will be cast aside (Scruton 1997, 461). Thus an ethical dimension comes into play in acts of interpretation. For Fredric Jameson that ethical dimension is more than a mere moralizing around interpretation; it is an often unremarked, but questionable, ideal that certain ways of coding the text are at once transhistorical, human, and natural (Jameson 1981, 59–60). This ethics of interpretation blinds itself to the political, historical, and social conditions that underpin our notions of the immutable self. But when Jameson opens *The Political Unconscious* with the warning "Always historicize!" it soon becomes clear that he has no interest in reviving historical codes of interpretation except to the extent that they illustrate how often a dominant ideology hides itself from the first readers of a text. In its use, a code as convention conceals its ideology. Jameson's historicized text is no hermeneutics of recovery but a hermeneutics of suspicion. When we bring the text back to life so that it can "deliver its long forgotten message in surroundings utterly alien to it," we do so in order to hear lost issues of economy, production, culture, and ideology (Jameson 1981, 19). Since both the text and its first readers may be blind to these issues, it is not a matter of reviving an aesthetic stance, or rediscovering a conventional interpretation, except to the extent that those revivals bear witness to that very blindness.

We are left with multiple stances on the conventions of codes and the competency involved in their use and development. We hope to study our own conventions of interpretation, or we hope to uncover historical ones. We accept these conventions as ways of understanding a text, or we view them with a suspicion that they hide an ideology. We view ourselves as more capable than our ancestors with texts, or we view the dead as the true inheritors of an unproblematic meaning. The text in the past is stable, or it is shifting. And so we cannot speak of a code of interpretation but only of codes of interpretation. A theory of a code is a theory of history.

2

A topic is a semiotic code that associates a conventional label with a constellation of musical signs. Topics of musical discourse have become an accepted part of the study of eighteenth-century music, while recent research pushes their scope back to the seventeenth century (Barnett 2002). In addition, Raymond Monelle (2000) and Robert Samuels (1995) develop topics in nineteenth-century music, and it is surely the case that much twentieth-century music relies on topics as well. Monelle openly defines a topic of musical discourse as a semiotic code, calling it "essentially a symbol, its iconic or indexical features governed by convention and thus by rule" (Monelle 2000, 17). Kofi Agawu (1991) studiously avoids the word *code* in his semiotic interpretation of topics until a discussion of how we might extend topical theory to the study of Romantic music; nevertheless, his exposition of topics is consistent with a theory of codes. For example, Agawu defines a topic as a musical sign whose "signified is designated by conventional labels" (Agawu 1991, 49). Agawu's inclusion of a provisional universe of topics in his discussion is also allusive to theories of codes (30). Codes are sign systems that earn their sense within a universe of other codes.

Within a universe of codes there is an economy of the musical sign that allows it to participate in more than one topic. The diminished-seventh chord, for example, figures in the code for *Sturm und Drang* as well as that for *ombra;* the topical fields around this chord narrow in the presence of other signs within a musical text. A sign is empty until placed within a code, and often the economy of signs within a universe of codes demands interpretive effort of the reader. For example, the last movement of Schubert's Piano Sonata in C Minor, D. 958, begins with the theme shown in Example 3.1. The $\frac{6}{8}$ meter, the persistent triplets, and the iambic rhythm of the right hand are musical signs that belong both to the topic of the horse and to that of the tarantella.[10] We cast about in the musical text for other signs that might narrow the topic to one or the other. Tarantellas in nineteenth-century piano music tend to be marked Presto or Vivace; they have a salient virtuosity often including scalar passages; tarantellas are sectional and may include modal mixture; they may appear as the final movement of a larger work, as in Weber's Sonata in E Minor, Op. 70 (Schwandt 1980). None of this is as helpful as it might appear. Schubert's movement has its moments of difficulty, but it evinces little overt technical display. Although the tempo of the movement is only Allegro, a performer may well decide to take a topical clue and push the music toward a more frenzied pace. As for modal mixture evident later in the theme, it is also a sign within Schu-

Example 3.1. Schubert, Sonata in C Minor, D. 958 (1828), IV

bert's musical idiolect, his stylistic code. Lacking conclusive evidence to fix a topic within this text, we turn to an intertext. Schubert's celebrated references to the horse topic in "Erlkönig" and "An Schwager Kronos" suggest that topic in the sonata. In addition, rhythms similar to those of the sonata's opening theme appear in Schumann's "Wilder Reiter." The cultural intertext around Schubert's sonata suggests alignment with the horse topic. When pressed to choose one topic for the first theme of the sonata movement, we discover that topical discourse requires interpretive efforts that go beyond a simple mapping of musical signifiers onto signifieds. Decoding and interpreting are interrelated acts (see Hatten 1994, 33, 269–73).

If both of theses topics in the first theme of Schubert's sonata were clearly defined, we might safely invoke Hatten's conception of musical metaphor, which brings together two previously unrelated topics in an integrative meaning at a higher level (Hatten 1994, 162–72; 1995). In another economy of signs the town of Taranto has given its name both to the tarantella and to the tarantula, possibly giving rise to the now discredited idea that the dance was used to cure the bite of the arachnid. The misconception goes back at least to the seventeenth century, and Erich Schwandt (1980) cites eight songs by Athanasius Kircher (1601–1680) that were written to cure tarantism. Allowing the deathly threat to remain within the code for the tarantella allows for a reading of topical interplay within Schubert's sonata movement, in which the horse, the dance, and the threat of death come together in a new pertinence. Remembering that these signs often point to expressions, and that the topics are about neither the horse nor the dance, but about the thrill of a journey by horse or the ominous excitement of a dance warding off death, we arrive at an expression of a threatening yet thrilling journey. Inevitably such a reading brings us back to the intertext with Schubert's "Erlkönig," and that connection will inform a more detailed interpretation of this sonata movement in

Chapter 4. Strictly, though, in Hatten's terms the theme from the sonata is no metaphor since neither topic is clearly defined. Rather, both topics are invoked metonymically as the economy and emptiness of topical signs allow the coexistence of more than one topic within the same musical figures.

The question of how we uncover topics is one to which Monelle turns before developing a perspective on topical discourse in nineteenth-century music.[11] Praising Leonard Ratner's study of eighteenth-century topics, Monelle both questions a methodology that turns first to theorists contemporaneous with a musical text and wonders at the extent to which Ratner has really found documentation within such texts. Nonetheless, Monelle broadly accepts Ratner's model in which the study of topics ultimately is "based on an observation of the music, not on a reading of the books, which is surely the right way to do music theory" (Monelle 2000, 27). Monelle's reading of Ratner's work uncovers how often the "American master" trusted first his own competency in defining the topics of musical discourse. The rediscovery of a topic, a code of communication, begins with such a belief in one's interpretive ability before turning to a fuller cultural study of the code in question. In essence, uncovering and developing codes in musical texts requires first a leap of interpretation based on experience, or what Charles Peirce called *abduction*.

Abduction is insight, an interpretive leap that hopes to account for phenomena by bringing together what no one before has thought to bring together (Peirce 1955, 304). Peirce, who had an affinity for trichotomies, situated abduction within a field of logic that included deduction and induction. In Peirce's model, which concerns itself with structuring scientific thought, we begin with data and abduct an informed hypothesis:

> The first starting of a hypothesis and the entertaining of it, whether as a simple interrogation or with any degree of confidence, is an inferential step which I propose to call abduction. (151)

Given this hypothesis we deduce a plausible consequence that would arise if the interpretation were true. Finally, through scientific experimentation we induce support for that hypothesis, confirming it until an unaccountable phenomenon requires another logical act of abduction.[12] For Peirce, abduction is the only way to explain how scientific thought can proceed from the known to the unknown. Facing the unexplained, the scientist must make an imaginative leap in the formation of a hypothesis.

Though Peirce developed his trichotomy of logic as a model for science, his concept of abduction is suggestive for semiotics and interpretation as well. David Lidov offers the example that, given a message and a code, we can deduce a meaning with certainty. Lacking a code, however, we might induce one if we notice that certain signs in a message are understandable with modification to a previous code. But if inductive methods are unsuccessful, we must abduct a code, by positing a hypothesis (Lidov 1999, 202–203). Lidov's example has the unfortunate implication that interpretive codes are stable, and therefore deductive. For some codes this is undoubtedly true, but for many we must face not only Nattiez's warnings against assuming a stable correspondence between the poietic and esthesic levels but also the problems inherent in an economy of signs. Still, Lidov's example suggests a methodology for the study of topics as codes. Given a sign without a code, we make a leap of interpretation and abduct one. Given the interpretive hypothesis that comes from abduction, we search for examples of like signs in other texts that will inductively validate that hypothesis. If we are careless, we might take an inductively verified code to be a monument of meaning and view it as a deductive route to an interpretation that lies beyond question.

Eco abducts Peircean abduction for his study of semiotic codes, and Hatten borrows it as well for an insightful discussion of style expansion, couched within his theory of markedness and correlation (Eco 1976, 129–33; Hatten 1994, 257–68). For Eco, abduction explains how we deal with what he calls *overcoding* and *undercoding*. In the first instance the interpreter of a text challenges an existing code in order to advance a more comprehensive one. In the second instance the interpreter of a text faces signs that are uncoded and must hypothesize a code in order to make those signs understandable. Both of these maneuvers involve abduction. Hatten fleshes out Eco's theory by describing a semiotic sequence of events in which a listener competent in a style hears a unique token (sign), interprets its significant features, and abducts a meaning. Further, when the novelty of that token is set as a marked opposition within the style, it becomes a new type, a code (Hatten 1994, 261–62). The extension that I propose here is that abduction involves forming an intertext. As we ponder the unknown sign, we seek its intertext throughout the repertoire. As we develop a code for that sign, we surround it with its likeness in other texts.

We gain a glimpse of the way intertexts inform our coding of music by studying an e-mail thread that ran through the Society for Music Theory list during a two-week period in June 2003.[13] Paul Rinzler began the thread in question by asking members if they were aware of any precedents to a progression in the Beatles' song "Hey Jude." The ensuing "Hey Jude" thread included fifty-one posts contributed by twenty-six members of the SMT list, among whom were many with a publication presence in the study of pop music. The tone of the thread is a model of civility, in which contributors acknowledge differences of opinion without recourse to ad hominem attacks. Rinzler asks the members to respond with the earliest instance of a I-↓VII–IV–I progression that appears in the closing vamp of "Hey Jude." Ostensibly he expresses a motivation to reinforce the artistic greatness of the Beatles by imagining that they have originated the progression, though he admits that it is likely that more knowledgeable listeners will correct his assumption. In addition, Rinzler expresses that a second motivation for the question wonders at the extent to which the "Hey Jude" progression might be involved in psychological/ affective responses he had to the closing vamp as a teenager. We might reframe Rinzler's question, characterizing it as an appeal to establish the rarity, or markedness, of the "Hey Jude" progression. If the progression were unique, it would be proof of the Beatles' artistic originality, and it would be an instance of an undercoded sign requiring abductive hypothesis for its meaning. If the progression were one of many, it would be a token of a musical topic, a code suggesting a meaning. In the presence of what he took to be a striking harmonic phenomenon, Rinzler sought an intertext.

Jonathan Bernard and Harold Owen quickly offer precedents to the progression, citing The Who's "I Can't Explain" and Orlando di Lasso's "Bon jour mon coeur," respectively. The range of these opening responses illustrates divergent strategies of competency: we hear a work within a style and seek its intertext historically, or we hear a work canonically and seek its intertext transhistorically. The latter approach has associations with canon formation because it tends to situate artworks within a historical totality.[14] Though later postings tend to favor examples within the style of "Hey Jude," a number of posts refer to music outside of the style. An intertext of nearly thirty works includes allusions to the progression in everything from Jimi Hendrix's "Manic Depression," to Richard Wagner's *Parsifal,* to European folk songs of the seventeenth century. The historical and stylistic breadth of the intertext around "Hey Jude" underscores a tension among the posts as contributors consider the extent to which syntactic codes for classical music are appropriate for understanding the harmonic practice of the Beatles. Tim Sullivan, for example, offers persuasive emic evidence that the harmonic code of the tonal repertoire distorts "Hey Jude" because pop musicians use the guitar, which allows for different harmonic norms than the piano.[15] Tim Hughes adds that the concept of key is highly fluid in popular music. Walter Everett, though, responds with evidence that "Hey Jude" was composed at the piano; in addition, he argues that any understanding of tonal function ought not limit itself to the outlook of the composer.

Most of the posts to the "Hey Jude" thread consider syntactic codes in understanding the vamp progression, with some consensus taking its striking feature to be the subtonic harmony, $\flat$VII. Theories suggested in the thread situate that chord within blues codes, modal codes, or within tonal ones (the chord as a secondary subdominant, or as an instance of mixture). When Daniel Wolf finally turns the discussion toward the psychological effect of the progression, Rinzler responds with "Daniel Wolf wins the prize," because no previous post has considered the affective motivation behind his opening question. Picking up this issue, Daniel E. Mathers suggests that the closing section of "Hey Jude" falls within a musical topic that he calls "let it all hang out." Having moved to the semantic level, Mathers brings in an intertext with the chorus "Let the Sunshine in," whose effect rests on a different harmonic progression, by which the minor vi moves to the major I. Despite harmonic differences, "Let the Sunshine in" and "Hey Jude" share plagal progressions, leading Mathers to hypothesize that the subdominant pole of much rock music lends itself to a "super-relaxed character" in tune with the "waist-down oriented posture of rock . . . rather than the . . . dominant-driven bearing of Classical ballet." Again we see a tension between different stylistic codes as the "Hey Jude" progression shows itself as relatively unmarked within rock music, but marked within the style of classical music, though even this interstylistic markedness fails to account for the increasing use of subdominant harmony in the nineteenth century (see Bailey 1985b, 119–21). Within the style the markedness of the "Hey Jude" progression rests on its ritual repetitions throughout the closing vamp, a feature it shares with "Let the Sunshine in." In addition, Rinzler admits that the context of listening to "Hey Jude" in the 1960s predisposed him toward an altered consciousness while attending to the vamp progression. Though we might be attracted to a theory of codes that concerns itself only with the text, we soon find it difficult to ignore the cultural and ideological contexts that influence our coding of the text.

From this lively e-mail thread on the "Hey Jude" progression, we learn how issues of intertext, competency, style, methodology, and insight are woven into our coding of music. In the presence of a sign that appears to us as unknown, special, unusual, or striking, we are motivated to form an intertext that will contextualize that sign and place it within a code. In Chapter 4 I shall revisit this issue within a theory of strangeness borrowed from Riffaterre. If we are successful in forming that intertext, we face the possibility that the sign in question already functions within an established topic, or code. If we fail to align this intertext with such a topic, we must abduct one. An insight lends us an interpretation that we confirm or deny by returning to the intertext, or considering cultural conditions of the text, or even reconstructing the poietic processes of its composer. We may alter an existing code in the understanding of this sign, or we may form a new code. At first, though, there is an intertext. A semiotic code is an intertextuality.

The historical range of a code as intertext remains open, especially for a late-capitalist society that often views artworks as so many commodities to be traded in the marketplace. In the "Hey Jude" thread we see how readily competent listeners cross styles and centuries in order to understand the closing progression. Even attempts to contain the intertext within the pop style encounter resistance, as those with multiple competencies bring their skills to bear on the text. We may see this historically unbounded intertext as a positive sign of our interpretive freedom, a token of the Barthesian world where we celebrate the *jouissance* of a text open to our playing with signs. Or we may worry, as does Jameson, that "as texts free themselves more and more from an immediate performance situation, it becomes ever more difficult to enforce a given generic rule on their readers" (Jameson 1981, 106). In this thread, however, I find it striking that given the freedom to say anything about "Hey Jude," none of the contributors is willing to let that freedom roam unbound. No matter the code, stylistic or interstylistic, the contributors remain unsatisfied with the interpretive results, rather more content to move back and forth across codes in order to come to terms with the harmonic progression.

A code begins with a catastrophe against meaning, as the reader/listener confronts an unknown sign and abducts an interpretive hypothesis. A code ends with a catastrophe against time, bringing together texts across history so that they might tell us what a sign means. But as a code violates time, so it reawakens time, showing us both its disjunctions and moments of reprise, and questioning whether any moment can be an unbroken plenitude that closes off the past and the future. The contributors to the "Hey Jude" thread may struggle to confine the intertext or to open it to a canon, but that struggle alerts its contributors to the sense that time is both a totality and a fragmentation. Just as intertextuality opens a text, so it opens time and wonders how a historical period could ever be inviolate. A code as intertext brings together bits of time in the making of a narrative called history.

As semiotic codes, topics invite intertextual connections among musical texts. Agawu and Samuels are clear on this point, while Monelle implies it in describing how codes develop as composers borrow indexical and iconic signs from other texts (Agawu 1991, 19, 25; Samuels 1995, 13; Monelle 2000, 16). Hatten, on the contrary, is unwilling to grant intertextual relationships to the "general use of typical patterns or templates that are part of the anonymous heritage of a stylistic language" (Hatten 1994, 196–97; see also Hatten 1985). Aware that current literary theory extends intertextuality to interaction among codes, Hatten nevertheless expresses a need to confine it to "straightforward instances of appropriation from other works or styles" for the time being in music semiotics (Hatten 1994, 197).

Musical topics are types that are instanced by tokens. In Peircean semiotics a type is an ideal, a conceptual category, a class whose reality is cognitive. A token is a member of that class, an instance with a perceptual ontology.[16] Sonata form is a type, and the first movement of Mozart's Sonata in B♭ Major, K. 333, is a token of that type. A token may be a representative for its type, but it cannot represent its type. Though we can point to Mozart's sonata movement as a token of sonata form, we cannot know the richness of sonata form by that token alone. Like types, musical topics are formed by culling potential tokens to find common attributes. A musical topic brings together the scattered signs in diverse musical texts and forms of them a conceptual category. When Monelle develops the topic for the noble horse in music of the nineteenth century, for example, he reaches for portions of Wagner's "The Ride of the Valkyries," Reichardt's "Erlkönig," Schubert's "Erlkönig," Haydn's *Die Schöpfung*, Brahms's "Keinen hat es noch gereut," Schumann's "Wilder Reiter," Mendelssohn's *Songs without Words*, Cowen's *Thorgrim*, Tchaikovsky's Fifth Symphony, Auber's *Le cheval de bronze*, Brahms's First and Third Symphonies, Elgar's *Pomp and Circumstance*, and works by d'Indy, Sousa, Franz, Musorgsky, and Berlioz (Monelle 2000, 45–63). The topic for the noble horse is an intertext within which these portions of texts function as tokens. From any one of these texts, a listener might abduct a code for their interpretation, seeking inductive validation for that code by reconstructing its intertext. From our position the problem of that intertext is that nothing prevents us from expanding it beyond the historical and cultural horizons of the individual tokens, so that meaning becomes open to the ideologies of another time and place. An intertext begins by pointing to meaning and ends by scattering meaning.

When we consider whether a musical sign is a token of a type, we compare that sign to that type as an ideal. But, as Hatten notes, we move smoothly from the ideality of the type to the reality of the token (Hatten 1994, 45). Because a topic is an intertext, it allows us to compare musical signs with other tokens from the same topic. Often such maneuvers take on the persuasive rhetoric of confirming an interpretation by summoning another token. For example, in a hermeneutic analysis of the third movement of Beethoven's *Hammerklavier*, Hatten claims that some simple, triadic drops in the second theme express resignation (18). Hatten's support

"Arrival" six-four

Example 3.2. Beethoven, *Hammerklavier,* Op. 106 (1818), III

for this claim comes in the form of an intertext that he forms between this theme, the opening of Beethoven's song "Resignation," WoO 149, and a melodic line from the Agnus Dei of Beethoven's *Missa Solemnis.* The intertext here is poietic, suggesting a topic within the composer's idiolect that associates triadic drops in the major mode with expressions of resignation. Though Hatten's discussion is brief, it suggests an elaborate network of signs more nuanced than a simple mapping between a triadic drop and an expressive resignation. The triadic melodies are situated within pastoral topics that form opposition with representations of the tragic. Rather than assert that the theme in question from Beethoven's *Hammerklavier* is a token of a type, or a code for resignation in that composer's works, Hatten brings together two tokens from the beginning and end of Beethoven's career, standing as synecdochical representatives for the entire type.

The intertext in this case is rather closed, though Hatten might well have pursued tokens from the works of Beethoven's contemporaries. More telling, though, are moments when he forms intertexts beyond Beethoven's moment in history. For example, in the same hermeneutic analysis of the *Hammerklavier,* Hatten describes a transcendental quality that he hears in a major six-four chord, which he likens to so-called *salvation six-four* chords in the music of Franz Liszt (Hatten 1994, 15). Example 3.2 shows the passage in question from the *Hammerklavier,* and Example 3.3 shows a token of the salvation six-four in Liszt's Sonata in B Minor. The intertext here is transhistoric, reaching beyond the bounds of Beethoven's time. The major six-four in Beethoven borrows the transcendence of the six-four in Liszt. Of course, one might reverse the intertext in support of a poietic argument that the first anticipation of Liszt's expressive language appears in the works of Beethoven. But when Hatten points to Liszt from the standpoint of Beethoven he uses a later code so that we might understand its pre-echo in Beethoven. This type of intertext threatens the hermeneutics of recovery and flouts the linear structure of time in order to understand works of art from a later historical standpoint.

Hatten cites Walter Robert, Professor Emeritus of Piano at Indiana University, though surely not a witness to Liszt's cultural era, as the source for the term *salvation six-four* (Hatten 1994, 298, n4). Hatten also associates the terms *elevated* and *transcendent* with the six-four, though he settles upon the more neutral term *arrival six-four.* The only other token that he offers is a cadence in the first movement of Beethoven's Piano Sonata in A Major, Op. 101, where a series of diminished-

"Transcendent" six-four

Example 3.3. Liszt, Sonata in B Minor (1854)

seventh chords moves to an augmented sixth before resolving on the major six-four chord. Opposition between the diminished seventh and the major six-four gives the latter chord an "expressive connotation of transcendent resolution" (15). Finally, in Hatten's coding such six-four chords need not resolve cadentially; it is enough that they appear at a point of arrival.

Curiously appropriate that Hatten should turn to Liszt when reaching for an expressive link outside of Beethoven's music, if only for the coincidence that Liszt championed Beethoven's late sonatas and gave a performance of the *Hammerklavier* made famous in a published review by Berlioz.[17] But Hatten's allusion to Liszt, even without a direct reference to a token within his works, clarifies the expressive content of Beethoven's *Hammerklavier*. The token I offer from Liszt's sonata in Example 3.3 appears after a Gretchen-like variation of a theme in the second key area, which has just dissolved into warbling trills and *dolcissimo*, fioritura cadenzas that also feature major six-four chords.[18] The textural sweep of the final cadenza passage builds quickly to the first arrival six-four on the bass G. This chord functions as a consonant six-four, initiating a middleground descent in the bass, which stops at F/E♯ before resolving on F♯ to support a first-inversion triad, reconfirming D as the second key area in m. 239. As with the tokens from Beethoven's works, a diminished seventh precedes the arrival six-four chord; however, unlike those tokens, this one entails no sense of an effort to overcome a tragic state, since the previous material is sweetly alluring. Within the broader outlines of the sonata, though, such moments of transcendence might be read as part of a struggle-triumph paradigm common to Liszt's music (see Hamilton 1996, 16–20). The salvation of this passage asserts itself in the rhetoric of outburst and open virtuosity.

The virtuoso style belongs to the public sphere, which in this case forms an opposition with the private sphere of the second theme. Virtuosity garners mixed and changing responses in the nineteenth century, inviting a rich cultural code that prohibits simple mappings of signifiers to signifieds. Late in the eighteenth century, unbridled virtuosity might meet critical evaluation linking it to excess and musical emptiness.[19] Though there is a growing taste for virtuoso display in the early nineteenth century, particularly in Paris, Liszt's career as a composer was plagued by the opinion that the dense virtuosity of his works was merely superficial brilliance (Hamilton 1996, 53). Still, the virtuoso style of the 1830s was at the center of avant-garde music, and although Liszt expressed a desire to break his "virtuoso chrysalis" in order to give "full flight" to his musical thoughts, the virtuoso style was the very vehicle of his compositional language.[20] Virtuosity is the means to a social transcendence, by which the pianist becomes marked as an artist with special abilities, often implying as well a heightened faculty of insight and interpretation, as evinced by Berlioz's review among many others. Virtuosity aligns itself with interpretive power, inscribing the score with the quality of a secret message that only gifted insight can decipher. Virtuosity must be public, visible, in order to earn the pianist the status of a seer with unique abilities. It is all too easy to align virtuosic transcendence with bourgeois triumph, where the hard work and diligence of practicing the mechanisms of the piano result in a marketable aura that casts the pianist as a public figure outside the social order. But the Lisztian virtuoso as hero rarely enters the negative outlook of a Wagnerian metaphysics, in which the artist's transcendent vision thrusts him so far from social/political life that he can only long for redemption at a distance (see Samson 2003, 181). Liszt's insights hope to bring society along; his virtuosity must be public to do its social work. Virtuosity not only leads to transcendence, it signifies transcendence. The work transcends its models; the performance transcends physical constraints; the audience receives transcendent visions. Virtuosity signifying transcendence is a breaking of boundaries. As such we can see how a social order might be threatened by virtuosity and might characterize it pejoratively as empty spectacle; as such we can see how a composer could gamble artistic strength on virtuosity and wield it for avant-garde music.

During the passage in Example 3.3 Liszt breaks the boundaries of the first transcendent six-four. After a pedal G supports the rising chords of mm. 209–12 as in a gathering of forces, the music bursts forth into a higher transcendence with the arrival six-four on F♯ in m. 213, anticipating the type of breakthrough (*Durch-*

bruch) that Adorno reads in Mahler's First Symphony (Adorno 1992, 5–6). Liszt's sonata ups the ante, apparently attempting another arrival six-four by taking a second pass at a pedal with registral expansion, this time on the F♯ in mm. 217–20. But here the gathered force reaches a diminished-seventh chord, initiating some furiously virtuosic music that exhausts itself before returning to D major. The example lends abundant possibilities for the coding of the arrival six-four. The chord may be set within a virtuoso passage that marks it as transcendent, suggesting special insight, the breaking of boundaries, the avant-garde, spectacle, or even empty display. That virtuosic transcendence celebrates the composer/performer as elevated, beyond the social sphere, a seer possessing unique insight. A hermeneutics of suspicion might take the chord as proof of a political unconscious that is blind to the fact that no one escapes the reach of social, cultural, and economic ideologies and necessities. The idea that anyone transcends these realities is the illusion that perpetuates them. Such a reading would find supporting signs in the tonality of this passage. Prior to the first transcendent six-four, the sonata had entered the second key area, D major, and though the passage in question enters some deeply chromatic regions, ultimately it returns to D major. In the codes of suspicion, transcendence must fail and fall back on the dominant ideology.

Chopin's rhetoric relies more deeply on situating the arrival six-four as a transcendent release of harmonic tensions, in keeping with the syntactic coding that Hatten outlines. Example 3.4 shows a pair of arrival six-four chords from the putative development section of Chopin's Ballade in G Minor, Op. 23.[21] The passage begins in E♭ and undergoes a chromatic ascending sequence before landing on the distant F♯-minor six-four in m. 154. I call the minor form of the arrival six-four a *tragic six-four*, an evil twin in ironic opposition to the salvation and transcendence of its major-mode sister. Leading to the first arrival six-four, the ascending chromatic sequence with its diminished-seventh chords indicates anxious striving or struggle, but the promise of salvation is thwarted briefly with entrance of that minor six-four chord. The tragic moment does not last long, however, since a chromatic descent in the bass leads through another diminished seventh, thence to an augmented-sixth chord that resolves on the arrival six-four in m. 158. Chopin highlights the transformation from tragic to redemptive with a polonaise rhythm in the left hand of mm. 154–57, as if the Polish cavalry has come to the rescue. The expressive logic of the brief passage is infused with dramatic energy. An anxious struggle (the ascending sequence) leads to a tragic moment (the first arrival six-four), and a second effort transforms that failure into a resolving salvation (the second arrival six-four). Binding the passage is the bass, which moves from the local tonic, E♭, down through C♯, C, and C♭, to land on the dominant, B♭. Because the tragic six-four on the bass C♯ appears as a passing chord, its affect only briefly darkens a section that ends in triumph. As with the passage from Liszt's sonata, the moment of salvation is public, coming in this case in the midst of a virtuosic waltz section. Though Chopin too relies on loud dynamics to punctuate the six-four chords, the piling of dissonance, the chromatic descent, and the interruption of a tragic six-four give the final arrival an aspect of achieved transcendence. Complicating the issue of virtuosity in this passage is Chopin's curious career since he

Example 3.4. Chopin, Ballade in G Minor, Op. 23 (1836)

eschewed performances at public concerts while in Paris. As a result, the muck of
empty display rarely adheres to Chopin's compositions, and his role as a seer rather
gains status through a view of him as the otherworldly voice murmuring secrets
out of public view.[22] Though difficulties in Chopin's ballades often approach the
Lisztian level, at times his music is not virtuosic but rather signifies the virtuosic.

The tragic form of the arrival six-four makes a dramatic appearance at the climax of Chopin's Fourth Ballade as well. The passage is shown in Example 3.5,
which begins with a moment of putative victory as an ascending chromatic sequence establishes D♭ major with a satisfying full cadence. A D♭ pedal through this

passage underpins an attempt to hold on to the climax and its attendant implications of the plenitude of presence. But D♭ is colored by the augmented triad in m. 192, leading to the vi chord of m. 193; and, when B♮ forms an augmented sixth with the pedal D♭ in m. 194, we know that all is lost, because this interval must find its resolution in an octave C that will direct harmonic motion away from D♭. As expected, in m. 195 the music lands on an F-minor six-four chord, underscored by hypermetric placement, textural change, phenomenal accent, and an embellished arpeggio. This tragic six-four stands in opposition to the major-mode success of the earlier music, as if a persona has reached a terrible recognition. The six-four chord turns out to be the structural dominant that will shift tonal focus away from D♭ major and back to F minor for a fiery coda. As the expression of the ballade makes its affective turn with this tragic six-four, the drama of the passage gains intensity from the arrival of the structural dominant at that very moment. The tragic six-four in this case comes after an apotheosis of the second theme of the ballade, whose earlier appearance evinced a clear pastoral topic. The chord thus stands in opposition to a dramatic trajectory that appeared to be moving toward transcendence. Arrival coincides with a moment of suffering, questioning the efficacy of the previous pastoral material.

Pastoral discourse inscribes oppositions between retreat to the countryside and return to the city. Descriptions of the countryside and its people may be highly idealized, to the extent that they represent notions of a lost golden age, or a land and time that never really existed.[23] Contemplation of this distant Arcadia is a retreat into the misty past that may be countered by a longing for some distant future when we might recapture that golden age. But that retreat into Arcadia must be balanced by a return to the real world with lessons learned, otherwise pastoral narrative becomes mere sentimental escapism. Higher levels of pastoral narrative question the wisdom of an Arcadian retreat or wonder at the illusion of re-creating that pristine world. Thus signs for death often associate themselves with the pastoral genre. The tragic six-four in the pastoral topic is a terrible realization, a moment of *peripeteia* that asks us to witness a paradise lost. Because reversal can work both ways, the transcendent six-four can equally be a sudden change for the better, when redemption comes at the moment when all should be lost. A reading of Chopin's Fourth Ballade might take the tragic turn at the climax to be a critique of any pastoral discourse that hopes to find escape in an illusory, pristine natural world.

Pastoral is the home topic as well for a tragic six-four in Tchaikovsky's ballet *Sleeping Beauty*. Act 2, from which the passage in Example 3.6 is taken, centers entirely on Prince Désiré, since the end of act 1 witnessed Princess Aurore touching the spindle that brought sleeping death. Act 2 opens with tokens of the hunting topic, establishing Prince Désiré's virility as well as pointing to the pastoral that forms the topical background for most of the act. Within the pastoral setting, the prince's capacity for heroic action is located distinctly where it can do no good, and much of the narrative action of act 2 is directed toward motivating the prince to leave the Arcadian woods and find the courtly site where Princess Aurora sleeps. That motivation comes from the Lilac Fairy, who appears before the prince, tells

Example 3.5. Chopin, Ballade in F Minor, Op. 52 (1843)

the story of the princess, and conjures up a vision of Aurora. Example 3.6 is the moment when the Lilac Fairy first appears before Prince Désiré. The melody and its bass pedal fit within the governing pastoral topic, and although act 2 shows the prince the way to the sleeping beauty, the simplicity of the melody in Example 3.6 points not to the princess but to the Lilac Fairy herself, as it is her leitmotiv throughout the ballet. Tchaikovsky has been careful from the start to portray Princess Aurora as strong and piquant; her famous "Rose Adagio," for example, closes with signs for heroic victory. During the passage in question, the fairy reviews the narrative's progress and previews the happy ending to come. From the stable tonic, D♭, at the melody's opening, the bass begins a chromatic descent that passes through the chromatic mediant, E major, and its chromatic submediant, C major, both of which enter on six-four chords. The C-major six-four in m. 58 sounds suspiciously like an arrival, but the contrary motion in the outer voices suggests a growing stature beyond this point, promising a more purposeful and higher transcendence. The expressive content of the passage changes swiftly with the augmented-sixth chord in m. 60 that resolves to the G-minor six-four in m. 61. The outer-voice expansion continues with a chromatic descent in the bass, and the passage meets its true point of arrival in the tragic six-four at m. 64, which is also the structural dominant. The tragic six-four has a familiar dynamic rhetoric as the brass glare with a triplet fate motive. Tchaikovsky has resorted to the hyper-emotive triple *forte* only twice in the ballet prior to this point: first at the end of Princess Aurora's "Rose Adagio," and then as the treacherous Carabosse drops her disguise after the princess falls to her presupposed death. The end of act 2 will see one more triple *forte* as Prince Désiré approaches the sleeping beauty.

Only one moment in the ballet exceeds these for dynamics and orchestral strength, and that is at the end of act 1, when the Lilac Fairy appears in order to cast her magic spell, bringing sleep to the members of Princess Aurore's castle. At m. 147 of this act's finale the structural dominant of E major is bolstered by a quadruple *forte*, but as the dominant reaches its moment of resolution, the music breaks through to a C-major six-four chord. The transcendence of this arrival is underscored by the brass and percussion before entering upon a leitmotiv for the fairy's magic spell. Transcendence in this case is not the result of human effort, but of grace granted from a magical naturalism (Lilac Fairy). In lieu of prior dissonances to underscore a sense of resolution at the moment of arrival, Tchaikovsky relies on direct modulation to the chromatic submediant, a magical change of perspective, to give the six-four chord the desired transcendence. In opposition to this moment, the tragic six-four in act 2 is deeply dark and menacing. Hyper-emotive dynamics not only punctuate these moments but also bring together the narrative events of the ballet: the princess's strength, the evil fairy's treachery, the good fairy's spell, the good fairy's retelling, and the prince's kiss.[24]

Even a deeply chromatic language in the early twentieth century may rely on an arrival six-four chord as a sign of transcendence. Example 3.7 is from the end of the exposition of Griffes's Sonata (1918), in which the composer uses a synthetic scale with potential for tonal allusions. It is tempting to read the augmented 2nds in this scale as signs for the exoticisms common to Griffes's other works. For an interview in *New Music Review and Church Music Review* of October 1917, for example, Griffes opines that frequent use of the augmented 2nd and of pedal points is characteristic of "Oriental music."[25] Descriptive titles, like *Five Poems of Ancient China and Japan, Komuri uta,* and *Noge no yama,* make clear the associations in Griffes's music, while the early reception history of these works attests to critical evaluation, at least, that accepted their musical signs of the East. In a review of a concert of music by Stravinsky and Griffes, for example, Sigmund Spaeth writes:

> Of the two [Stravinsky and Griffes], Mr. Griffes adhered the more closely to the traditional scales of the far East, and in general made his effects the more intelligible and hence convincing. This American composer has already given proofs of his ability to appropriate and revitalize the oriental spirit.[26]

Example 3.6. Tchaikovsky, *Sleeping Beauty* (1889), act 2

We might read the sonata, however, as a gesture toward absolute music that hopes to subsume the exotic within the project of modernism, thus neutralizing topical allusions. Early reception of the sonata failed to hear its alignment with Griffes's other East-inspired works and focused instead on its modernist and impressionistic tendencies. The simple second theme of the sonata unfolds with an accompaniment of open fifths in a slow harmonic rhythm suggesting the pastoral topic, though Griffes's reference to the pedal point, quoted above, may indicate a poietic motivation to signify the East. During the passage in Example 3.7, the contrary motion and thickening texture build to a climactic repetition of the second theme over the arrival six-four in m. 46. The major chord above the bass is embellished in the left hand with a falling half-step motion, A–G♯, forming apparent augmented triads. Such embellishments of a major triad have become common in movie scores of the science-fiction and fantasy genres, especially in the presence of a hero topic. Though it is possible to project this code back to Griffes's sonata and hear the arrival six-four as a sign of magical and heroic transcendence, the augmented triads also belong within an earlier code for anxiety, questioning the power of that transcendence to have a lasting effect. Salvation does seem dashed with the dissonant repeated chords of m. 50 and the ponderous bass octaves that enter a measure later to conclude the exposition of the sonata. Read as pastoral or as exoticism, or even as a nameless Other, the second theme makes a pass at transcendence that is undercut. In the midst of affirming a musical modernism that appropriates for rational development pitch sources outside of the diatonic western scale, the second theme questions that modernism by dashing its journey to transcendence.

With each of these examples we see that Hatten's neutral term *arrival* marks the one syntactic element crucial to its recognition: the six-four must appear at a grouping boundary to be heard as a culminating point. Even the F♯-minor six-four in Chopin's First Ballade comes at the end of a group that completes a sequence. That small group is subsumed at a higher level into a larger one marked by the bass descent from E♭ in m. 150 to B♭ in m. 158. That the second arrival six-four appears on the dominant of the local key lends it greater stability; but adding to its power to dispel the earlier tragic moment is that it comes at the end of a larger group containing the earlier six-four. The same examples also illustrate Hatten's claim that the arrival six-four need not resolve within the normative syntax of the cadential six-four. In the example from Liszt's sonata the arrival is on a consonant six-four, and in the example from Griffes's sonata tonal function at the foreground level is largely absent. When the arrival six-four coincides with a structural dominant, as in Chopin's Fourth Ballade and Tchaikovsky's *Sleeping Beauty,* the effect gains enormous emotional intensity. Leading to the climactic moment may be a growing expanse of register as the outer voices move in contrary motion. A sense of transcendent arrival benefits from increased dissonance in the moments prior to the six-four, often in the form of diminished-seventh chords or an augmented sixth.

On the semantic level the arrival six-four is coded with signs for virtuosity, transcendence, salvation, or, when the chord is in the minor mode, darkness and tragedy. These arrivals are grandiose events, underlined by extremes in dynamics, scoring, and register. Trumpets sound, choirs sing, and the heavens open up before us, or the netherworld reveals its engulfing darkness. As the six-four arrives, the piled-up dissonances resolve in a flash. Thus transcendence and salvation are associated with sudden realization, while the code for virtuosity brings in signs for insight, special faculties, and the avant-garde. Opposition between the six-four chord and surrounding material is crucial to the emotional impact of these passages. Coming after the apotheosis of a pastoral theme, the tragic six-four in Chopin's Fourth Ballade is a sudden realization of the naked truth that all is lost in spite of an earlier triumph. Following the calm beauty of the Lilac Fairy's theme, the six-four in

Example 3.7. Griffes, Sonata (1918), I

Sleeping Beauty is tinged with a tragic reversal of fortune. The home topic for many of these examples is pastoral, whose generic oppositions inscribe both an untroubled joy in the natural world and a reminder of the death that awaits any who try to remain in that world. Prince Désiré may be refreshed in his journey to the forest, but he must return from the untroubled woods, because a sleep unto death awaits the awakening of his kiss. The tragic six-four here and in Chopin's Fourth Ballade asks us to witness a paradise lost. The arrival six-four can equally be a sudden change for the better, when redemption comes at the moment when failure seems inevitable.

In order to abduct a code for transcendent and tragic six-four chords, I have cast the net wide and collected tokens ranging culturally and historically from Paris of the mid–nineteenth century to New York of the early twentieth century. This transhistorical code may be well beyond what Hatten intended when he made reference to Liszt's music within the hermeneutic-semiotic analysis of Beethoven's *Hammerklavier*. Nonetheless, however carefully Hatten has avoided bringing tokens from the style of Liszt into direct confrontation with Beethoven's sonata, it is still the case that from the open horizon to the future that was the *Hammerklavier* for listeners in Beethoven's time, Hatten has directed attention narrowly to a code for transcendence in Liszt's time. The resulting hermeneutic problem is well known: whereas our perspective allows us to organize the past into codes of interpretation, the perspective of those in the past is one in which all the future is openness and potentiality, where any sign might one day take on an unpredictable significance.[27] Listeners in Beethoven's time might well have abducted a code for transcendence upon hearing these arrival six-four chords in the *Hammerklavier*; sidestepping the normative syntax, these chords are undercoded and lend themselves to interpretive effort. But as these chords in their time have an open horizon to the future, their meaning only narrows in the presence of texts in that future that pick up the undercoded sign and lend it a new significance. Thus, to the extent that Hatten points to a later coding of signs in order to interpret the *Hammerklavier*, his project exceeds the boundaries of reconstructing the competency necessary for understanding Beethoven in his own time.

We do Hatten's work a disservice, though, if we critique it on the grounds that it exceeds its self-proclaimed historical limit. Although we would be naive to think that we can wipe time away and reveal the undiminished text in all of its youth for a reading untainted by the future (Jauss 1989, 200–01), we would be equally naive to think that such a project is the one that Hatten's work really hopes to fulfill. Identification with the text in its original historical position is only the first step in a hermeneutics that realizes that texts can be understood only by taking account of their consequences. The text situated within its first historical horizon speaks in dialogue with the same text situated within a canonic horizon that necessarily reclassifies it in contemporary terms, while "often finding in it previously unrecognized significance" (204). A horizon is a limit, and our efforts to understand a text within its first horizon must reach the point where a boundary breaks and we transcend that limit in our search for meaning. Jim Samson reaches a similar, though more pragmatic, conclusion when he argues that an analytical perspective that views the text within a canon is just as useful as a historical perspective that recovers only that text's original causes.[28] More than model the competency of listeners hearing Beethoven's music in his time, Hatten has negotiated a dialogue of historic and canonic horizons that brings to the *Hammerklavier* a new significance. This dialogue, hidden by efforts to confine intertextuality and to eschew direct reference to tokens within Liszt's style, accounts for how we can read Hatten's work both as modeling something long known to us and as discovering something new.

Hatten's analysis transcends the historical to lend us insight; it is hermeneutic in that it whispers a secret.

4

As Eco reminds us in some later work that fights to recover the lost boundaries of interpretation, "the ultimate secret of Hermetic initiation is that everything is secret" (Eco 1992, 32). Codes, topics, and types give us intertexts, whose signs, instances, and tokens allow us to move from the puzzling configuration in one text to its secret answer in another. But as we utter that secret, we often find that meaning has moved into another text and another, until we too have moved from horizon to horizon across time and culture. At the moment when we ask what a text means, we risk tearing it from its historical position, and the moment we speak the secret of that text, we risk exposing our failure to realize that these secrets do not rest long enough for us to utter them unequivocally.

The inscrutable six-four chord in the second movement of the *Hammerklavier* promises to tell us a mystery if we can answer the question of what it is. We find its intertext in Liszt's sonata, showing us a vision of transcendence. Texts by Chopin and Tchaikovsky usher in the evil twin to that transcendence, suggesting that its existence points to a narrative paradigm of reversal for better or worse. Finally, Griffes's sonata begs us to wonder whether any quest for transcendence can find a lasting moment far from the threat of suffering. But finding ourselves in early-twentieth-century New York, we are far afield of the first horizon of Beethoven's text. The six-four chord in the *Hammerklavier* has none of the overtones of virtuosity and dynamic power that mark its brethren throughout the intertext. Hatten brings us back to the first horizon of the sonata and aligns the quiet light of its transcendence with abnegation, a spiritual resignation and acceptance of a tragic situation. His interpretation surely rings true to our imaginings of Beethoven's suffering. In the light of the intertext, though, the abnegation suggested by the enigmatic six-four chord in the *Hammerklavier* is also an answer to a questioning about transcendence that appears in later texts. Transcendence is no willed and sudden burst of power that can save the day, but a still resignation in the face of tragedy. The six-four in the *Hammerklavier* signifies transcendence while it answers a question about transcendence.

Paul de Man argues that "few historians still believe that a work of the past can be understood by reconstructing, on the basis of recorded evidence, the set of conventions, expectations, and beliefs that existed at the time of its elaboration" (de Man 1982, xi). But to admit that we have already crossed the boundaries of time that disallow our ability to hear a text in the first freshness of its origin is no excuse for abandoning the past in favor of our own codes of understanding. Even if we refuse to follow Jameson in his Marxist analyses of texts, we can still take heed of his warning that ignoring history places us in the discomfort of witnessing an uncanny text that arises from the past and appears in a time where it is alien, speaking a message that no one can fathom (see Jameson 1981, 74–102). Often, though, a text is an alien in its own time; it speaks with uncoded signs that seek readers yet to come, who will make the interpretive leap necessary to make sense of the text (see Jauss 1982, 25–28). Contemporaries of Liszt heard his sonata as an empty display with a dismaying tangle of notes. Tchaikovsky's *Sleeping Beauty* earned mixed critical responses that questioned whether the music interfered with the dance, whether the child's fairytale was appropriate for an adult audience, and whether the magnificence of the production hid an artistic emptiness (Wiley 1985, 189–92). It is only later that these texts find an audience as their signs become coded within other texts. It is only in retrospect that we see a text as timeless. A text, though, is not a timeless essence, nor is it a prisoner of its historical period; a text is a stream of events searching for readers who will make sense of it by bringing to it other texts.

When the reader makes sense of the text, she must fight the urge to view it as read. She must consider that her reading fails to account for the signs of the text in the fullness of their meaning. The reader must return to history and learn to hear the text again as strange. We revisit the *Hammerklavier* and imagine that the six-four chord is still uncoded and unfamiliar. We take it as offering an answer to a question that we can only guess. In this way we open the text again to the possibility of transcending another boundary and finding its code in the signs of a text yet to come.

4   Bloom, Freud, and Riffaterre: Influence and Intertext as Signs of the Uncanny

> When you read a canonical work for the first time you encounter a stranger, an uncanny startlement rather than a fulfillment of expectations.
>
> —Harold Bloom (*The Western Canon*, 3)

1

Like many useful distinctions, the one between semiotics and hermeneutics, the how and what of meaning, breaks down as soon as scholars try to occupy a critical position. Without becoming entangled in the problems of what texts mean, semioticians have seen themselves in the business of revealing *how* texts mean. Writing of semiotics, Jonathan Culler reminds us that "confronted with a plethora of texts that communicate various meanings to their readers, the analyst does not pursue a meaning; he seeks to identify signs and describe their functioning" (Culler 1981, xvii–xviii). Anyone familiar with the practice of semiotics, though, must be struck by how often semioticians cross this imaginary boundary between the how and the what of meaning. After all, who can resist the appeal to interpret signs, especially in the complicated sign systems that are literary, artistic, and musical? Robert Hatten finds the combination of semiotics and hermeneutics common enough to mark a stage in the development of musical semiotics.[1] But where we can accept Hatten's deft structuring of the field, we must not infer from it that music has taken the initiative in combining semiotics with hermeneutics. From Roland Barthes to Umberto Eco, analysts of culture and literature took that initiative some time ago.[2] Among their number we also find Michael Riffaterre, whose *Semiotics of Poetry* (1978) offers a theory of intertextuality and its impact on interpretation. I shall soon be co-opting Riffaterre's work in order to understand what I take to be uncanny startlements in some musical texts. To arrive at a hypothesis of how intertext and influence mark texts with strangeness that channels our interpretive energies, I shall surround his work with writings by Harold Bloom and Sigmund Freud. Like Bloom, I find these strange passages to be uncanny, and so it is to the uncanny that I first turn.

2

One can hardly approach the uncanny without considering Freud's famous essay "Das Unheimliche."[3] Ostensibly written to analyze uncanny effects in nineteenth-century German literature, Freud's essay begins in a manner worthy of literary criticism by discussing the etymology of *unheimlich* and its near equivalents in nine other languages.[4] The English word *uncanny,* which refers to anything supernatural or beyond the normal, bears only an uncomfortable relationship to the German *unheimlich,* which refers to the weird, the sinister, and, as we shall see, the terrifying in the sublime. Intimations of our mortality, untimely and ghostly, run more deeply in the German cultural context of *unheimlich* than they perhaps do in the Anglo-American context of *uncanny.* In the German context we imagine *der Doppelgänger* pursuing us with the threat of a death foretold, or we see the tremor of fear in Schubert's forsaken traveler as he spies *die Krähe* circling overhead. Though Freud claims it "is long since he has experienced or heard anything which has given him an uncanny impression," it is easy to agree with Lawrence Kramer that Freud's method of scientifically examining the creeping dread of nineteenth-century German literature was also his way of mastering the fear of death.[5]

Of considerable interest to Freud is the relationship between the root word *Heim* (home) and its cognates *heimlich* (hidden), *unheimlich* (uncanny), and *Geheimnis* (secret), which will contribute to his oft-quoted definition of the uncanny as "that class of the terrifying which leads back to something long known to us, once very familiar" (Freud 1958, 369–70). Exploring this problem, Freud turns to analysis of tales by E. T. A. Hoffmann, of which "Die Elixire des Teufels" (The Devil's Elixir) will lead to a fruitful discussion of *der Doppelgänger.* In an early mental stage the ego interprets formation of the double as an insurance against its own destruction, a denial of death; but in later mental stages the ego takes the double as a "ghastly harbinger of death" or a "vision of terror" (387, 389). Closely allied to the manifestation of a double is the ego's propensity for self-observation. The ego splits in order to see itself. As such, the *unheimlich* double threatens univocal subjectivity. This transformation of the double from a sign of immortality to one of the impending death of the ego results from a failure of repression:

> [I]f psycho-analytic theory is correct in maintaining that every emotional affect, whatever its quality, is transformed by repression into morbid anxiety, then among such cases of anxiety there must be a class in which the anxiety can be shown to come from something repressed which *recurs.* (394)

The word *anxiety* appears almost as a repetition compulsion here in Freud's text. And since he also associates repetition compulsion with the uncanny, one again suspects that Freud attempts through the essay to master his own anxiety over death. His rationalization tells us that, like the double, the uncanny is something that was once known to us, but has been repressed and forgotten; in a later mental stage any reappearance of the repressed material seems new and terrifying. The ego has failed to master itself, and this failure of repression blooms into a heightened dread of death.

In the end Freud must settle upon multiple explanations for the uncanny, among which is the aforementioned problem of repetition compulsion:

> It must be explained that we are able to postulate the principle of a repetition-compulsion in the unconscious mind, based upon instinctual activity and probably inherent in the very nature of the instincts—a principle powerful enough to overrule the pleasure-principle, lending to certain aspects of the mind their daemonic character. ... Taken in all, the foregoing prepares us for the discovery that whatever reminds us of this inner repetition-compulsion is perceived as uncanny. (391)

In Freud's terms, repetition compulsion is a primal activity of the mind; he later compares it to the working mind of a child. As an instinctual activity, repetition compulsion may take on a demonic character that we perceive as the uncanny. Again we see that a once familiar working of the mind in childhood may take on an uncanny effect when it returns in a later mental stage. In one of the ironies of Freudian thought, repetition compulsion is also a psychic defense used to repress unwholesome thoughts from the conscious mind. Repetition and repression are the mind's mechanisms for clearing space in order for the ego to function. But failure of these mechanisms results in morbid anxiety. Thus repetition both conjures up the uncanny from the primal mind and forces the uncanny back down to the subconscious. The mind traps itself in cycles of repetition. As we shall see later, repression, return, repetition, and anxiety will have consequences for theories of influence and intertextuality.

The few musicological approaches to the uncanny resonate with Freud's analysis. In a discussion of Schoenberg's uses of tonality within his twelve-tone compositions, Michael Cherlin, for example, addresses directly Freud's conception of the uncanny as the return of something once familiar (Cherlin 1993). Borrowing Bloom's theory of influence, Cherlin's analysis is reminiscent of Joseph Straus's *Remaking the Past* (1990), wherein the vestiges of tonality, that father figure for the early twentieth century, reappear as ghostly reminders in atonal music. Joseph Kerman also references Freud in a study of the final movement of Beethoven's quartet Op. 131. Though admitting that Freud is unavoidable in any discussion of the uncanny, Kerman warns against too facile a mapping of Freud's conception onto the music.[6]

Descriptions of the uncanny in music resort to many of the same signs that Freud uses. We see references to *ghastly, horrifying, eerie* (Cherlin 1993), *disorienting, ogre-like, aberrant, eccentric, grotesque, mechanical* (Kerman 2001–02), *miming, empty gestures* (Kramer 2002), *absence, otherworldly, death, Dionysian, Other* (Kurth 1997), and *strangely new but familiar* (Tovey 1978, quoted in Kramer 2001–02).[7] In order to develop the idea of the double in German culture, Richard Kurth's discussion of that *Ur*-text for the uncanny in music, Schubert's "Der Doppelgänger," brings in Nietzsche's conception of the Dionysian. We learn that the Dionysian is "the nightmarish encounter, sublime in its desolate solitude ... the dark double of bright Apollonian apparitions of the divine" with a power to induce self-forgetfulness, intoxication, and the destruction of the individual (Kurth 1997, 9–10). Again we see how the uncanny threatens the ego. And in the word *sublime* that functions in this argument, I am reminded of Daniel Chua's reading of an opposition between the beautiful and the sublime in nineteenth-century musical thought, wherein the idea of the absolute vacillates between visions of music as beautiful, the self-sufficient form of tonal structures, and as sublime, the formless power of a Schopenhauerian Will that threatens subjective annihilation.[8] The sublime here is terrifying in its dual oneness and emptiness, aligning it with the ghastly Other of the uncanny.

In these texts we have the making of a semiotic code for *das Unheimliche*, which I picture as the web of signs in Figure 4.1. The interconnection between the signs in this figure is more complex than can be pictured clearly in two-dimensional space, and the number of signs that can be shown is limited as well. As such, lines that appear to lead nowhere in the figure imply that other signs may be brought into the orbit of the uncanny. In addition, as we saw in Chapter 3, this code must be viewed as hypothetical and open to revision. The signs for this code have been culled from writings about German literature and music in the nineteenth century, with one foray (by Cherlin) into twentieth-century music. Our closest witness to the cultural context of these artworks is Freud, who nevertheless writes a century after E. T. A. Hoffmann penned the tales that are the object of his essay. As such, any claims about this code apply not to responses contemporaneous with those passages deemed uncanny, though we might embark on studying such a code, but to responses from our own time. In terms of music the code is heavily linguistic in that it accounts for verbal signs that particular listeners have engaged in their cross-domain mappings of literary/psychological attributes onto musical ones. To that extent the *unheimlich* (hereafter synonymous with *uncanny*) surrounds itself with signs numerous enough for rich coding. In purely musical terms, however, the uncanny is undercoded because writings have been less direct in pinpointing its musical signifiers. Faced with this situation, we move into those strategies of intertextual abduction that were the focus of Chapter 3.

To begin, the uncanny in nineteenth-century German music is related to the topic (code) of *ombra* in the eighteenth century, with its familiar tremolos, chromatic lines, Neapolitans, and diminished-seventh chords. Leonard Ratner suggests that *ombra* in the eighteenth century includes gods, morality, and punishment as means of arousing awe and terror, and he submits Mozart's *Don Giovanni* as an example (Ratner 1980, 24). Though awe and terror remain with the uncanny in the nineteenth century, there is a sense from Freud's analysis that the object of that fright, indeed of the supernatural itself, is not some outside force, like a god, but an inner force that splits the ego. Minus the sense of gods and punishment, we still hear the same signifiers for the uncanny that once stood for *ombra*. The Neapolitan in Schubert's "Die Krähe," which marks that *wunderliches Thier* as supernatural, and the diminished-seventh chords that underscore the traveler's trembling at the thought of the grave (*Grabe*) are signs for the uncanny split of the ego, allowing the traveler to see phantom wings.

We find other intuitions about the uncanny in descriptions of nineteenth-century

something repressed that returns (Freud)

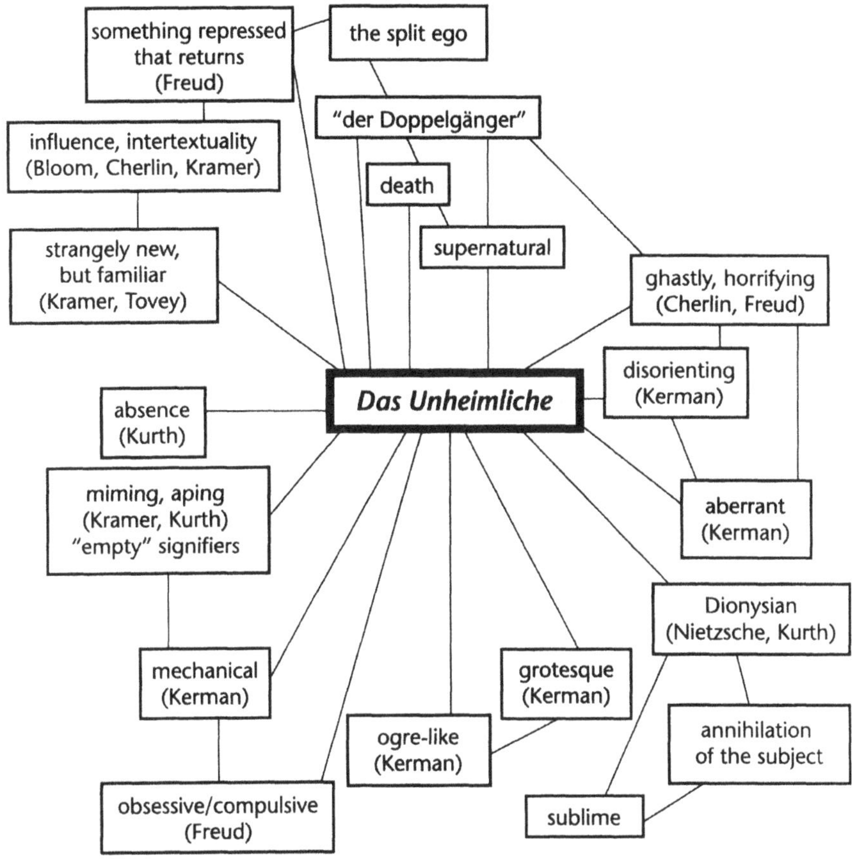

the split ego

"der Doppelgänger"

death

influence, intertextuality (Bloom, Cherlin, Kramer)

supernatural

strangely new, but familiar (Kramer, Tovey)

ghastly, horrifying (Cherlin, Freud)

Das Unheimliche

disorienting (Kerman)

absence (Kurth)

aberrant (Kerman)

miming, aping (Kramer, Kurth) "empty" signifiers

Dionysian (Nietzsche, Kurth)

mechanical (Kerman)

grotesque (Kerman)

annihilation of the subject

ogre-like (Kerman)

obsessive/compulsive (Freud)

sublime

Figure 4.1. Code for *Das Unheimliche*

instrumental music. Peter Smith, for example, characterizes as *unheimlich* the E♮'s in the opening of the Brahms Piano Quartet in C Minor, Op. 60, shown in Example 4.1 (Smith 2002). Although he eschews further comment, Smith may hear the E♮'s as *unheimlich* because they fall outside the prevailing harmony. Pizzicato makes salient these pitches, which disturb the calm, sustained dominant of mm. 27–30. Typical is the recoil from those notes in m. 31, where an outburst on a dominant-ninth chord responds to the *unheimlich* E♮'s. Though we might read this outburst as defiant in face of the doubtful opening, a Freudian reading hears the dominant ninth as the terrifying recognition that something long forgotten has recurred. A sudden energy bursts forth as the musical persona reacts to the uncanny. A voice-leading sketch in Example 4.1 shows that the E♮'s participate in a 3-line over the dominant; but the parallel fifths in this passage, barely hidden by syncopations and 6–5 motions, add to the disorienting gloom. In particular those 6–5 motions result in apparent chords, enharmonic to minor triads in second inversion, that signify a

Example 4.1. Brahms, Piano Quartet in C Minor, Op. 60 (1875), I

supernatural eeriness in mm. 22 and 24. The entire passage brings together many common signifiers in the musical code for the uncanny: chromaticism, enharmonicism, the strange note or voice-leading. In addition, we find that the uncanny is associated with a code for outburst as the persona makes a terrifying recognition with the sudden energetic impulse on the dominant ninth. Finally, that we lend these *unheimlich* E♮'s a tonal meaning in a Schenkerian middleground makes us participants in the same kind of *Wissenschaft* with a vengeance that Freud brings to his essay. We try to find a rational explanation for the dread that rides the surface of the music, and in so doing we recover our sense of mastery over death.

If the strange note can signify the uncanny, the famous C♯ in m. 7 of Beethoven's *Eroica* could be read as an *unheimlich* apparition, haunting the hero's journey at its very onset. Scott Burnham writes that programmatic interpreters of the *Eroica* inevitably stumble on this C♯ as they realize that something less than expeditious has befallen the hero (Burnham 1995, 4–5). If the hero creates himself from nearly nothing, emerging as a primal force from the overtones of the opening E♭ chords, what can we make of the chromatic C♯ that seems so far removed from the triadic melody in the tonic that signifies a self-possessed ego? The difficulty is not just that the note in question is *a* chromatic pitch but *that* chromatic pitch, a raised 6̂, the leading tone to the leading tone. Schenker, too, considers this problem, writing, "the bass, surprisingly, has C♯ instead of D♭" and postulating progressions that might have earned coherence through that alternate D♭, which would point downward to 6̂ in support of a subdominant chord (Schenker 1997, 11). But C♯ must move up. And when it does, a syncopation in the upper voices leaves in its wake a G-minor six-four chord. Here is the darkening thought, the tremor that reacts to the uncanny C♯. Schenker writes of C♯'s drive back up to D that it "communicates itself to the treble, which now also rises in a *cresc.* to the neighbor note a♭2 . . . The fifths indicated by oblique lines in the Foreground Graph are avoided by means of syncopation" (ibid.). In other words, the underlying harmonic progression moves directly from the chord with C♯ in the bass to the dominant with D in the bass—the G-minor harmony of m. 9 is an apparent chord that results from the staggered motion of the upper and lower voices. As with Brahms's Piano Quartet, an apparent chord may signify the uncanny.

Narrative interpretations for the *Eroica* are well enough known that I shall not rehearse them here, except to say that the C♯ calls into question the subjectivity of the hero at the very moment that he forms himself from the chord of nature. His psyche is lost momentarily in the apparent G-minor chord before he can summon his strength in the first of many large-scale patterns that Burnham reads as "statement—liquidation—stronger statement" (Burnham 1995, 5). G minor will return to open the finale of the symphony, where it is blazoned with a more optimistic affect; and another G-minor chord reaches the status of a real *Stufe* in Schenker's sketch, which shows III (G minor) as a space filler on the first-level middleground of the final movement.[9] The hero manages to integrate into the ego his reaction to the opening uncanny C♯ and to forestall psychic disintegration. Wagner took that same C♯ to be the first note of modernity, and that note was really an uncanny one, threatening the heroic in the act of creating it, questioning modernity in the midst of affirming it.[10]

The interrelationship between the uncanny and subjectivity appears in Beethoven's *Appassionata* as well. Example 4.2 shows the transition from the second to third movements of this sonata, leading to the first theme proper of the final movement. The second movement, with its distant key of D♭, chorale texture, plagal successions, and registral ascent, brings to the sonata a spiritual and transcendent calm, safe from the stressful outbursts of the opening movement.[11] But the diminished-seventh chord in m. 96, substituting for an expected cadence on the tonic, is an uncanny tremor disrupting the still composure of the second movement. The *fortissimo* repetition of that chord in m. 97 is the terrible recognition that the turbulent character of the first movement has returned. This chord and its compulsive repetitions into the opening of the third movement have the enharmonic potential to redirect the tonal focus of the sonata away from serene D♭ major and toward stormy F minor. The chord is spelled as the vii°7 of F minor, but within D♭ we hear it enharmonically as vii°7/V, a chord more common in music encoding the tragic. In Mozart's *Requiem*, for example, vii°7/V at cadences brings to the music an *ombra* topic, especially in Ratner's conception as a sign of fear in the face of punishment and retribution. In the passage from the *Appassionata*, because B♭ is set in the bass,

Example 4.2. Beethoven, *Appassionata*, Op. 57 (1805), III

we might also hear the vii°⁷ as a substitute for vi in D♭, so that its function wavers between dominant (vii°⁷/V) and pre-dominant (substitute for vi). Functional ambiguity remains with the chord when the third movement commences in F minor. With B♭ in the bass we can hear the chord of mm. 1–12 as a pre-dominant, acting as a space filler to the dominant C of m. 13.

In response to the uncanny interruption at the close of the second movement, the musical persona splits its energies among the various textural lines of the finale. If we agree with Kramer that "melody has become the Western trope of self-expression par excellence," bringing us in contact with the naked subjectivity of another, we may wonder just where is the melody that represents subjectivity in the final movement of the *Appassionata*.[12] Is the subjectivity written into the perpetual sixteenth-note figuration that fuels most of the movement, or in the supporting bass notes that first appear in mm. 21–22 before a more melodic occurrence in mm. 26–28, or in the dotted-rhythm motive that first appears above the figuration at the end of m. 28? In face of a similar problem in the first movement, where textural, rhythmic, motivic, and dynamic changes play against the formation of a single coherent subjectivity, the music pulls together a long-breathed melody for the second theme, though this moment of self-possession suffers its own uncanny interruption and dissolution in a Neapolitan before a structural dominant and creeping chromatic line lead to the agitated closing theme. But no such melody coalesces from the texture of the final movement until possibly the coda, where a frenzied chorale texture supports an extended melodic line, appearing too percussively and late in the work to redeem the struggle of the movement. Instead of unfettered melody, the last movement offers the compulsive repetition of its motives. Though the return of the first movement's topic was signaled only briefly by the vii°⁷ chord at the end of the second movement, that uncanny harmony was enough to unhinge the subjectivity of the sonata. The subject is shattered in its own defiant attempts to form itself out of cataclysm. The deeper code for the outer movements is a heightened *Sturm und Drang,* but signifiers for *ombra* and the uncanny, especially the use of diminished-seventh chords and the Neapolitan, color this code in the *Appassionata*. Again we see that enharmonicism and a harmonic vocabulary borrowed from the *ombra* topic can signify the uncanny.

Fear and trembling over the destruction of the ego often reaches to signifiers for death, so that death's code is tightly woven into that for the uncanny. Among many examples is the final portion of the "Song of the Wood Dove" from Schoenberg's *Gurrelieder,* where the Wood Dove witnesses the grief of King Waldemar over the death of his beloved Tove at the hand of Queen Helwig. In the passage shown in Example 4.3 the Wood Dove describes the bells that ring the death knell (*die Glocke Grabgeläute tönte*) and then sings a refrain about how far she has flown to find grief and death (*Weit flog ich, Klage sucht ich und den Tod*) before concluding with the realization that Helwig has slaughtered Tove (*Helwig's Falke war's, der grausam Gurres Taube zerriß!*). As the climax of this song of sorrow, the passage is filled with signs for death. Though Schoenberg sets the song in B♭ minor, this section rests firmly in the subdominant, E♭ minor, which, in opposition to a key on the dominant side, darkens the moment when the Wood Dove will finally utter the word *Tod*.[13] The subdominant, E♭, alternates in the bass with its own subdominant, A♭, supporting a chromatic chord. The full majesty of the orchestra punctuates the word *Tod* with another E♭-minor chord before turning to an upper-neighbor embellishment that sets forth a C♭-major triad, whose brightness only makes more disheartening the return to E♭-minor and A♭-minor chords in the following measures. The final phrases of the passage replay an eerie orchestral refrain that is crushed by the sudden return of the tonic, B♭ minor, played with horrifying force in the low brass.

Example 4.3. Schoenberg, "Song of the Wood Dove" from *Gurrelieder* (1912)

But musical signs for the uncanny add detail to this climax of the Wood Dove's song. Though we might read the steady rhythm and walking bass as indexical signs for a funeral march in this context, the staccato in the winds lends a mechanical aspect to the alternating chords leading to the climax. The section seems an ironic parody of a phrase some twelve measures before, where the Wood Dove describes a monk ringing the evening Angelus, during which the music evokes a religious topic with plagal successions evenly paced in B♭ major. As the Angelus turns to a death knell in the climax, so B♭ major turns to its dark subdominant, E♭ minor, where the plagal successions now include a chromatic chord over A♭. That chord is strange in its configuration, including D♮ and C♭ as members of vii°^{7} in E♭ minor, and a frozen nonchord tone, G♭, held from the previous harmony. Enharmonic to vii°^{7} on the root A♭, the chord in question wavers in function between a dominant and a pre-dominant, offering another sign of the uncanny. To the mechanical staccatos in the winds of this passage, the strings soon add tremolos, underscoring anxiety. The whole section moving to the climax has something of the ogre about it.[14] Death marshals its uncanny force to release a terrifying vision of the sublime in the harmonies that follow utterance of the word *Tod*. And in her final phrase, as she releases the crucial secret that Helwig is Tove's murderer, the Wood Dove speaks a poetic symbol for Helwig, the word *falcon* (*Falke*), as the Neapolitan unfolds in another uncanny sign. In the mechanical repetitions, the strange chord, the tremolos, the Neapolitan, we can read signs of the uncanny code coloring death in this music.

Coming at the end of the first part of *Gurrelieder*, the approximate midpoint of the work, the song of the Wood Dove is the dramatic and expressive crux of the cycle. That the poet Jens Peter Jacobsen chose to distance Waldemar's grief by making it the object of observation on the part of a bird adds poignancy to the depiction of Tove's death. The assonance between the name Tove and the German for dove, *Taube*, in addition to the symbols of the song, describing Tove as a dove in opposition to Helwig as a falcon, allows for an interpretive strategy that makes the Wood Dove a transfiguration of Tove, who describes the memory of her own funeral.[15] But the grief in her song is Waldemar's. His subjectivity is shredded by the loss of Tove, leaving him mute to describe her death. Instead, his mind finds voice in the song of a bird. By the end of the cycle, Waldemar's split ego will result in open descriptions of his insanity.

In these few musical examples, ranging from the music of Beethoven to that of Schoenberg, we can make an intertextual abductive hypothesis about the musical signs surrounding the uncanny. To the signs for the *ombra* topic (tremolos, diminished-seventh chords, Neapolitans) we can add enharmonicism, strange uses of chromaticism, odd voice-leading, and mechanical repetitions of musical material. The uncanny is associated with signs for terrible recognition, anxiety, dread, death, and the sublime. In the wake of the uncanny, we may read narratives of the dissolution of subjectivity, the ego's heroic reintegration in face of that threat, or the ego's defiance in spite of it. And in a narrative that I develop in the next section, we may even read the signs of the ego's total collapse.

3

Freud's definition of the uncanny as a class of the terrifying arising from "something repressed which *recurs*" holds promise for a hermeneutics of narrative in music (Freud 1958, 394). However, taking Kerman's words of warning to heart, we must be cautious about too facile a mapping of Freud's conception onto music.[16] Easily enough we can find in the *Eroica* recurrences of the C♯, or its enharmonic double, D♭, that lead to dark sections of that symphony, where we could argue for the uncanny return of something repressed. In mm. 102–103 of the second movement, for example, a Neapolitan arpeggiates down to the bass, D♭, signaling the return of the funeral march in C minor after the review of military honors bestowed by C-major fanfare in the previous section. We revel in these miraculous reappearances of a chromatic pitch at important expressive moments in the music. But if we are to force Freud's hermeneutic model onto this passage, we must argue that C♯/D♭ has been repressed in some way, and that its return brings an uncanny effect that is heightened by comparison to earlier events involving that same chromatic pitch. Working against such a reading for this section of the *Eroica* is an expectation of the return of the funeral march in a genre whose three parts are the march itself, military fanfare, and a return of the march. Though the D♭ does darken the mood in preparation for the march's return, adding perhaps a suggestion of *ombra*, it is difficult to argue for the type of terrifying recurrence consistent with Freud's analysis of the uncanny.

The final movement of Schubert's Sonata in C Minor, D. 958, at first does promise to fit Freud's conception, though I shall argue that in the end the work falls short of this narrative paradigm. Example 4.4 reproduces part of the retransition leading to the recapitulation of this sonata-rondo movement. After a major scale embellishes the dominant, an iambic rhythm on octave G's prolongs that harmony, hinting at the return of the first theme, which shares that rhythm. Each occurrence of the opening theme has been in a soft dynamic range, so that we expect the quiet octave G's in mm. 417–20 to knit themselves seamlessly into the fabric of the recapitulation. Shattering the presumed calm of this transition, though, is the *unheimlich* chord of mm. 421–22, an inverted minor Neapolitan that clashes acutely with the previous G's. The chord shares musical features of the uncanny. First, it is an apparent chord, resulting from a double upper-neighbor embellishment of the VI chord that comes in m. 424. Second, its three chromatic pitches strangely intrude upon the prevailing harmony. If we hear this chord as uncanny, it is at once the terrifying and the recoil from the terrifying, like an unseemly supernatural cry from beyond. We might leave the matter as it stands and hear this passage as another musical sign in the uncanny code.

But to hear this section according to the narrative possibilities implied by Freud's essay, we first need to move backward from the minor Neapolitan in m. 421 and search for its early manifestations. Example 4.5 shows portions of the first theme, in which the Neapolitan appears as part of an ascending chromatic 6–5 sequence in mm. 28–35, where accents on weak beats jostle the steady triplet figures in the

Example 4.4. Schubert, Sonata in C Minor, D. 958, IV (end of development)

left hand. By m. 39 the Neapolitan is hammered in the lower register and embellished by its own vii°⁷, suggesting something more ominous than what was hinted in the earlier measures. At last, beginning in m. 49, the minor Neapolitan makes its first entrance on the scene, and when its major-mode sister answers in mm. 53–56, the putative brightening of the chord only adds irony to the theme. We are not convinced that all will be well. Even when this extended first theme turns to the major mode in mm. 67–92 (not shown in the example), one questions whether the gloom has truly lifted, especially since the theme ends with a tonic pedal alternately supporting augmented-sixth chords and Neapolitans. This whispering major version of the first theme is a token of Schubert's propensity to whistle past the cemetery.

The minor Neapolitan becomes an issue already with the second theme, which Schubert sets in C♯ minor. The semitonal relation between the keys of the first two themes suggests an instance of what Robert Bailey calls *expressive tonality,* though his examples generally involve transposition or sequence of a single theme.[17] Certainly one suspects a poetic motivation for the key of C♯ minor, which comes in place of the minor dominant, G, or the mediant, E♭. Within a Freudian narrative, the minor Neapolitan, enharmonic to C♯, already threatens the deep structure of the music, though the exposition does manage to end on the mediant after modulation down a major third to A minor and up by a sequence of thirds to C minor and E♭ minor. C♯/D♭, however, is largely absent from the movement after the second

Example 4.5. Schubert, Sonata in C Minor, IV (first theme)

theme of the exposition; D♭ major makes only a brief appearance during a sequential passage near the end of the development. One might say that C♯/D♭ is repressed through the second half of the exposition and most of the development, so that the recurrence of D♭ minor as an apparent chord in the passage of Example 4.4 is uncanny in the Freudian sense. When the rondo theme makes its final appearance after the recapitulation, the minor Neapolitan makes its presence felt again; and while earlier occurrences of this theme concluded with a softening response in C major, this final version remains solidly in the minor mode and whimpers away in the final dozen measures before two *fortissimo* chords seal the fate of the sonata.

The question, though, is to what extent we can claim that the return of the minor Neapolitan prior to the recapitulation is the recurrence of something repressed. William Kinderman strikes the right note in writing that "the poetic evocation is perhaps less of a dance than of a ride on horseback, thrilling and yet strangely ominous" (Kinderman 1997, 161). And Kinderman's later suggestion that this movement bears expressive resemblance to Schubert's "Der Erlkönig" gains potency when considering the horse topic that was discussed in relation to this movement in Chapter 3 (ibid.). Already within the first theme, Neapolitans both major and minor, augmented-sixth chords, weak-beat accents, and the horse topic are signs of the supernatural with the potential for uncanny return. And when an extended melody in B major begins the development, we have the choice of hearing it either as an idealized alternate to the spooky reality of the exposition or as an ironic lisping from the Erlking himself. But, paraphrasing Kerman in his analysis of the uncanny in Beethoven's Op. 131, it is not so much that the minor Neapolitan has been repressed in Schubert's sonata as that it has merely gone away for a while (Kerman 2001–02, 158). And if we wish to argue that the development section manages the unique psychic struggle of repressing the uncanny signs and the Erlking's enticements only to have them burst forth with frightful clangor in the retransition, we still have that common hermeneutic problem of dealing with the nearly literal return in the recapitulation of all the material from the exposition. Though Freud's vision of the uncanny gives us insight into the psychology of Schubert's C-minor sonata, in the end we must either abandon his conception or ignore large portions of the sonata altogether.

One text that follows more closely the Freudian paradigm for the uncanny is Chopin's "Funeral March" Sonata, Op. 35. In Chapter 1 I touched briefly on Wayne Petty's analysis of this sonata in terms of the anxiety of influence (Petty 1999), and I shall return to the question of influence later. Like Petty, Barbara Barry hears the echo of Beethoven's sonata Op. 111 in the diminished-seventh interval that introduces the first theme, some of which is shown in Example 4.6 (Barry 2000, 3). Whether or not we choose to hear reference to Beethoven's last piano sonata in the ponderous octaves that open Chopin's sonata, we can hear signs for the uncanny in the chord that answers these octaves in m. 2. Chopin asks the performer to cross an enharmonic abyss from the D♭ of m. 1 to C♯ in m. 2 and back to D♭ in m. 3. What can we make of this odd notation, and how shall we understand the chord of m. 2? Example 4.6 shows that the chord in question has at least two tonal meanings. First, it is enharmonic to a D♭-minor chord, functioning as ♭iii⁶ in B♭ minor. Odd as this harmony may be, it gains tonal coherence upon repeat of the exposition, whose closing theme ends in D♭ major, pausing on a dominant seventh in that key before returning to the exposition.[18] In this context the D♭ octave of m. 1 resolves the dominant from the close of the exposition. As that octave moves down to E, enharmonic to F♭, the mode shifts to minor, and this mixture is affirmed with the chord in m. 2, enharmonic to i⁶ in D♭ minor. In this case, though, one

Example 4.6. Chopin, "Funeral March" Sonata, Op. 35 (1840), I

wonders why Chopin notates as C♯ minor the chord of m. 2, and an answer to this question concerns how that chord resolves in the following measure. The E♮ in the bass of m. 2 functions as a leading tone to the dominant, F, in m. 3. As such, the chord in m. 2 has a second tonal meaning as an altered vii°⁷/V, where G♯ functions as a chromatic passing tone. Neither interpretation for the progression is wholly satisfactory. Chopin confronts us with a chord that is both/neither C♯/D♭ minor. The enharmonic riddle so soon in the text opens a rift in tonality through which we glimpse an uncanny world.

Much of the first movement involves itself in exorcising that uncanny beginning. The first theme, for example, is generated from a single rhythmic motive, repeating unabated for nearly thirty measures. Such motivic concision is unusual for themes in Chopin's larger works. As such, recalling Freud's analysis of the uncanny, we hear a repetition compulsion forming in response to the opening measures, as if the theme can cleanse itself of the otherworldly effect. The first break in the compulsive cycling of the rhythmic motive appears only four measures before the second theme, where a brief transition moves to the key of D♭ major. With this second theme Chopin offers an alluring alternative to the unpromising ontological reality of the introduction. A chorale topic blooms into a nocturnal one as a new psychology develops in a trope typical of Chopin's mature style. In his larger works, Chopin often sets a second or third theme as a nocturne, chorale, or pastorale, marking it through his melodic gift as a desired emotional state. The same theme often returns as an apotheosis near the end of the work.[19] Examples include the Polonaise-fantasie, Op. 61, the Barcarolle, Op. 60, and the Fourth Ballade,

Op. 52. As Chopin is associated particularly with the nocturne, we may even hear the second theme of this sonata as a metaphor for his own subjectivity, as if he has written his psychology into the text.[20] The second theme of the sonata blossoms over an extended parallel double period, and the following closing theme even suggests triumph in opposition to the discouraging opening theme.

But the development section shatters that triumph and devotes all of its energy to the diminished-seventh interval and the compulsive rhythmic motive from the first theme. The act of psychic repression seems more thorough and distressing here, with a particularly anxious section appearing in mm. 138–54, where for the first time both the diminished seventh and the motive from m. 9 of the first theme appear in counterpoint. As expected, the development moves at last to the dominant, F. But after a descending chromatic line in the upper voice and a repeated F in the bass herald the sonata's double reprise, the recapitulation commences directly with the second theme in the tonic, repressing a return of the obsessive first theme. An aesthetic motivation for the missing theme may be that since it generated all of the material for the development, the first theme would be tiresome if brought back to initiate the recapitulation. As such, one could argue that Chopin makes the reprise of the first theme coincident with the development, telescoping that formal section with the recapitulation. In fact, Chopin resorts to the same ploy again in his Sonata in B Minor, Op. 58. But recomposing the transition so that it retains D♭ and leads to the first theme reveals no fatal flaw in the structural balance of the work if it adheres rigorously to sonata form. What does change in such a recomposition is the expressive content of the sonata, wherein the dramatic efforts of the development seem to be for naught. Chopin's version leaves us with the impression that the psychological pains of the development lead us back to that glorious alternate reality promised in the second theme of the exposition. In Freudian terms, repression earns the right to own that new reality.

Much of the second theme proceeds as it did in the exposition. During the closing theme, though, a minor tremor threatens tonal stability as repeated chords in mm. 222–25 are supported alternately by C♯ and D♭ in the bass, replaying the enharmonic rift that set the sonata on its way. The parallel section in the exposition centered on E in the bass, so that both pitches from the diminished seventh in m. 1, D♭ and E, return at crucial expressive points in the sonata. Having closed this tonal rupture, the music heads for a final cadence, whose success is interrupted by the unexpected recurrence of the first theme in the bass. I find this sudden return to be the most uncanny in this movement, because the failure to repress the obsessive first theme comes just as an emotional triumph seems certain. Signs of heightened anxiety fill this passage, which is reproduced in Example 4.7. The now ominous theme appears in the bass of m. 231, where it supports a dominant of the subdominant in $\frac{4}{2}$ position. Hatten writes of the V$\frac{4}{2}$ that the resolution of its bass downward is indicative of yielding (Hatten 1994, 56–63). The upper voices in this case, however, will not yield to the usual resolution nor, by implication, to the uncanny theme in the bass. Instead, the upper voices are urged upward by half step to diminished-seventh chords with the power to counter the normative syntax and raise the music up by sequence. When these diminished sevenths resolve, they do so by

Example 4.7. Chopin, "Funeral March" Sonata, I, uncanny return

common tone to land on another V$^4_2$, supported again by the first theme in the bass. Finally, in m. 236 Chopin thwarts the $^4_2$ chord altogether, treating it like a common-tone augmented-sixth chord, whose B♮ resolves upward to C. This new voice-leading at last represses the unhappy motive in the bass, and the first movement ends with a triumph tinged by modally mixed subdominants.

Looking forward to the "Funeral March," we discover the ultimate failure of that final act of psychic repression that occurred in the closing measures of the first movement. In the bass of this march is the B♭–D♭ motive from the head of the opening movement's first theme.[21] The once churning motive is now an incessant bass, above which a neighbor, F–G♭, forms apparent VI chords in second inversion. Those apparent major triads on weak beats, emptied of their power to signify a benign result, add a ghoulish color to the march. The trope of death here is kin to the uncanny code, and as if the failure of repression were not enough, the narrative of the sonata ends with a fourth movement in which we witness the disintegration of subjectivity. This final movement offers no theme, no center of consciousness, for our contemplation. The chromatic lines, played in whirling monophonic octaves, rush by too quickly for even a secure sense of harmony.[22] The ego of the sonata, which first sprang into obsessive compulsive action in recoil from an enharmonic rupture, succumbs at last to that terrifying uncanny world.

As a whole, Chopin's "Funeral March" sonata more nearly fits Freud's conception of the uncanny than did Schubert's sonata. Signifiers for the uncanny, from the enharmonic uncertainties to the obsessive first theme, fill the opening of Chopin's text. After each attempt to repress that uncanny beginning, the terrifying effect returns with renewed force, leading finally to the crumbling consciousness of the last movement. Schumann rather famously complained of this work that Chopin had only gathered together four of his strangest children and called them a sonata in order to bring them into view. Charles Rosen opines that, despite this review, Schumann must have been sensitive to the sonata's power (Rosen 1995, 283). One wonders if Schumann sensed that what Chopin had really gathered was a poetic force in service of a penetrating narrative. Bloom complained, less famously but more recently, that Freudian readings of Shakespeare are less compelling than Shakespearean readings of Freud (Bloom 1994, 371–94). We venture a guess that the same might be said of Freud in relation to Chopin, whose sonata shows us that mastery of the fear of death has no strength against our last consequence.

4

Strangeness has been a theme throughout this exposition of the uncanny in music. The word forms a densely woven intertext with ideas ranging from those of the Russian Formalists, for whom strangeness was a mark of poetic language, to those of Ludwig Wittgenstein, for whom it was merely the condition of everyday language (see Perloff 1996). Victor Shklovsky, among the more important Russian Formalists, discusses defamiliarization as a strategy in which writers take quotidian objects, occurrences, and beliefs and make them strange and unsettling (see Shklovsky 1965). We come across a notion of strangeness as well in Bloom's wonderment at the texts in the western canon:

> I have tried to confront greatness directly: to ask what makes the author and the works canonical. The answer, more often than not, has turned out to be strangeness, a mode of originality that either cannot be assimilated, or that so assimilates us that we cease to see it as strange. (Bloom 1994, 3)

Later, in the passage that appears as this chapter's epigraph, Bloom tells us that a canonical work is like an encounter with a "stranger, an uncanny startlement."

Strange it is that Bloom should choose the word *uncanny* while reflecting upon canonical greatness. Riffaterre, to whom we shall soon turn, would call Bloom's statement an ungrammaticality, because the word *uncanny* falls outside of its use in the lexicon of common language. We expect the phrase *uncanny resemblance*, but *uncanny startlement* is itself a startlement, unless we read Bloom's text within the intertext of Freud's conception of the uncanny, where the familiar is transformed through the anxiety of repression into a recurrence, strangely horrifying. From the Freudian perspective, Bloom's notions of the anxiety of influence are nothing short of the anxiety over an uncanny startlement, a strangeness, a ghoulish specter that comes when the writer realizes that what she takes to be originality in her work is merely the double, the recurrence, the *influenza* of another work, threatening the artistic ego with death. The emphasis on writers, though, is paired in Bloom's work with a focus on the text, which feels the anxiety of influence as well. We may add that the reader too feels this anxiety. The reader comes upon a text, which she takes to be original; she is struck by a strangeness that ought to stand as the mark of that originality, only to realize that what she took to be new was really the double, the intertext, from another work.

It is in this sense that Cherlin describes as uncanny Schoenberg's use of tonality in his twelve-tone music (Cherlin 1993). The claim is not that Schoenberg resorts to tonality in order to signify the uncanny, though we might learn to hear such evocations as signs in such a code within atonal music; rather the claim is that, when we recognize tonality in Schoenberg's twelve-tone compositions, we confront the startlement that what ought to have remained in the past has recurred. For Cherlin, these gestures of tonality are "evanescent," mere specters of tonal music that have been emptied of meaning because they fail to gain middleground status in the pitch structure of these works (369). For Bloom, though, these failures of repression make for a strangeness in the language that is more than a matter of syntax. To remember is to call forth a ghost, and to hear music or read a book is to confront the specters of another's memory. To listen or to read is necessarily to invoke the uncanny. The uncanny is an intertextuality.

In his own confrontation with the uncanny, Riffaterre makes of it a hermeneutics for poetry. For Riffaterre, poems are transformations of what he calls a *matrix:* a hypothetical, simple, and literal sentence. As the reader attempts to interpret a poem in terms of its matrix, she comes upon points where the text fails to make sense. Riffaterre calls any such point an *ungrammaticality,* a term that covers everything from lapses in syntax to uses of rhetorical figures that resist interpretation. The neologism might be considered unfortunate for its unsonorous nature, except that it is an ungrammaticality of its own, inviting interpretation. In a passage about the interrelationship between intertextuality and ungrammaticality, Riffaterre speaks the word already marked as central to Bloom's theory of influence:

[T]he embedding in the poem of textual borrowings . . . creates a new hierarchy of words, a new grammar whose very novelty or strangeness makes it harder to ignore or bypass. (Riffaterre 1978, 165)

Here again is that word *strangeness*, directing us back to the writings of Bloom and Freud, teaching us that an ungrammaticality is an uncanny startlement. Echoes of the uncanny appear in another discussion of the poetic matrix, where Riffaterre explains that "the text functions something like a neurosis: as the matrix is repressed, the displacement produces variants all through the text" (19). The passive voice in this statement makes it unclear where the act of repression lies. For Bloom there is no doubt that it lies with the writer. Generally, though, Riffaterre tries to redirect the energies of the writer and the reader back into the text. For Riffaterre, then, the act of repression happens within the text, and it is at just those moments when the text fails to repress its origins in another text that strangeness, an ungrammaticality, appears as an uncanny startlement.

How this formulation governs our hermeneutic efforts is the focus of Riffaterre's theory of the text and its readers. As the reader attempts to discover the matrix of a poem, she goes through two types of reading: heuristic and hermeneutic. Our early efforts with a text are heuristic, during which we read both with the assumption that the text will make sense and with an alertness to ungrammaticalities, those points where the text fails in this regard. Our later efforts with a text are hermeneutic, during which we try to interpret these ungrammaticalities by creating intertextual links with other texts, because "any ungrammaticality within the poem is a sign of grammaticality elsewhere, that is, of belonging in another system" (Riffaterre 1978, 164). Ungrammaticalities are hermeneutic windows that signal the reader to look to another text for meaning. While it has become a commonplace in literary criticism to claim that the intertextual nature of writing threatens stable interpretation, Riffaterre's theory marks intertextuality as the enabler of meaning in regard to strangeness.

We read in Riffaterre a desire to rein in unruly intertextuality and place within the text the power to control interpretation:

> [T]he text's hold on the reader's attention is so strong that even his absentmindedness or, in later eras, his estrangement from the esthetic reflected in the poem or its genre, cannot quite obliterate the poem's features or their power to control its decoding. (22–23)

By placing semiotic weight in the text, Riffaterre would seem to bracket off the role of the reader in making sense of the text. At this point, however, the distinction between the how and the what of meaning resolves the tensions in what would otherwise be an untenable proposition. In another passage it becomes clear that while the text may control how the reader proceeds, it may fail to control what meaning the reader makes of these ungrammaticalities:

> Implicit intertextuality is highly vulnerable to the erosion of time and cultural change, or to the reader's unfamiliarity with the corpus of the elite that bred a particular poetic generation. But even when the intertext has been obliterated, the text's hold on the reader is not affected. The fact that he is unable to decipher the hypogram of reference immediately does affect the content of his reactions, but not his perception of the grid of ungrammatical or nonsense phrases. They function as buoys marking the positions

of a sunken meaning. If retrieval is blocked, this denial of the reader's right to lan-guage as communication is not taken lying down. The reader looks elsewhere for a meaning, as well as for the reason why the text is playing tricks with language. (136)

To the extent that a reader is separated from the cultural/historical contexts that surround the production of the text, she might not bring to her reading the in-tertexts that would allow her to decode ungrammaticalities in the way that the writer and her contemporaries might have decoded them. Faced with ungram-maticalities, though, and lacking the same context, the reader will make her own intertext in order to discover a meaning, no matter how far that meaning may stray from any intended by the author. The reader makes a leap of interpretation. Thus texts control how a reader proceeds to make meaning—the reader makes intertexts; but though texts may constrain what meaning the reader makes, those readings are relative and variable with time and culture.

Like Freud's essay, Riffaterre's semiotic theory seeks to master the uncanny. In-stead of reining in the dispersal of the subject, though, the theory celebrates it as the first condition of poetic meaning. Turning to music, we shall see that Riffaterre offers a strategy rich with implications for hermeneutic analysis. In the next sec-tion I focus this strategy on an intertextual interpretation of Brahms's Intermezzo in A Major, Op. 118, No. 1.

5

It is strange to think that we could ever exile Brahms's music to that place where the buzz of structures hums loudly enough to block out word, image, story, philosophy, emotion, and meaning. An old gossip concerning Liszt, Wagner, and their putative adversary, Brahms, seems to have held its grip on research well into the twentieth century, so that we could almost believe that the younger composer from Hamburg had achieved nothing more than his modest aspiration to become a Kapellmeister, writing music whose merciless logic made moot the programs that supplemented the works of his two dynamic elders. Research over the last decades has formed a new image of Brahms. Michael Musgrave reminds us that Brahms's intellectual curiosity went beyond an appetite for eighteenth-century figured-bass treatises and reached into areas of literature, history, art, and philosophy, even in-cluding an acquaintance with some writings of Wagner's beloved Schopenhauer.[23] Robert Bailey and David Brodbeck both reveal a Brahms unafraid to quote the mu-sic of the New German School.[24] Dillon Parmer sheds welcome light on the song quotations and secret programs in Brahms's instrumental music, opening the her-metic seal that protected the composer's output from the supposed squalor of extra-musical associations (Parmer 1995; 1997). And the power of that seal seems forever vanquished when Robert Fink proposes a Freudian reading of Brahms's First Sym-phony that sees its anxious chromatic lines as the transformation of repressed de-sire (Fink 1993). Whether or not we are willing to accept this new image, we must wonder how Brahms's music could ever have been misconstrued as absolute.

However we answer this question, we are still left with the dual problems of deciding what Brahms's music means and how it encodes that meaning. Flooded by strange details in a work like his Intermezzo in A Major, Op. 118, No. 1, we may find problems rich enough for that well-known gambit in which the theorist heralds the text's resistance to analysis in order to heighten a sense of victory upon taming the music's strangeness. But, as Riffaterre shows, problematic passages signal intertexts as clues to meanings that might be lost if we were to become too intent on rationalizing the ungrammatical. In what follows I shall undertake those two types of reading that Riffaterre describes: a heuristic one that points to strangeness in Brahms's intermezzo, and a hermeneutic one that forms intertexts in the pursuit of meaning. In the hermeneutic reading it is not my aim to propose a definitive, or even a singular interpretation for the intermezzo. Though there is much evidence that the *Sechs Klavierstücke,* Op. 118, meant more to Brahms than a mere display of musical structures, and that this multipiece made a particularly emotional impact on Clara Schumann, I shall try to avoid the peculiar act of claiming to read minds that took their everlasting rest long ago.[25] Instead of proposing what this intermezzo *does* mean, I shall be occupied with what it *can* mean, especially when an ecology of pieces surrounds it.

Heard freshly, Brahms's music startles us with uncanniness, opening a world where we are alien. Example 4.8 is an annotated score of the Intermezzo in A Major. Faced with strange details, we may at first undertake a heuristic reading in which we seek the familiar before probing these hermeneutic markers. The text's expressive content unfolds in a rounded-binary form whose tonal center, A, remains unclear through much of the music. In light of this tonal uncertainty, a coda equal in length to each of the three formal sections seems a necessary supplement for the confirmation of the tonic.[26] The only other key confirmed by an authentic cadence is C major, which is established at the end of the first formal section. C colors the tonality of the intermezzo in what Patrick McCreless, borrowing from Ferdinand Saussure, might describe as its *syntagmatic* and *paradigmatic* roles (McCreless 1991). That is, C acts both syntactically as a goal of tonal motion and associatively as a referential sonority in the intermezzo. For example, despite some tonal ambiguity in the opening measures, the bass line of the first section traverses an unremarkable path from and to C. Appearances of C in its paradigmatic role are marked by asterisks in Example 4.8. A striking instance occurs in m. 20 at the end of the B section, where a C^6 chord substitutes for an expected dominant on E in the bass. In addition, one of the climaxes in mm. 23–24 arpeggiates another C^6 chord.

About the motivic material, we are already a bit less sure. Thematic content seems to spin out of an opening three-note motive, forming a simple, stepwise descent. Some instances of this motive are shown in Example 4.8. The motive appears in diatonic and chromatic forms; it is combined with its mirror form in the B section and undergoes a classic Schoenbergian liquidation in both A sections, where it becomes a simpler two-note pattern. The opening motive in the upper voice of m. 1 is answered by the tenor octave E, accented in m. 2; the answer comes again in the next two measures.[27] In the B section, where the putative three-note motive combines with its inversion in mm. 10–11, both forms of the motive are answered by accented octaves in m. 12. The slurs, however, cut across these four-note groups,

Example 4.8. Brahms, Intermezzo in A Major, Op. 118, No. 1 (1893) and the change of register into the fourth note of each group makes us question the motivic structure. Shall we hear it as a three-note motive with an answering fourth note, or shall we hear it as a simple four-note motive?

Analytic problems become more difficult as we explore details of the music. The first of these concerns a tonal ambiguity inscribed in the first measures. Edward T. Cone has written about this problem, arguing that although a retrospective hearing establishes the harmony of m. 1 as an A-minor chord in first inversion, this fact is not obvious during a first hearing, when the apparent dominant seventh on C may delude the listener into thinking that the piece will continue in F major.[28] Further, because the A-minor chord in first inversion seems an unsatisfactory starting point, we may learn to hear it as an abortive attempt to resolve a root-position C-major triad with a 6–5 resolution of pitch-class A down to G. When pitch-class G does arrive in m. 3, it does so over a change of bass, converting G into a dissonance. Schenker addresses this problem of harmony, if indirectly, when he argues that the entire intermezzo is an expanded auxiliary cadence, starting on III (C) and moving through V (E) to I (A).[29] Schenker's position, therefore, would be that mm. 1–2 establish a C-major triad.

A second analytical problem involves the intermezzo's hypermetric structure. The annotations in Example 4.8 show that the first four measures establish an unambiguous two-bar hypermeter, while the remaining six measures suggest both a two- and a three-bar hypermeter. More difficult is the hypermetric pattern of the B section. Although mm. 11–16 reestablish the two-bar hypermeter, the remaining five measures of the B section resist rhythmic interpretation. The heavy accent in the middle of m. 19, coupled with the main motive in diminution, suggests that the downbeat has shifted to the middle of the bar. Brahms accomplishes this shift in the three-beat groupings of mm. 18–19. Complicating this issue is a chromatic ascent in the bass from A_2 to E_3, which begins in m. 17 and cuts across the hypermetric interpretation shown in Example 4.8.

The final analytical problem that I wish to address concerns the closing cadence of the intermezzo. In mm. 36–37 the last functioning dominant appears as a vii°$^4_3$, embellished by an accented passing tone in the upper voice. The voice-leading out of this diminished seventh is odd by most accounts, since none of its pitches resolve properly in the tonic triad of m. 38. The leading tone in the tenor resolves in the bass; the tritone-forming fifth, D, resolves in the tenor; and, although the seventh, F, does resolve in the proper register, it begins in the alto and resolves in the soprano. A combined motivic and Schenkerian perspective might argue that this passage involves the last use of the four-note motive, forcing the B in the soprano of m. 37 to move down to E in the soprano of m. 38. Smoothing over this voice-leading problem is the chord in the final measure, where C♯ appears in the soprano. A look to Schenkerian voice-leading would argue that E_4 in m. 38 is really an alto voice, while C♯$_6$ in m. 40 is a register transfer of the true soprano. The final three measures unfold the two upper voices of the tonic triad, so that there is a proper resolution of these voices on a deeper level. This solution says nothing about the bass voices, though, and a complication is the plagal motion in the bass, which moves from A in m. 35 to D in m. 36 and back to A in m. 38. This plagal reference undermines the dominant function of the diminished-seventh chord. We saw a similar problem in Schoenberg's "Song of the Wood Dove," and we shall see in this case that the uncanny effect will be the startlement that points to influence.

In Riffaterre's terms a heuristic reading of the intermezzo has uncovered ungrammaticalities in the text. A musical-structural approach would send us scrambling to the deepest levels of tonal structure within the text to find connections that can make sense of these instances of strangeness, and at some points I have suggested the directions that such an approach might take. In the interest of a hermeneutic reading, however, we may view these ungrammaticalities as points that form intertexts to spur interpretation. Among the ungrammaticalities of the intermezzo, I find the most striking to be the final cadence. From the dominant pedal in m. 30 to the final tonic in m. 38 we can hear references to several types of closing gestures, forming intertexts with music from the eighteenth and nineteenth centuries. For example, when the dominant pedal of the coda moves to the tonic A in the bass of m. 34, the supported harmony is a subdominant instead of the expected tonic, alluding to a harmonic maneuver familiar to much Baroque music. Variants of this closing harmonic motion are common in the preludes of Bach. In the C-major prelude from *WTC* I, for example, a closing dominant moves to a V^7/IV that acts as a tonic substitute before a move to IV prepares a return to the dominant. The entire harmonic progression appears over a tonic pedal. When such progressions appear in the minor mode, Hatten interprets them as style expansions on the Picardy third, because the raised third in V/IV prepares the listener for the major tonic of the final cadence (Hatten 1994, 39–43). In addition, since the subdominant region is marked as relaxed or calm in opposition to the tension of the dominant region, progressions like these entail a sense of prolonged relaxation from the dominant, so that the tensions of the work do not resolve all at once with a single tonic. A token of this type appears in the closing progression of the A-minor prelude from *WTC* I. Again the cadential dominant moves to V^7/iv, acting as a tonic substitute. After moving to iv over a tonic pedal, the harmony returns to a dominant, in this case vii^{o7}, before resting on the final tonic chord. Example 4.9 maps this type of progression beneath the intermezzo's final cadence, revealing Brahms's trope on this well-known close. Here the dominant-pedal E extends through the V^7/IV, so that the subdominant coincides with the move of the bass to the tonic A. There is also an expansion of the subdominant with mode mixture in a gesture that I shall explain shortly. Finally, the diminished-seventh chord is embellished with the same motive that permeates the intermezzo, though more striking is the bass motion to the subdominant D at the same moment. The refusal to align the bass with the well-known cadence adds a poignant tension to the text at just that point where we expect the calming influence of the subdominant region.

A second cadential intertext for this passage concerns the modally mixed subdominant in mm. 34–35, summoning a progression that Robert Bailey calls a near cliché of late-nineteenth-century music (Bailey 1985b, 119). Example 4.10 shows two variants of this plagal cadence with mixture. In the first, from Schumann's *Fantasie*, Op. 17, a tonic pedal supports both major and minor forms of the subdominant. In the second, from the final measures of Wagner's *Götterdämmerung*,

A. "Bach" Cadence

a: V⁷ V⁷/iv (iv) (vii°⁷) I♯

B. "Schumann/Wagner" Cadence

a: (IV) (iv) (ii°⁶₅) I♯

Example 4.9. Intertext of closing progressions around Brahms intermezzo

this cadence type is expanded with an upper-voice ascent from $\hat{1}$ to $\hat{3}$, accompanying a harmonic succession from IV to a mixed ii°⁶₅ back to I, all over the same plagal bass that characterizes Brahms's intermezzo. Example 4.9 aligns such a progression beneath the intermezzo's final cadence. Because of its associations with church music, the plagal cadence can be a sign of religious feeling, or spirituality, and the mixed subdominant in the cadences of this intertext adds poignancy. In the case of the *Fantasie,* this mixed plagal cadence is perfectly chosen. If we take the final movement to be an expression of tenderness, then this cadence expresses a spiritual yet pained love, the *Herz und Schmerz* of so much nineteenth-century German poetry.[30] As for the cadence in *Götterdämmerung,* it is a token of a type found throughout Wagner's music and post-Wagnerian instrumental genres, where it participates in a *Weltanschauungsmusik* that cycles around a Schopenhauerian redemption through love/death.[31]

Comparing the plagal cadence at the bottom of Example 4.9 to the final measures of the intermezzo, we find that once again the bass motion cuts across the usual configuration. Where we expect a tonic pedal or a movement in the bass from $\hat{1}$ to $\hat{4}$ with the latter scale step supporting all of the subdominant chords, Brahms delays the move to $\hat{4}$ until the final portion of the subdominant. More disruptive is the apparent chord beginning in m. 36. A search within the boundaries of the

C: I   (IV)   (iv) I   Db: IV   iv   "ii⁶₅"   I

Example 4.10. Plagal cadences in Schumann and Wagner

text suggests that the closing measures are a mere echo of the opening motive, so that pitch-class C at the downbeat of m. 36 is an accented passing tone with no harmonic meaning of its own. In this reading the odd voice-leading of the chord into the final tonic is nothing more than the result of another completion of the four-note motive, as B in the upper voice leaps down to E. But recalling that the apparent chord in m. 1 functioned in the tonal ambiguity of the intermezzo, we may wonder if Brahms has been equally savvy with the chord at m. 36. In fact, if we include pitch-class C into the harmony of that measure, we hear an apparent "Tristan" chord. That apparent chord in the intermezzo, echo of the voice of Brahms's adversary, is more ghostly than we may first guess. Though the first chord of Wagner's *Tristan* has been the focus of much attention, most commentators proceed to view one or more of its pitches as chromatic alterations.[32] The chord's ontology rests on a combination of the length that Wagner accords it in the opening measures, the number of times it appears in the opera, and the preoccupation with which theorists obsess over its structural meaning. The "Tristan" chord is a supernatural force without harmonic corporeality, and its apparent materialization in the intermezzo rings with its magic power.

The intertext between the intermezzo and *Tristan* is stronger for those very problems of tonality that I mentioned earlier. Bailey writes that the prelude and first act of *Tristan* gain their tonal meaning from a double-tonic complex around A minor/C major, and that complex is implicit in the first two statements of the "Tristan" chord, which resolve respectively on the dominants of A and C (Bailey 1985b, 121–26). Brahms tropes this indirect exposition of the A/C complex in the first measures of the intermezzo, where the apparent chord is at once both A minor and C major. We recall, as well, that C-major triads substitute for the dominant in the B section of the intermezzo. Even the bar form, the Schoenbergian sentence in the opening of Wagner's prelude, finds its uncanny double in the A section of Brahms's intermezzo. These pieces of evidence form an intertext that may send us scrambling for clues of influence. We know, for example, that Brahms owned and studied Wagner's scores, even correcting parts in his personal copies. To his closest friends Brahms claimed to be the best of Wagnerians, because he admired the operas without entangling himself in the cult of personality. But in relation to the opening of *Tristan*, Jan Swafford writes that Brahms had an abiding distaste for

Example 4.11. Wagner, *Tristan und Isolde,* final cadence

the work, claiming that though he studied Wagner with enthusiasm, "if I look at that [*Tristan*] in the morning, I'm cross for the rest of the day." Yet Swafford finds echoes of *Tristan* in the second intermezzo, Op. 117, and in the song "Mein wundes Herz," Op. 59, No. 7 (Swafford 1997, 423).

It is tempting to read these connections from Bloom's perspective and make some claims about Brahms's anxiety of influence, under which he awaits for the safety of Wagner's death to quote *Tristan.* We might even point to a relationship between the close of the intermezzo and that of *Tristan,* whose final cadence is shown in Example 4.11. Here is the mixed subdominant, leading to the apparent ii°⁶₅ chord, resolving directly to the tonic without reference to a dominant. Leading to the subdominant is the "Tristan" chord, acting here as an altered secondary dominant; and it is this progression of harmonies that points out the trope in Brahms's language. For Brahms the "Tristan" chord will not be tamed as a mere adjunct to a well-known cadence type but will retain its strangeness, interrupting the iv chord before it can resolve into the final tonic. And here, in Bloom's terms, is the crucial swerve that makes Brahms the champion of an artistic agon. Semiotically, Brahms's blow to Wagner is more insidious, though, as he turns the "Tristan" chord from a sign of *ratio difficilis,* an expressively pure token that is perfectly in accord with its content, to a sign of *ratio facilis,* a token of a broader conventional code whose replication runs across the repertoire.[33] Within its opera the "Tristan" chord is that perfect matching of signifier and signified into a magical sign whose meaning we know without recourse to a learned code. But when Brahms both repeats and tropes that sign, scattering it from its source, he makes of it a mere token of a type, a part of a code whose meaning rests upon convention, that deadly word for the modernist artist.

But such analyses are only interesting if they can rise above a mere contest between the hallowed dead. Otherwise, to worry about the canonical strength of Brahms as compared to that of Wagner is nothing but a harmless amusement. More than offering clues to artistic anxiety, the intertext plays into the matrix of the intermezzo. Put directly, because strangeness in Brahms's intermezzo points to Wagner's *Tristan,* and because *Tristan* is about desire, so too is the intermezzo. The desire signaled by the "Tristan" chord finds its double in the intermezzo and spreads through all of the apparent chords in Brahms's short text. Now the various analyti-

Bloom, Freud, and Riffaterre 105

cal problems become marked passages, imbued with meaning. The tonal ambiguities of the text come to signify the melted ego in love; and the shifting hypermeters
play into the neurotic rhythms of near madness. Even the motive, whose identity
is split between versions with three or four notes, becomes analogue to the divided
subject, losing itself in those sighing appoggiaturas.[34] If the two works speak of
desire and longing, though, it is clear that their conceptions of these emotions are
quite different. The constant rhythmic motion of Brahms's work is in opposition
to the static, near mystical depiction of desire in the opening of Wagner's prelude.
The disruptive "Tristan" double in the final cadence of the intermezzo shows us as
well that this text will have nothing to do with Schopenhauer's negation of will
and desire in that happy transfiguring death that Wagner so aptly portrays in the
final appearance of the "Tristan" chord. The intermezzo fights the deathless love
and loving death that promise redemptive annihilation in Wagner's text. Still, like
the cycling in Wagner's operas, the pieces of Brahms's Op. 118 look back in time
to the simpler significations of love in the second intermezzo, and the evocations
of the past in the Romanze, only to meet death again in the oddly familiar reference
to the "Dies Irae" that opens the final intermezzo, set in distant, dark E♭ minor.

6

As the strange note of the supernatural, the Freudian narrative of menacing recurrence, and the ungrammatical sign of intertextual meaning, the three
forms of the uncanny that have filled this chapter resist thorough separation. The
final chord of Schoenberg's "Song of the Wood Dove," for example, evokes the
uncanny with that strange skip in the bass from B♭ to G♭ in its last measures (Example 4.3). But that strange note is also an ungrammaticality. Where we expect
the B♭-minor triad to be prolonged by a chordal skip to F in the bass, we hear instead the startlement of G♭. Forming an intertext with Chopin's "Funeral March,"
we hear in the bass that same G♭, embellishing as an upper neighbor the chord tone
F in prolongation of a B♭-minor triad. The final chord in the "Song of the Wood
Dove" shares B♭ minor with the "Funeral March" and refers by synecdoche to the
eerie G♭ upper neighbor. Schoenberg's text fails to repress this detail as the sign for
death, and so G♭ strangely intrudes upon the final harmony. With awful force the
orchestra releases a specter of the memory of death. The Chopin sonata itself plays
through a Freudian narrative, until we consider whether its first interval bears an
intertext with Beethoven's sonata Op. 111 and hear the subjective extinction in
Chopin's text as ironic reply to the transcendence in the final movement of Beethoven's sonata. We hear the ungrammaticality in Brahms's intermezzo as a clue to its
meaning, only to recall that, as an apparent chord, the harmony of m. 36 is a signifier in the code for the uncanny. And the chord *is* uncanny once we hear it as the
ghostly form of a Wagnerian harmony.

If the enharmonic note, the apparent chord, the strange harmony, the ungrammaticality, the intertextual recognition can all signify forms of the uncanny, then
we run the risk of finding signs for that code at every turn. The uncanny devours

music from the inside, replaying the catastrophe of signification unbound. Kramer suggests that we learn to write music far from the anxiety of those ghost stories that seem to be the only ones we can tell in music (Kramer 2002, 286–87). His advice would mean that the only way of mastering the fear of death implicit in our confrontations with the uncanny is to recognize and accept that we the living are ever surrounded by the voices of the dead.

5 Narrative and Intertext: The Logic of Suffering in Lutosławski's Symphony No. 4

Artistic creation may be thus viewed as a hunt for human souls resulting in a cure for the most acute of human sufferings, a sense of loneliness.

—Witold Lutosławski (Notebook)[1]

In the first place, the plots that configure and transfigure the practical field encompass not just acting but suffering, hence characters as agents and as victims.

—Paul Ricoeur (*Time and Narrative* I, xi)

1

Moments signifying suffering are frequent enough in Lutosławski's music that we might view him as both agent and victim in the narrative of his compositions. As with Chopin, Lutosławski's life lends itself to the biography theory of musical narrative, in which tragic events miraculously inscribe themselves into the fabric of the music. The violent death of his father, the terror of the Nazi work camp, the repression of the Soviet regime, and the very history of Poland lend ample events for us to read as narratives in his music. This conflation of biography with music can run both ways, leading Tadeusz Kaczyński and Charles Bodman Rae to read ascending gestures in closing sections of Lutosławski's compositions as iconic signifiers for an ascent to heaven, as if one must compensate for the scant evidence of religious belief on the part of this Polish composer by searching in his music for signs of an unremarked faith.[2] Having no motivation to align the historical figure we name Witold Lutosławski with Polish Catholicism, I read those same ascending gestures as iconic for a scattered consciousness, as if subjectivity fails to cohere in the aftermath of a tragic event. One can barely avoid, however, the conclusion that ideology invades either interpretation of these musical signifiers.[3]

Roger Scruton writes about the biography theory of musical expression that it is "so evidently erroneous that it would be pointless to refute" (Scruton 1997, 144). Scruton here refers particularly to the notion that a composer writes her state of mind *into* the music. Edward T. Cone's idea of the musical persona allows us to rescue interpretation from such problematics of the biography theory (Cone 1974).

In Cone's conception we hear the expressive states of music as if projected from a subject, a consciousness, which is a mask worn by the composer. We may hear the music as if flowing from a single subjectivity, or we may hear the expressive states of multiple musical characters, but in either case we must take the same care in separating the persona of a composition from its composer as we do in separating the narrator of a novel from its author.[4] In so doing, we come perilously close to the death of the author, that slogan of a poststructuralist thought that seems intent on banishing the illusions of humanism. Though the perpetrator would seem to be Roland Barthes's essay "La mort de l'auteur" (1968), it is uncertain whether we could place the blame for the author's death solely on this text. Michel Foucault's "Qu'est-ce qu'un auteur?" (1969) argued many of the same issues and was published contemporaneously with Barthes's essay.[5] Foucault traces the death of the author back to Beckett and Nietzsche, though one might also consider the Russian Formalists, whose focus on literary structures foreclosed consideration of the author's biography. A related concept is W. K. Wimsatt and Monroe Beardsley's *intentional fallacy*, which ironically has strayed from its intention to address the aesthetic evaluation of poetry and has become instead a warning against reading the author's mind in search of a text's meaning.[6] No one authored the death of the author; it is a discourse that floats in the air.

Raymond Monelle argues that Barthes's "The Death of the Author" has been misunderstood by traditional critics, who see in it nothing more than an Escher print in which texts write themselves (Monelle 2000, 158). The pragmatic motivations behind Barthes's essay included challenging the notion that a single meaning for a text resides in its author, questioning the extent to which the author is also the narrator of a text, and reinvesting interpretive energy into the reader as the site where meaning takes place. Barthes's untangling of the various conceptions of the word *author* is in line with strategies of contemporary philosophy and literary criticism, which often seek to reveal that what we take to be natural, commonsense ideas are really the products of discourse.[7] Foucault, too, uses the strategy in order to divest the authority that we grant the author when we grope for meaning. He considers four author functions (Foucault 1977, 124–31). First, the author is a legal concept. The author owns her work and, to some extent, its manner of reproduction. To claim her rights on a work, the author must highlight its originality, its boundaries against other works. Thus, though not stated by Foucault, the problem of influence coils itself around the definition of the work and its concomitant implications of ownership and compensation. Authors have a vested interest in denying not only claims of influence but also arguments that intertextuality reduces the work to a collection of citations and allusions. Second, the author function varies with history and is not a constant of all discourse. One finds it difficult to imagine, for example, that musicians in the medieval period concerned themselves with real-life figures who authored plainchant in the same way that musicians in the nineteenth century concerned themselves with the real-life figures who authored symphonies. Third, rather than arising spontaneously, the author function results from a complex discourse around an individual and her works. The composer of a symphony, the painter of a landscape, the writer of a novel become authors only when their names enter a discursive space resulting in texts that depict them as historical figures, ascertain the works they have authored, describe their artistic style, etc. Finally, the author is scattered in texts. The search for an author sends us to a diversity of works, manuscripts, letters, documents, drafts, etc. The author is an intertextuality.

Binding these various functions into an apparent unity is the name of the author, a proper noun lending agency to sentences that might otherwise languish in the indeterminate and bureaucratic passive voice. Thus there was a real-life figure named Witold Lutosławski, who resided in Poland, ate meals, played the piano, paid bills, formed personal relationships, composed music, and so forth. There are biographical texts whose sentences refer to that historical figure called Witold Lutosławski. There is a name, Witold Lutosławski, that groups together a collection of compositions with titles like *Mi-Parti, Chain 1,* and *Trois poèmes d'Henri Michaux.* There are legal documents that refer to the compositions of a Witold Lutosławski and detail how the person so named will be compensated for the sale and performance of those works. There are texts that describe features of these works, allowing us to define a style in compositions by a certain Witold Lutosławski. There are texts that uncover structures in these works and tell a compositional narrative in which an agent called Witold Lutosławski combines intervals and set-classes to form chords called *harmonic aggregates.* From documents, books, articles, music, conversations, rumors there is the composer that I imagine in my mind who shares the name of the historical figure we call Witold Lutosławski. The proper noun Witold Lutosławski is the nexus around which texts form with which we come to interpret the proper noun Witold Lutosławski. Witold Lutosławski is an intertextuality.

Of the author functions in this intertext, the author as transcendental signified deserves attention for its impact on the interpretation of texts. The term *transcendental signified* has become common coin in postmodern thought, requiring the obligatory reference to Jacques Derrida's *Of Grammatology* (1974).[8] The vexing problem of signs is that nothing binds a signifier to a signified in a stable and unquestionable structure that can fix meaning. "There has to be a transcendental signified for the difference between signifier and signified to be somewhere absolute and irreducible," writes Derrida in a withering critique of the belief in the authority of meaning (Derrida 1974, 20). He locates the illusion of a transcendental signified within a metaphysics of presence that values the spoken word over the written one. Interpretation stumbles over aporia in the text and reaches back in search of the author's voice, whose author(ity) can guarantee meaning. If we could stand in the presence of the author, interpretation might stop at the endpoint of her voice, where the signifier and the signified could meet in the fullness of a determinate meaning. We need not have Derrida's acumen with the texts of western philosophy, though, to wonder how it could ever be the case that a semiotic system so open to the vagaries of time, culture, and the arbitrary connection between signifier and signified could suddenly find resolution in the presence of the author. To such wonderment, responses take the form of a quest to read the author's mind in search of the clues that will bring interpretation to a close. One of the strategies of interpretation is to revive the author as a presence, to search through documents in pursuit of a text that will clinch the case and validate a reading of her work.

In this quest the author and her work often stand in a reciprocal relationship, interpreting each other by mutual guarantee. Thus the historical figure Pyotr Tchaikovsky narrows the strange harmonic devices in the last three symphonies to codes for homosexuality, while the appearance of fate motives in these same works testifies to Tchaikovsky's feelings about that sexuality (Jackson 1995). Thus the fact that the historical figure Johannes Brahms read *Parerga und Paralipomena* allows us to view the *Vier ernste Gesänge* as a response to Schopenhauer's philosophy, while the joyous character of the final song shores up a claim that Brahms objected to the deep despair of that philosophy (Beller-McKenna 1994). Further, that the historical figure Johannes Brahms studied Wagner's scores supports an argument that there is a *Tristan* double in the final measures of the Intermezzo, Op. 118, No. 1, while the strange voice-leading of that chord tells us that Brahms would have nothing to do with a Wagnerian love-death (Chapter 4). The circularity of this strategy conveniently reduces the open text and its author to self-endorsed truth. But postmodern poetics is suspicious of meanings that reach a fixed point. Linda Hutcheon writes that "among the many things that postmodern intertextuality challenges are both closure and single, centralized meaning" (Hutcheon 1988, 127). When authors, texts, and readers become intertexts, they all participate in the scattering of meaning. In response to the polyvalent text we may wish to reserve the right to recapture a lost stability. In Chapter 1 we saw how Barthes reserved the term *work* for a physical document tied to the real-life author. We may endeavor to recover that document by reconstituting the conditions of its creation and the mind of its author. However, the moment we ask what that work means, we cease our dealings with it as a work and commence our struggle with it as a text, a "methodological field" open to pathways of interpretation, whose outlines shift with time and culture (Barthes 1981, 39). And as another text to be interpreted in the intertext around a work, the author has no transcendental power to close interpretation and fix meaning in place.

Released from its author, the text comes close to that collection of free-floating signifiers that so worries some who wish to make an interpretive claim. But even viewed far from the shadow of the author, the artwork as text and intertext resists interpretation. Whenever offered the freedom to make a text say just anything, we must confront those details that refuse to submit to unfettered critical subjectivity. In pursuit of an object of interpretive study, then, we seem pinned between two conceptions of the artwork, whose problematics leave us questioning our methodology before we even begin: the closed work, whose author is the transcendental signified establishing a singular meaning; and the open text, whose signifiers roam freely in the never-ending play of a language game. In such situations the middle road promises to mediate: the work comes off as less closed than we might first appreciate, and the text becomes open only within limits. Eco puts this succinctly as a "dialectics between the rights of texts and the rights of their interpreters."[9] Interpretations often resort to unremarked dialectics between dual conceptions of the author, the artwork, and the methods of analysis. A consideration of the text will resort to a discussion of the work; a conception of the author as persona will turn to the author as transcendental signified; an analysis of the text's meaning will take up problems of the conditions of that meaning. Though the vigor of our institutions does appear to rest on the fact that we can never settle matters of interpretation, confusion might be diminished if we were to be clear about our stance regarding the author/persona and the work/text.[10]

Much of the remainder of this chapter will be devoted to a narrative reading of Witold Lutosławski's Symphony No. 4 (1992) as a text. I shall have occasion to refer to other texts that invoke Lutosławski as interpreter of his own works. Though I shall try to bring these texts together in an effort to recover the composer's position, I view his interpretations as neither authoritative nor transcendental but as open to agreement, refutation, counterargument, misunderstanding, or outright denial. The narrative I read in the symphony will also refer to an intertext of other narratives and other music without worrying over claims about influence. That narrative tries to respond to the question What intertext do I bring to an interpretation of the text called Lutosławski's Symphony No. 4?

2

Lutosławski likely would have found distasteful the narrative analysis that follows. From a substantial intertext of his words about music, we find enticing hints of a dramatic and narrative sensibility that nonetheless is downplayed by a care to define narrative in purely musical terms.[11] Regarding the formal processes in his music, for example, Lutosławski offers:

> "Dramaturgy" . . . is very serviceable, although it has not come into use in the West. . . . It is significant because it reflects things which the term 'forms' does not fully cover. I would also introduce the concept of "akcja" (action), which, with its dramatic and literary implications, is narrower than "dramaturgy." (Nikolska 1994, 76)

But at the moment when those words *dramaturgy, action,* and *literary* might lead us to suspect extra-musical narratives, Lutosławski turns our attention back to intramusical processes:

> By "action" I understand a purely musical "plot"—not what is described as programme music. . . . That is to say, a chain of interrelated musical events. (ibid.)

In these texts, metaphors for drama, narrative, psychology, and emotion struggle against statements that deny extra-musical content. In reply to a question about the marking *funèbre* in the score of his Quartet, for example, he declares:

> The term *"funèbre"* isn't meant to suggest any hidden non-musical content. I use these descriptive terms at points which demand special interpretation. I want to achieve a particular expression, colouring or way of performing. The word *"funèbre"* tells the performer which particular effect I'm hoping for more emphatically than the word *"grave"* would. But as I've already said, this isn't meant to be a work of funereal character . . . it merely indicates the kind of interpretation required. (Kaczyński 1984, 18)

One strains to resolve the tensions in this statement—to understand how an indication for a funereal interpretation during performance captures a desired musical expression which is at the same time not funereal.

Such tensions are particularly evident in Kaczyński's published conversations with Lutosławski. With every composition under discussion, Kaczyński turns to the question of musical meaning, to which Lutosławski vacillates between descriptions of dramatic content and claims against the extra-musical. Finally, answering his interviewer's mildly programmatic interpretation of the Cello Concerto, Lutosławski loses patience:

> I'm horrified to see how one can be carried away by my careless mention of the dramatic conflict between the solo part and the orchestra. I must immediately use the reins on this galloping imagination which prompts you to interpret the work as an illustration to some macabre spectacle. This was never my intention. (Kaczyński 1984, 63)

Lutosławski exercises his composerly authority over the Cello Concerto, closing interpretation at the moment that its reader, Kaczyński, flexes his imagination. But even this foreclosure finds little resonance in the composer's later statement that "everybody has a right to receive the music in his own particular way, if he finds it fulfilling"—that is, one assumes, everybody but a musicologist, whose published accounts of this music might wrestle away in full view the composer's authority over his work (90). As if to make his position clear at last, Lutosławski concludes:

> You have often maintained in these conversations that non-musical associations and descriptions of the so-called content are indispensable to wider audiences. I am not so sure this is the best method of educating a listener. If you take him away from music itself to meanings beyond it, you might lead him astray, deprive him of authentic reactions by suggesting your own to him. . . . And that is why I view any discourse about the so-called content of a composition with some scepticism; to my mind this content is absent. (91)

We hear the voice of Hanslick in this final remark, which, in the face of so difficult a subject—balancing the rights of the composer and the listener, determining the relationship between music and its content, defining what we mean by meaning—resorts to outright denial of the extra-musical. Music must mean nothing but music, the self-sufficient system of sonic signifiers in endless denial of those signifieds that threaten to point elsewhere.

How shall we read these texts in which Lutosławski discusses musical meaning? We might take an attitude of suspicion and argue that, as a successful composer, Lutosławski had every motivation to uphold a position that grants autonomy to music and authority to its composer. One imagines a Lutosławski who secretly believes in the narrative, dramatic, and emotive content of music, but who feels constrained to tow the line in favor of absolute musical narratives, whose structures of pitch, rhythm, and form point only to the creative power of its composer. Another account might see the contradictions in these texts as the mere symptoms of the problem of absolute music. This view is no less debilitating with regard to Lutosławski, who, as a product of musical training steeped in the German tradition, accepts an ideology that removes from music its signifying endowment.[12] A closely related problem surrounds the term *program music,* which is often the nexus of confusion, since it may refer to representation, or narrative, or expression, or a combination of these ideas (see Scruton 1983, 41–61). Lutosławski's denials of extramusical content may have been directed particularly at representation, leaving open the possibility of music's expressive capacity. As such, an indication of *funèbre* in his Quartet allows for an expression of grief *as if* at a funeral while denying the representation of an actual funeral. A third account might contextualize these reactions within the musical history of mid-century Poland, where the government imposed an aesthetic calling for composers to write music with overt programs and socialist content. Lutosławski may have denied extra-musical meaning as a way of distancing himself from an unpleasant musical past. A more humane interpretation of these texts might accept their contradictions as the understandable result of even the most organized human intelligence, which by its nature suffers the conflicts, self-doubts, and reconsiderations that ultimately cancel a unified consistency.

To the question of what Lutosławski really believed regarding musical meaning in general, and musical narrative in particular, we must first respond by asking what *we* believe about these subjects. That we are storytellers, *homo fabulans,* has contributed to our capacity to narrativize music, hearing stories in it and telling stories about it. In Chapter 2 I reviewed some of the dramatic metaphors for pitch that animate both Schenker's and Lewin's music analyses. Nearly every text on music theory resorts to such metaphors in an effort to tell stories about structures.[13] Pitch in particular often becomes a character in a musical drama, where obstacles stand in the way of an objective, whether it be returning to the home key or participating in a motive. Music theory's absolute dramas of musical structure have a compelling power in our discourse, and we might conjecture that when Lutosławski defines *akcja* as "a purely musical plot" he aligns his conception with that discourse, enlivening musical structure by accounting for it narratively. Engaging that discourse for his music, we come to hear textures invading one another, or see registral blocks floating across an imagined musical landscape in defiance of the gravity of pitch centers.[14]

Controversy begins when we move from telling stories about music to hearing stories in the music. Much of the dispute about musical narrative comes from a literal and narrow definition of that term as the representation of characters who perform a sequence of actions. For music to tell a story under this definition it must have a power of representation that few are willing to grant. Thus Jean-Jacques Nattiez complains, "I may well hear a march in Mahler's Second Symphony and imagine that it concerns a group of men, but I don't know which men" (Nattiez 1990a, 244). And Lawrence Kramer warns, "any theory of the relationship between music and narrative must start with the cardinal fact that music can neither be nor perform a narrative" (Kramer 1995, 99). Overstated claims about music's power to tell a real story often result from confusion over the extent of representation in music—its capacity to imitate the sounds of a limited number of real-world objects. Crucial, though, is Scruton's observation that when music imitates birdsong, for example, "the musical line is not about the birdsong" but about "the birdlover's emotion as he is carried away by the song" (Scruton 1997, 127, 129). Monelle clarifies this point semiotically, arguing that, when music imitates the sound of a bird, that imitation may well be interpreted as an iconic sign, but the bird that music imitates is indexical to what are often the real signifieds of the music: spring, nature, joy (Monelle 2000, 19). We may well hear a march in Mahler's Second Symphony and imagine that it is an iconic sign for a real march, but we may also hear that march as indexical to other signifiers: military industrialism, regimentalism, national pride, fear. Music may make gestures of imitation, but it soon returns to itself, carried away with the emotional responses to the object of imitation. Music "appropriates being"; it does not represent the world but devours the world to make of it music (Adorno 1992, 71).

Nothing in music allows it to point unambiguously to the actions and characters necessary for a narrative. As if anticipating such an objection, though, Theodor Adorno responds, "It is not that music wants to narrate, but that the composer wants to make music in the way that others narrate" (Adorno 1992, 62). Adorno's response is directed particularly at the music of Mahler and makes no sweeping generalization about all musical narrative. Still, his characterization of Mahler's music suggests a willful misreading, in which we add that it is not that music wants to narrate, but that we want to hear music in the ways that we hear a narration. We want to hear stories. Structuring these perspectives, we can borrow Nattiez's semiotic tripartition and position musical narrative on three levels.[15] On the poietic level, a composer may wish to write music that narrates, focusing on musical attributes that she believes will signal that narration. On the immanent level, the music may have such attributes, regardless of whether the composer intends to write narrative music. On the esthesic level, a listener may want to hear music as she hears a narration, regardless of composer intent or musical attributes.[16] Because music has a limited capacity to represent, most observers now dismiss the ability of music to narrate a real story on the immanent level. These real stories take the brunt of Lutosławski's rejection of extra-musical meaning. The marking *funèbre* in his Quartet ought not confuse us into believing that the work is about a real funeral, though Lutosławski overstates the case when he denies even a funereal expressive character for this music.

For many who study musical narrative, it is the expressive/dramatic content of music that is the real object of analysis. The impulse to narrativize music is a motivation to find the expressive logic within both the individual composition and the repertoire that supports it. In the work of Robert Hatten (1991; 1994), Gregory Karl (1997), and Fred Maus (1988), among others, narrative analysis eschews the mapping of a particular story of actors and actions onto the music and, rather, concerns itself with describing expressive states evoked by the music and the ways that their unfolding implies a narrative. The term *expressive* covers primarily affective meanings (sadness, apprehension, etc.) but may also cover dramatic situations or ideas (outburst, transcendence, etc.). With regard to this type of narrative analysis, Lutosławski's comments on his music appear contradictory. While he refers to the dramatic content of his music, he also denies whatsoever anything extra-musical.[17]

3

Aristotle gives us our first theory of narrative in his *Poetics,* where we learn that plot, an imitation of action, is its most important feature. Aristotle teaches that a good plot has a beginning, a middle, and an end, that it has a proper magnitude, and that it gains unity through probable connections between events. Plot is unified, economical action. For many, causality differentiates plot from story. E. M. Forster defines story as "events arranged in their time-sequence," and plot as "a narrative of events, the emphasis falling on causality" (Forster 2002, 71). Paul Cobley defines story as "all the events which are to be depicted," and plot as "the chain of causation which dictates that these events are somehow linked" (Cobley 2001, 5). Examining the phenomenology of narrative, Paul Ricoeur adds that plot pulls us along in anticipation of future events that lead to a decisive final act. Because plots so often resort to detours and obstacles to delay conclusion, we review events to find the logic of their connection: the ordering of events need not be predictable, but it must be acceptable upon reflection. Thus a teleology governs our involvement with plot as we look forward to events and backward to their relation.[18] Described as such, plot makes for easy cross-domain mapping from a literary sphere to a musical one. Ricoeur's account of our involvement with plot rings with the echoes of Schenker's account of music (though admittedly of a tonal variety): we are pulled along tonal pathways, and we anticipate events to come, encountering detours and obstacles which, in retrospect, have a logic of connection after all. Music is unified, economical action.

This unity of plot may give pause to those who would flesh out a theory of narrative. From the *fabula* (plot) and *sjužet* (discourse) of the Russian Formalists, to the dialogism of Mikhail Bakhtin's theory of the novel (Bakhtin 1981), to the five codes of Roland Barthes's *S/Z* (1970), literary theorists have long recognized that narrative is a mix of different types of writing.[19] The plot imposes its unity by crossing the boundaries of disjunction, hiding lapses in predictive logic, and binding different types of discourse. Emplotment brings together scattered events, temporalities, motivations, characters, lyric descriptions, secret thoughts, unintended consequences, and makes of them a narrative. Again, Ricoeur explains:

> By means of the plot, goals, causes, and chance are brought together within the temporal unity of a whole and complete action. It is this synthesis of the heterogeneous that brings narrative close to metaphor. In both cases, the new thing—the as yet unsaid, the unwritten—springs up in language. Here a living metaphor, that is, a new pertinence in the predication, there a feigned plot, that is, a new congruence in the organization of the events. (Ricoeur 1984, ix)

Plot, like metaphor, brings together unlike terms in the formation of meaning. When we hear a story, we not only attend to its teleology, we also ask, Why these events? Why this ordering? Why this beginning? Why this point of closure? The recognition that plot is an arrangement of events is the realization that the narrator is inscribed into the plot as a point of view, the one who has made this *particular* arrangement of events (Ricoeur 1998, 279–80). The whole question of *mimesis* (showing) and *diegesis* (telling), of whether the action is mediated by a surviving narrator or whether it unfolds before us, has no bearing on the question of whether music, drama, poetry, or painting can be narrative.[20] The requirement for a narrative is that we apprehend that the story might have been arranged in another way. Narrative is any showing or telling of events (Cobley 2001, 6).

If we wish to find in music a narrative impulse, we must look past the immediacy of the music as action, and attend to disruption, the clash of topics, and the mixing of genres in an intertextuality. In the opening of Mozart's Sonata in F Major, K. 332, for example, Agawu hears references to musette, aria, the learned style, and the minuet—a remarkable topical interplay that we might miss if we were to listen only for the action of tonal processes and formal design (Agawu 1991, 45). In the music of Chopin both Jeffrey Kallberg and Jim Samson hear a stunning mix of genres, where a nocturne may be cast in the style of a mazurka, or where the lyricism of a slow waltz may lead to the brilliance of a virtuosic passage within a ballade (Kallberg 1996, 3–29; Samson 1989). In the music of Mahler tonality and form strain to the breaking point at containing the disruption that ensues from the clash of styles and intertextual references. In such cases we might narrativize the music, seeing in the binding together of unlike terms an indication that the music wants to make itself in the way that others make a narrative. These disruptions of form, genre, tonal structure, and the way music is supposed to go have been the clues to musical narrative in other studies. Anthony Newcomb, for example, writes that when the character piece invades Schumann's larger works, as when the "Im Legendenton" section interrupts the first movement of the *Fantasie,* it is a sign of Schumann's desire to narrate in the ways that his favorite novelists do (Newcomb 1987). Though Kramer questions Newcomb's reading of another Schumann work, *Carnaval,* he argues that the apparent disorder of its fragments is a narrative cue (Kramer 1995, 101–105). Musical action often halts at moments of lyricism in much nineteenth-century music, which prompts Monelle to argue for a musical temporality mirroring that of the novel, where the progressive time of musical transitions is in opposition to the static time of lyric melodies (Monelle 2000, 115–46). Musical plot is more than the immediacy of action, it is the binding together of unlike terms into a new pertinence, an intertextuality.

We can hear such signs of emplotment early in Lutosławski's textural music, where the limited aleatory of an *ad libitum* often alternates with a metered *battuta* section. In the opening movement of *Jeux vénitiens* (1961), for example, Lutosławski first uses his so-called *ad libitum* technique, in which pitch, rhythm, articulation, and dynamics for the various instruments are notated, but the manner of coordinating the parts is left to the performers. *Ad lib* sections generally lack a common meter, and the players perform their parts as they would a cadenza. During an *ad lib* the conductor ceases beating time, suspending the baton for an indicated duration until the next section is cued. Most often Lutosławski unfolds a single harmony within an *ad lib* section, with each pitch-class fixed to a single register. The result is a stasis of pitch, texture, timbre, and register beneath a complex rhythmic surface. By contrast, the so-called *battuta* sections require the resumption of metered time, and coordinated performance. Lutosławski structures the first movement of *Jeux vénitiens* on a simple formal plan, in which a single *ad lib* alternates with three *battuta* sections.[21] Opposition between these sections could barely be more pronounced: the *ad lib* sections are set for winds, brass, and piano, displaying a rhythmic vitality close to chaos, while the *battuta* sections are set for the strings, sustaining a serene homophonic texture, whose soft dynamic makes barely audible the gradual changes in pitch. Punctuating each abrupt transition from one section to the next is a short, loud attack from the percussion, underlining the points of disjunction. The plot here is close to metaphor, bringing together two dislike terms whose only points of contact and continuity are those short jabs from the percussion. Centripetal and centrifugal forces are tied to those percussive bursts, which bring to consciousness the unlikely juxtaposition of these musical sections while joining them at the same time. We seek a correlation to this musical opposition: the *ad lib* is outward activity, while the *battuta* is inward contemplation; the *ad lib* is present, the *battuta* is past; the *ad lib* is chaos, the *battuta* is order; the *ad lib* is narrative action, the *battuta* is static evocation.

But like many narratives, even the simple one of *Jeux vénitiens* questions unity of plot in the midst of asserting it. The *ad lib* sections only feign activity as the unchanging harmonic background forbids meaningful musical motion. In place of directed pitch motion, there is purposeless activity. The *battuta* sections hide the slithering motion of their pitches behind the apparent calm of a rhythmic stasis. In place of lyric evocation, there is carefully executed musical action. The more committed we become to hearing *Jeux vénitiens* as a narrative, the more it deconstructs the foundations upon which it narrates itself. In the act of telling its story, *Jeux vénitiens* tells of how it became nothing in the act of telling its story. The function of this musical narrative is to undermine musical narrative.

Because we often catch narratives in the act of affirming or undermining the rules of their formation, the question of narrative function becomes inevitable. What psychological and social functions do narratives serve, and why do narratives so often deny these functions in the midst of affirming them? Reviewing responses to these questions, Cobley finds that narratives help us to organize experience, view humans as agents of action, and envision the ego as narrator of its own story (Cobley 2001, 21–28). Implicit is the notion that reality is a jumble of events, places, people, threats, and rewards that the human mind needs to organize in the temporal sequence of an emplotted narrative. Narratives are ways of making sense of the world. J. Hillis Miller discusses related issues involving the ways that narratives either reveal or create meaning. Concerning the latter, narratives have a performative function: rather than imitating the world, they are acts that create the world (Miller 1995, 69). This view of narrative owes a debt to speech-act theory, in which performative utterances act upon and change reality, as when a minister says, "I now pronounce you man and wife."[22] Narratives propose modes of being, reinforce or question cultures, promote or deny ideologies. Kramer has taken up this view of narrative for the cultural analysis of music, explaining:

> By regulating the underlying dynamics of the stories it encourages, mandates, or prohibits, a cultural regime perpetuates itself. . . . In this case, what the stories do—or fail

to do, sometimes wittingly—is the cultural work of modeling, of symbolically enacting and enforcing, the process of prescription and placement, or what [J. Hillis] Miller calls ordering and confirming. (Kramer 1995, 105)

These types of musical narratives are perhaps most familiar in the writings of the so-called new musicology, where the ways that music is put together mesh with cultural conceptions of gender, power, society, etc. Thus, according to Susan McClary, the listener's desire to hear a resolution of chromatic tension at the end of *Carmen* underpins the violent murder of Carmen, so that the audience can rationalize her death as not only necessary but natural, perpetuating a societal need of the nineteenth century to confine vigorously feminine sexuality (McClary 1991, 62–63).

If we are committed to a view of the text as an immanent expression of the intent of its author, we may misunderstand these stories about music, as if McClary were claiming to uncover a secret and intended program for Bizet's opera. Though these types of narrative readings often point to characteristics of the text in question, they are best read as claims about narrative function, not about authorial intent. A focus away from the author, however, does little to answer questions about how these narratives really promote or challenge the societal order in which they first find themselves. Much the same problem as well accrues to Marxist readings that hope to show how everywhere and at once the text is an expression of the economic conditions of its time. Marx himself understood the problem of accounting for the multiplicity of artistic forms that arise within the relatively slow rate of change in social and economic conditions up to the nineteenth century (see Jauss 1982, 9–16). Ironically enough, to say that every text knowingly or unknowingly drives social and economic realities that marginalize vast segments of society is to submit every text to a totalizing meta-narrative that so far has failed to account for the varieties of genres, forms, meanings; the difference between the accepted text and the alien one; the ways some texts resist interpretation; the historical trajectory of readers in confrontation with texts; and the degree to which texts are often misunderstood in their own time. To be sure, texts from the past can be blind to our ideology and are often blind to the ideologies of their time as well (see Jameson 1981). But the hard work of uncovering just how texts involve themselves in social realities deserves deeper involvements with the interrelationships between semiotics, sociology, power relations, epistemes, and ideology than narrative studies of music have shown so far.

Lacking a more subtle and nuanced theory of narrative function, I can only suggest some readings at that level for *Jeux vénitiens,* where we see that the text questions the unified ego, as its disparate parts find no integrative moments. Within the culture of its composer, *Jeux vénitiens* both supports and undermines the authority of the state: the individual lines freely pursue their rhythmic way within the strict confines of a single harmony that remains in stasis through the *ad lib* sections. The narrative collapse of the opening movement performs the act of undoing the extra-musical narratives and social/political programs that the state had demanded of its functional music in the years before 1956. We can hear *Jeux vénitiens* as ironic in that its composer, Lutosławski, imposes authority over John Cage's free aleatoric processes and allows the performers of an *ad lib* the freedom to assert their will in only a limited way. This text seeks to signify freedom but is blind to the way that it confines freedom.

Though these views of narrative function offer potential for readings richer than the ones I have outlined here, I shall turn again to Ricoeur and the epigraph that heads this chapter in order to arrive at a narrative reading of Lutosławski's Fourth Symphony. We the living are like characters skirting the edge of disaster in narratives. Acts of God, forces of nature, ill intent, happenstance, and consequences strike the characters of narrative with a force often akin to malice, so that they must find a way to respond to the reversals that threaten to make life meaningless. As characters become victims, emplotment of the events that bring about their misfortunes makes the function of narrative an account of suffering (Ricoeur 1984, ix). We can read these accounts didactically and literally. Isabel Archer, for example, suffers because she has miscalculated the motivations of her husband, whom she never would have met without her wealth, which she never would have inherited without the secret love of her cousin. The account of Isabel's suffering brings together her wealth, her husband, her cousin, and their secret motivations into a plot of causation. Isabel learns from her suffering, though Henry James stops the narrative short of telling us her final decisions, leaving us to ponder what lessons we can gain from her misfortune. But our readings need be neither didactic nor literal to account for suffering in the way that Ricoeur describes narrative. Emplotment itself makes suffering meaningful by replacing the accidents of time and place with a chain of causality that makes temporality human. Perverse strokes of chance become arrivals by design; events one after another become events one because of another; and moments of suffering become glimpses of the marvelous as they initiate the questioning that leads to our search for meaning in the order of a causal temporality.[23]

Musical narrative, so conceived, depends upon moments of disjunction, when unlike elements disrupt music's usual power to present itself as undivided action. Among the disparate events, one must recognize an instance of *peripeteia*, reversal. From this moment of suffering, one looks both backward and forward to find the expressive logic that emplots the *peripeteia*, joining it to the other musical events in a chain of causation that makes time human. Analysis of Lutosławski's Fourth Symphony will begin with that moment of suffering and show how it gains its signifying capacity through a code that runs through both his works and those of others. In search of the expressive logic that moves through disjunction to that moment, the analysis will bring to the symphony other musical narratives. Miller conjectures that since no story perfectly fulfills its function, another story is always necessary (Miller 1995, 72). Northrop Frye, in a phrase that by now sounds familiar, says that "Poetry can only be made out of other poems; novels out of other novels"; and, responding to that statement, Ricoeur writes that narrative structures are borne upon a tradition of narrative (Frye 1957, 97; Ricoeur 1998, 287). A narrative is read and understood intertextually with other narratives. To the Fourth Symphony, therefore, the analysis will bring not only other musical narratives by Lutosławski, but also narratives by Chopin, particularly his ballades. The choice would seem driven by Lutosławski's biography, and largely this is so. Lutosławski acknowledged that, among the Romanticists, Chopin was his only influence, and he made reference to the ballades as proof that Chopin was "a great innovator capable of developing a dramaturgically consistent—and profoundly impressive—musical action."[24] As must by now be evident, though, the analysis will make no claims that these particular works informed the act of composing the symphony, or that Lutosławski intended the musical action to be read in such a way. References musical, textual, biographical, and historical are the intertext through which I approach a narrative analysis of this symphony.

4

A prolonged outcry brings Lutosławski's Fourth Symphony to a climax at Fig. 85, close to the conclusion of the work, as the full orchestra repeats and then sustains a ten-note chord that fills five octaves of register space. Example 5.1 is a reduction of these measures, including an interval string that represents the ordered pitch intervals from the lowest to highest notes in the sustained chord. Perfect fourths and tritones predominate, no doubt contributing to the chord's harsh effect. Throughout Lutosławski's oeuvre we find such chords marking moments of outcry, anguish, despair, even death. An early example appears in *Musique funèbre* (1958), whose *Apogée* section begins with a loud, sustained, twelve-note chord, filling five octaves of register space before a collapse brings the full ensemble to a twelve-note cluster, set within a single octave. In Lutosławski's later music these twelve-note chords, or *harmonic aggregates,* become central to his organization of pitch, so the mere appearance of one is insufficient to signify outcry.[25] However, as with *Musique funèbre,* when outcry is signified, the harmonic aggregate is usually loud, and sustained, often within the frenzied activity of an *ad lib.* The collapse of register space, either to a chromatic cluster within an octave or to a single pitch, is also typical. In the climax of *Chain 1* (1983), for example, a wildly active *ad lib* section at Fig. 46 sets a seven-note chord that soon collapses to a single pitch, $B\flat_4$, before registral expansion brings in a harmonic aggregate, which itself collapses to a chromatic cluster. These moments when the entire ensemble contracts into a cluster or a single pitch suggest metaphors for darkness or a psychic implosion to deep despair.

As melody comes to the fore in Lutosławski's later music, and harmonic aggregates play a smaller role in structuring pitch, a single large chord may be enough to signify outcry.[26] In the third movement of his Piano Concerto (1987), for example, an eight-note chord with doublings, unusual in the composer's music, fills six octaves in the climax at Fig. 77. As is common for these outcries, the chord bursts forth powerfully across the entire orchestra, which sustains it in an extended moment of severity. Elsewhere, in support of a narrative informed by the anxiety of influence, I have interpreted this chord as a reaction to the voice of Bartók that we can hear in this same movement, but the chord may be read as outcry even without that framing reference (Klein 1999a). In Lutosławski's chamber and vocal music, even smaller collections may signify a dreadful event. Maja Trochimczyk notices,

Example 5.1. Outcry in Lutosławski, Symphony No. 4 (1992), Fig. 85

for example, that Lutosławski often uses chords with interlocking minor thirds to signify death (Trochimczyk 2001, 105). Callings these *doom* chords, Trochimczyk points to a prolonged tetrachord at the close of Lutosławski's *Tarantella* (1990), whose text begins with a reference to the whirling of life but ends with a description of the treading of death. This particular chord is set in a soft dynamic range, playing against significations of outcry and, rather, pointing to a dismal expressive atmosphere. But in other works Lutosławski sets such chords as dynamic jabs amid climactic sections. In the final movement of *Partita* (1984), for example, the climax is set as an *ad lib* section that begins with a chord of interlocking minor thirds and concludes with the piano hammering out repetitions of a similar chord.

When I claim that the climax of Lutosławski's Fourth Symphony is an outcry, I do so within an authorial intertext like the one sketched here. But we could open this intertext to outcry in music by Mahler, Beethoven (the opening of the Ninth Symphony's final movement comes to mind), Prokofiev (moments of terror in *Romeo and Juliet*), and many other composers. Familiarity with Lutosławski's works is no precondition for understanding a code that often includes harsh dissonances and screaming brass. The outcry in the Fourth Symphony also allows for *intratextual* connections. Far from initiating a new musical section through the disjunction of a sudden outburst, the chord at Fig. 85 concludes a section whose initiation comes at Fig. 73, where the harmonic aggregates shown in Example 5.2 interrupt completion of an optimistic melody. These earlier chords form a breach in the music as action and serve as one of many clues to narrative in the symphony. These chords have the now familiar signs of outcry: the harmonic aggregate, the loud dynamic, the full orchestra, the momentary stasis. Since these chords interrupt closure of the previous melody, they are the point of *peripeteia* for the symphony, the reversal of fortune that signifies suffering. Between the two outbursts at Figs. 73 and 85 there are two sections that perform the dramatic functions of recoil and pronouncement. In the first of these sections, Figs. 74–81, a direct response to the first outcry leaves the music bereft of the melodic direction that it had evinced previously. The various lines of this section oscillate across dyads for a number of

73

Interval String: 8 - 3 - 4 - 4 - 3 - 4 - 4 - 3 - 4 - 3 - 1   5 - 3 - 3 - 5 - 3 - 3 - 5 - 3 - 3 - 4 - 1
(low to high)

Accidentals apply only
to the notes they precede

Example 5.2. Lutosławski, Symphony No. 4, Fig. 73

measures before the strings and brass come together in a more purposeful melody, whose most recurrent interval is the falling semitone, which Trochimczyk hears within topoi of death, lamentation, and sighing.[27] The initial loss of melodic direction in this section is a recoil in the face of the tragic turn of Fig. 73. The musical persona loses itself momentarily before finding its voice to reassert melodic subjectivity.

This melody concludes on a sustained perfect fifth, long a signifier for emptiness or moral judgment. The strings and brass at Fig. 82 now move to a unison melody in a slower tempo, beginning on longer notes that commence the second section since the tragic turn. That the melody begins in the low register on a sustained note is metaphoric for a profound statement. And the exclusive use of tritones and semitones in the melody brings forth immediate connection to the *Musique funèbre*, whose twelve-tone row is made up entirely of these same two intervals. The singularity of purpose expressed by the brass and strings in unison brings in allusion to the chorus of a Greek tragedy, making a pronouncement upon the dramatic action. As such, this second section pronounces the deep consequences of the reversal of fortune. From the harmonic aggregate of Fig. 73 to that of Fig. 85, we can form a causative sequence of events: reversal leads to recoil leads to pronouncement leads to outcry.

This remarkable paragraph of music, what Rae calls the symphony's "decisive moment of culmination," is the narrative cue that asks us to look back upon the various episodes of the symphony and hear them one because of another rather than one after another (Rae 1994, 244). The usual methodology of formal analysis begins by charting the succession of musical sections as is done in Table 5.1, which considers textural, rhythmic, and melodic features to delineate the parts of this symphonic whole. In regard to the larger musical sections, although the symphony is ostensibly a single movement, every commentator agrees that it is set with Lutosławski's famous two-movement scheme, in which the first movement is generally short and episodic in relation to a longer and more directed second movement.

With regard to the second movement, commentators are also in agreement about the attractive quality of the harmonic texture that unfolds so carefully beginning at Fig. 53. In addition, Lutosławski, Harley, and Rae all point to the singing melody at Fig. 64 as the main thematic focus of the symphony (Nikolska 1994, 146; Harley 2001, 189; Rae 1994, 242). Though such a survey of formal sections and outstanding features represents an important stage in understanding the symphony, the results fail to answer questions about the dramatic effect of the climax. Why this ordering of events? Why this point of expressive reversal? What chain of causation leads through the episodes to the final measures of music? Attempts to find coherence in the formal sections of this symphony may resort to purely musical narratives. Andrez Tuchowski renders a finely detailed study of the voice-leading and registral connections that bind together this symphony's structural points (Tuchowski 2001). Rae offers the single observation that the constant $\frac{9}{8}$ meter in the second movement lends a rhythmic momentum that binds the episodes (Rae 1994, 239). Though simple enough, Rae's comment reminds us of similar observations by Alan Rawsthorne and Jim Samson that the compound duple meter in Chopin's ballades acts as a narrating presence, linking the musical scenes (Rawsthorne 1966, 43; Samson 1992, 86). But to hear this symphony as leading up to a culminating event is to place the text within a perspective of musical narrative that considers the expressive trajectory of the composition: it is to hear Lutosławski's Fourth Symphony wanting to tell itself in the ways that other music has told itself.

The expressive narrative of the Fourth Symphony plays within a tradition of the nineteenth century. Despite Lutosławski's avant-garde music of the 1960s, with the emphasis on texture, the denial of melody, and the intercutting of musical sections, his documented concern with developing a formal model whose expressive weight lies at the end, coupled with a mounting attention to melodic writing in his late works, suggests a tradition of narrative in this music. That tradition unavoidably points back to Chopin, and, as we have seen, Lutosławski admits to this connection. The narrative logic of Chopin's larger forms is governed by what Cone calls *apotheosis*, "a special kind of recapitulation that reveals unexpected harmonic richness and textual excitement in a theme previously presented with a deliberately restricted harmonization and a relatively drab accompaniment."[28] Cone considers apotheosis in Chopin's music to be an early version of what will become thematic transformation in the music of Liszt and Wagner, where a poietic impulse to narrativize music makes critical the desire to avoid exact repetition of a theme. If characters in a narrative change over time, then the themes that represent them or their emotional states must change over time as well. By the end of the nineteenth century, the recapitulation of a theme in an emotionally charged texture close to the end of a work is a near cliché, signaling a narrative that moves toward a final transcendence, salvation, or transformation. In Chopin's larger forms the theme that will reappear in apotheosis is often a nocturne or pastorale, whose simple accompaniment imbues it with the potential for a harmonic and textural elaboration. Though the nocturne in particular is associated with Chopin, a broader perspective might see these internal themes as metaphors for otherness. A gendered reading might view these themes as signifying the feminine and their apotheosis as an

Table 5.1. Lutosławski, Symphony No. 4, Form

Introductory Movement

Figs. 1–23				
Figs. 1–3	3–6	6–8	8–13	13–23
Opening Theme	*Ad lib*	Opening Theme Developed	*Ad lib*	Opening Theme Developed to Climax

Main Movement

First Theme Group Figs. 23–43						Second Theme Group Figs. 43–53			
23–25	25–27	27–31	31–32	32–39	39–43	43–47	47–51	51–52	52–53
First Theme	Texture and Tom-toms	Sighing Theme	Texture and Tom-toms	Development	Climax	Second Theme	Pronouncement Theme	Triplet Motive	Ascending Scale

Main Movement (cont.)

Texture Music and Apotheosis Figs. 53–73				Climax and Aftermath Figs. 73–92					Coda Figs. 92–97
53–56	56–59	59–64	64–73	73–74	74–82	82–85	85–86	86–92	92–end
First Aggregate	Second Aggregate	Solos and Transition	Apotheosis Theme	*Peripeteia*	Second Theme	Pronouncement Theme	Outcry	Solos *ad lib*	Coda

exaltation of feminine musical discourse (though defined by a man). However we interpret the theme marked for apotheosis, we can hear it as signifying a difference from the ontological reality of the surrounding musical material: it is past as opposed to present, interior as opposed to exterior, there as opposed to here, feminine as opposed to masculine, night as opposed to day.

The implication of apotheosis is that a musical persona has achieved a heightened emotional state. In rare cases, as in Chopin's Barcarolle, Op. 60, or Debussy's *L'Isle joyeuse*, the apotheosis simply exalts an emotional state that was evident from the beginning. Though we may hear hints of shadow in both of these works, there is little implication of a struggle that leads to the apotheosis: the Barcarolle's climax reinforces a perfectly fulfilled happiness, while that of *L'Isle joyeuse* brings the joyous state to one of ecstasy. Lacking any sense that there is a change of emotional state in these works, we may downplay a sense of narrative in this music. More often, however, the apotheosis comes in an effort to overcome an undesired state. Chopin's First Ballade, for example, begins with a dysphoric waltz marked with tragic possibilities by an imposing and profound introduction. The second theme of this ballade presents an alternate reality, a desired "as if" that stands in opposition to the opening waltz. When that second theme returns in apotheosis, one has the sense that the musical persona has overcome the darkness of the earlier waltz, and the tragic conclusion of the ballade rests on the eventual failure of that apotheosis. Broadly, the drama of this ballade begins with a somber state followed by a desired alternative whose eventual apotheosis promises realization, only to lead to a reversal that brings on a tragic conclusion.[29] Chopin's Fourth Ballade tells a story similar to the First, with a greater sense that the musical persona has really achieved through effort the apotheosis of the desired theme before reversal sends the narrative to a tragic end. The reversal in this case is close in expressive effect to that of Lutosławski's Fourth Symphony.

In Lutosławski's late music there is little question of a theme appearing first in an unadorned version only to return as apotheosis near the end of the work; unless we force the issue, this technique plays no part in his larger forms. Rather, the fact that Lutosławski gives us a theme at all can be the intimation of a narrative that plays into the tradition of apotheosis. The inevitable example is his Third Symphony (1983), which draws the listener into the famous *cantando* theme of Fig. 84 that moves to the climactic and optimistic end of the composition. No commentary on the Third Symphony can resist gushing over this melody, and for good reason. Rae calls the *cantando* "the most memorable thematic idea of the work," before describing its "potent" continuation and "triumphant delivery" (Rae 1994, 174–76). To be sure, the Third Symphony has other melodic ideas, one of which leads to an earlier, putative climax at Fig. 76. But textural music characteristic of Lutosławski's avant-garde period interrupts these other melodic ideas, lending reason to savor the long-breathed *cantando* theme when it finally arrives. Trumping the emotional effect of the theme is the celebratory gamelan music that enters at Fig. 99, accompanied at first by the full orchestra, whose punctuating chords gradually drop the lower register to uplift the music into its shimmering conclusion, leaving little wonder why the Third Symphony is one of Lutosławski's most popular compositions. The sense of apotheosis one hears in the *cantando* theme only gains potency when we hear the Third Symphony within the context of the composer's works up to that point. Though his textural music had found its own ways of telling and being, in retrospect one can hear the prolonged stasis of these textures as ways of clearing creative space, of pushing away a tradition that invested its poetic voice into melody. As the narrative path of the Third Symphony wends its way to the *cantando* theme, it recaptures that tradition of musical storytelling, empowering melody as the site of expressive fulfillment.[30]

In the Fourth Symphony the theme promising apotheosis begins in the upper strings at Fig. 64, shown in Example 5.3. Illustrating Lutosławski's predilection for additive techniques as each ascending line moves through one more whole step than did the previous line, the theme's reference to whole-tone collections becomes increasingly focused before a reversal of direction replays the additive technique in descending lines. The theme participates in a three-part texture, with the low strings and brass moving steadily in short notes, and the winds and percussion moving at the fastest rate. The three textures with their steady but individual rhythmic pacings lend an inexorable momentum to the symphony. Each repetition of the theme begins a whole step higher in quicker rhythmic values, indicative of an inevitable drive to the goal of apotheosis until the reversal at Fig. 73 interrupts completion of the third enactment of the theme. Until that interruption the symphony had clearly taken a hopeful turn, beginning before the main theme with a carefully unfolded texture at Fig. 53. Over the course of Figs. 53–59 the music unfolds a twenty-four-note chord in a stunning combination of tone colors signifying a nocturnal magic, as the texture begins in the upper register with the piccolo, solo violin, first violins, glockenspiel, and a small cymbal. The texture remains at first in the upper register, gradually adding oboe, second violins, vibraphone, and another cymbal before the lower register becomes active with the addition of lower strings, harp, and bassoon. Together the three groups form a harmonic aggregate, which is doubled at the octave with the entrance of three more timbral groups. The musical action from the unfolding texture through the main melody marks an expressive shift in the symphony from the dark opening measures to the promise of a brightening apotheosis.

That promise remains unfulfilled as the reversal and outcry of the symphony's climax halt completion of the main theme. The dramatic/expressive narrative here closely follows a moment of *peripeteia* in Chopin's Fourth Ballade that was discussed in Chapter 3 (refer back to Example 3.5).[31] In that narrative Chopin presents primarily two themes: a dysphoric waltz in F minor and a more hopeful pastorale in B♭ major. Shortly before the coda the pastorale returns in an apotheosis. Because the return of the pastoral theme in D♭ at m. 169 magically interrupts a cadence in the key of B♭ minor, an ascending chromatic sequence seems a necessary willed effort to earn the key of D♭ major. Though a satisfying full cadence in D♭ fulfills the promise of apotheosis for the pastorale in m. 191, a B♮ in m. 194 transforms the harmony into an augmented sixth with the power to pull D♭ down to C, the dominant of the home key, F minor. As expected, in m. 195 the music lands on a minor six-four chord, underscored by hypermetric placement, textural change, phenome-

Example 5.3. Lutosławski, Symphony No. 4, "apotheosis" theme

nal accent, and an embellished arpeggio. We have already witnessed the tragic effect of this chord in a discussion of the arrival six-four in Chapter 3. Having lost the triumph of D♭ major with the tragic six-four, the persona attempts to recover the earlier affirmation. Contrary motion in the outer voices following the reversal indicates a willed effort to gain stature in the face of the terrible implication of that tragic six-four chord. The entire passage ends on triple *forte* C-major triads, whose presumed triumph is ironic in light of their function as resolution of the earlier six-four chords. A homophonic passage that follows suggests a religious topic, while the relatively higher register narrows the expressive content to one of transcendence. The silences framing this passage lend that transcendence an air of the deus ex machina—that is, we may believe it to be too sudden and contrived. At best, the religious topic offers only brief respite before the final narrative action of the coda, whose fierce virtuoso passages leave little doubt to a tragic end or a defiant struggle.

Like Chopin's Fourth Ballade, Lutosławski's Fourth Symphony begins darkly but offers a happy alternative in the magical textures and striving main theme that come after the text's midpoint. But, as with the ballade, the implication of a bright and fortunate apotheosis reaches instead a terrible reversal before the coda. In the face of these circumstances, the closing section of the Fourth Symphony is as defiant as that of Chopin's Fourth Ballade. This reading parts company with those who read in the coda of the Fourth Symphony a "spirit of exuberance" or a "positive note" (Rae 1994, 245; Harley 2001, 189). These uplifting readings may be responding to intertextual references to the joyous close of the Third Symphony. Both works end energetically with repeated E's in the bass, above which the Fourth Symphony adds a chord that includes the major third, a likely signifier for a nontragic state. But in the two measures preceding these closing chords we hear descending chromatic lines in the string parts, accompanied by glissandi in the harps, which I read as iconic signs for sighing with their indexical associations to grief. Accompanying these descending patterns are chords with prominent tritones and semitones, the signifiers for mourning in Lutosławski's compositional language. In addition, the first measures of the coda take up a theme from the opening of the main movement, which we shall see has tragic allusions as well. On the whole, it is difficult to hear much optimism in the coda of the Fourth Symphony, which retells the narrative of Chopin's Fourth Ballade.

Even the quiet homophonic passage that follows the tragic turn in Chopin's ballade finds a correlate in the solo *ad lib* sections of Figs. 86–92 that follow the climax of the Fourth Symphony. These quiet solos are all that remain after the full force of the catastrophic chord at Fig. 85; they bring to mind Lutosławski's oft-quoted statement about his method of writing past the climax of a composition:

> The building up to a single climax in the music is of course nothing new; what is perhaps my original contribution—and I think it is important for the understanding of my music—is the *way out* of the climax. This is closely bound up with my technique of "aleatory counterpoint": gradually the music rises to a sort of (apparently) traditional climax . . . suddenly one of the musicians and then others and still others realize, as I imagine, that "there is no use continuing it any more," and they start playing something else, each one going his own way. The musical culmination is collective, the way out of the climax is individual. (Nordwall 1968, 95)

In the Fourth Symphony these solos in the aftermath of the climax resort to replaying motives from the first part of the main movement, all of which feature prominent half-step motion. Particularly affective is the group of three violin solos at Fig. 89, whose canonic glissandi down through three half steps are reminiscent of the *funèbre* section of Lutosławski's Quartet. In the hushed wake of the reversal in Chopin's Fourth Ballade, the persona sought hope in the religious hymn topic that preceded the coda. But in the midst of the outcry in the Fourth Symphony, the collective forces give up, leaving the individual to recognize and replay the return of the sad expressions that opened the symphony. In both musical narratives a final silence before the coda lends the persona a chance to collect energy for the defiant conclusion.

To review, the climax of Chopin's Fourth Ballade moves from the apotheosis of a desired emotional state to a reversal, to which the persona responds with a willful struggle to recapture the apotheosis; in the face of failure the sudden quiet of a hymn topic finds no success before a pause allows the persona to prepare for the tragic coda. The climax of Lutosławski's Fourth Symphony follows a similar dramatic path. An optimistic theme, introduced by a prolonged texture with significations for a magical otherness, promises an apotheosis that leads instead to reversal, an ominous pronouncement, and a culminating outcry; from this climax the persona collapses into a remembrance of an earlier dark state before a pause lends time to prepare for the defiant coda. Within these twin narrative sequences, two moments of disjunction mark sites of suffering that provoke our search for causative links between musical events. The first of these, the moment of reversal, has been our focus from the start. But the second of these, involving the sudden quiet moment after the climax, clarifies subtlety of difference between the two dramatic texts. While the odd appearance of the hymn topic in the Fourth Ballade might be read as an appeal, or a moment of reflective resignation, the terrifying loneliness of the solo *ad libs* in the Fourth Symphony that sing their song of grief out of the shadow of the orchestra's awesome force allows little room for an encouraging ending. We shall see later that the implied narrator of the Fourth Symphony knows from the start that the story must end tragically.

The implication of the musical narrative from the apotheosis to the last measures of the Fourth Symphony is that the main theme before the climax has been an alternate reality to an undesirable expressive state. The short introductory movement, to which I shall soon turn, sets up the dark mood of the symphony, and when the main movement follows without a pause, we are inclined to hear its opening theme within a similar expression. Example 5.4 shows this first theme from Fig. 23, played by violins with responses from the English horn, featuring the half-step intervals prominent throughout the symphony. The descending triplet patterns are the symphony's earliest iconic signs for sighing, and such signs become more obvious at Fig. 27, where extended glissandi in the strings are again reminiscent of Lutosławski's Quartet. The main theme or its triplet motive returns throughout the first half of the symphony, making a marked entrance at Fig. 51 just before the expressive transformation by the textures of Fig. 53. In addition, both the main theme and the sighing glissandi will play their roles in the solo *ad libs* that follow the climax. The first part of the main movement comes to a climactic point at Figs. 39–41, where *ad lib* sections briefly take over as the piano launches into a passage that resembles the cadenza in the third movement of Lutosławski's Piano Concerto (Rae 1994, 240). That passage from the concerto led to an outcry from the orchestra, and within this intertext Fig. 41 of the symphony has a similar dramatic function. The main movement from Figs. 23 to 42 evokes a distressed emotional state that leads to outcry.

A second theme for the main movement, beginning at Fig. 43 and shown in Example 5.5, responds to that climax with a melody that maintains the insistent and mournful half steps of the earlier theme but involves them in a larger pattern that begins each phrase a half step higher, suggestive of striving. The effort to break away from the dark expressive state is weighed down, however, by pedal tones on B_1 and $A_{\flat 2}$ in the low strings. This same theme returns after the reversal in Fig. 73, though in that instance it takes some time to coalesce. The second theme thus takes on a function of response in the face of outcry. In the first instance, though that response fails to uplift the expression of the symphony, leading instead to another utterance of the first theme in Fig. 51, the sudden turn to a bright texture in Fig. 53 casts light back upon the second theme as an event along the path to a more fortunate alternative. In the second instance, however, the second theme fails utterly, concluding on the fateful pronouncement of Fig. 82 that makes manifest a grim reality that will find no answering transformation.

The progress in the main movement, from the sighing theme and its development in its first half to the optimistic texture and theme of its second half, suggests that the Fourth Symphony is a token of the darkness-to-light narratives common to music of the nineteenth century. The reversal at the end of the symphony turns tragic the narrative as darkness overcomes that light. That there are two moments

23

Accidentals apply only
to the notes they precede

Example 5.4. Lutosławski, Symphony No. 4, main movement—first theme

43   44

45

Accidentals apply only to
the notes they precede

Example 5.5. Lutosławski, Symphony No. 4, main movement—second theme of outcry in the main movement, though, and that each is answered by the same theme suggests the possibility of reading the symphony as a telling and retelling of a story, wherein the first half of the main movement tells of a progression from darkness to outcry, and the second half tells of a progression from light to outcry. In support of a double narrative, we might note that the bright texture of Fig. 53 comes almost too easily, since nothing in the music up to that point suggests a gradual transformation. In the brief first movement we find evidence as well of a narrative that wants to tell and retell. Though this relatively brief movement retains the refrain structure of Lutosławski's other large works, the lyric melody that forms the first refrain testifies to a dramatic and narrative function already in the opening measures. More than fulfilling the objective in Lutosławski's earlier works of engaging the listener, this music will tell the story of the symphony in advance.[32]

The first movement opens by unfolding a C-major triad in first inversion, shown in Example 5.6. Rae hears in this chord and the first theme in the solo clarinet a similarity of expression to the sober middle movement of Lutosławski's *Partita* (Rae 1994, 238). In addition, the first-inversion sonority makes an intertextual allusion to the paradigmatic chords that open opera recitatives. The slow unfolding of a major triad in first inversion in the first measures of both Chopin's First Ballade and Beethoven's *Tempest* sonata marks instances when instrumental music borrows this operatic paradigm to signify the entrance of a persona who narrates (see Berger 1996, 68–70; Hatten 1994, 174–84). The Fourth Symphony tropes this harmonic signifier for narration by extending the inverted C-major chord with an inverted B major, from which the clarinet begins its solo line. Pulsing E pedals in the bass and cello weigh down this opening theme until its interruption by an *ad lib* section creates a set of oppositions: the opening *battuta* appears in the middle and low registers while the *ad lib* appears in the highest register; the *battuta* features a harmonic background of tetrachords against a single solo, while the *ad lib* features the aggregate against multiple solos; the rhythm of the *battuta* is steadily paced, while that of the *ad lib* shimmers with activity. The lightly textured upper register in strings and harps loans the *ad lib* resemblance to Bartók's night music, and that connection becomes stronger when the brass and clarinet at Fig. 5 play a short figure with canonic imitation that runs through an interval cycle in a manner similar to Bartók's contrapuntal procedures.[33] The allusion to Bartók's night music marks the *ad lib* as an alternate reality to the somber opening theme. A number of additional interpretations are possible as well: the two sections may map onto a temporal sequence of present and past; they may map onto a spatial opposition of exterior versus interior; they may map onto a psychological ontology of reality versus imagined alternative. Finally, we can understand this *ad lib* section as a pretelling of the magical texture that will appear at the midpoint of the second movement, and forging this connection is a trumpet solo at Fig. 4 of the first *ad lib* that bears remarkable similarity to a trumpet solo in the texture at Fig. 59 (see Rae 1994, 242).

The thematic *battuta* appears three times in the first movement, interrupted twice by refrains of the *ad lib*. Already with the continuation of the theme at Fig. 6 the bass begins to pull free of the pedal point that anchored the first section. At

SYMPHONY No. 4

(1992)

Witold Lutoslawski
(1913 - 1994)

Example 5.6. Lutosławski, Symphony No. 4, beginning

Fig. 13 the theme continues its development for the last time before reaching a climax that will move the music into the second movement. This final utterance of the thematic material in the first movement witnesses an expansion of register, an accumulation of orchestral forces, and a girding of the melodic line as it moves from solo instruments into the full violin section. The music gathers its strength for the events to come, almost overextending itself as the violins reach to a stratospheric E_7 before repeated chords bring the music to a climactic and frenzied *ad lib* at Fig. 20. In retrospect this *ad lib* is the symphony's first outcry, exhaling at Fig. 22 as the register and texture contract to make way for the first theme of the second movement.

The narrator of the Fourth Symphony anticipates the story to come, framing the tale of the symphony as a fait accompli, a causative sequence of events that takes place in the past. This forecast of the expressive path to come little impacts the pity and fear associated with the *peripeteia* of the main movement. Like the retelling of a myth for whose hero we cheer, we attend to the Fourth Symphony in the hope that perhaps this time the quest will not falter. The music as action draws us into the plot, particularly during the main movement's promised apotheosis, so that we can almost forget the narrator's warning of the inevitable reversal. As such, the outcry interrupting the apotheosis is a moment of realization and recognition, an instance when the persona as hero, the narrator, and the listener all remember at once that this story has already been told and can finish itself in no other way. The Fourth Symphony as an instance of *akcja* questions the possibility of action, wondering whether it can change the face of suffering. In lieu of that possibility, the Fourth Symphony offers only a causative sequence of musical events whose very logic lends meaning to suffering.

5

Lutosławski's Fourth Symphony makes its narrative of suffering out of other narratives, gathering references to outcry in *Musique funèbre,* the Piano Concerto, and *Chain 1,* branching out to music of Prokofiev, Mahler, Beethoven, and others unnamed. The symphony plays upon the idea of apotheosis in nineteenth-century music, retelling the tale of Chopin's Fourth Ballade and retelling itself along its narrative path. Lutosławski hoped that, in composing the Fourth Symphony, he might bring together human souls in a cure for that most acute of sufferings called loneliness. Precisely what he meant by this aspiration, we can never know, except to guess that he envisioned his works beckoning to those of like mind whose attention to his music would render a sympathetic response in accord with his intent. In the face of suffering, though, the Fourth Symphony calls not upon souls but upon texts, the most narrative of which account for suffering by casting time as more than a jumble of success and failure. Plot imposes its unity on that gathering and hides the reality that like its composer, now scattered in texts, the Fourth Symphony is an intertextuality.

Analysis of that intertextuality has commenced with a restaging of issues around Lutosławski's words about musical meaning. Although we may seek the voice of the author as a presence by animating texts and reconstructing the logic of a mind at work, these efforts can never meet a fixed point from which claims about the artwork can ring with echoes of a truth revealed. Our imaginings of the author are only one way into interpretation, and if we travel first by this route, we must be willing to transcend the authorial voice that promises to rid us of doubt in our endeavors to make sense of a text. This analysis of the Fourth Symphony began with Lutosławski, but it soon turned away from him as an authority who could bestow validity on its narrative claims. This analysis wishes to make no declarations that Lutosławski knowingly or unknowingly referenced Beethoven, or Chopin, or even his own earlier works in composing the symphony. At best, analysis that considers the author as historical figure can only allege an intellectual honesty in wondering how that once living authorial voice might have interpreted the tale it tells. But even in the absence of the author reconstructed from interviews, biographical material, and historical documents, the text is perfectly capable of signifying on its own. We can learn how that text signifies even if we do so away from the shadow of the author.

Attending too closely to the author can drown the intertext in a monologic reading that closes interpretation. Other threats to hearing the voices in a musical text are our absolute dramas of pitch, rhythm, texture, and form, whose appeals to unified structures can pull together moments of disjunction, topical play, and rhetorical shifts. Tonality in particular may evoke an aura of inexorable progress within which we fail to notice a surface fractured by the intrusions of other texts. Though it may be easy to view tonality, or rhythm, or form as monolithic forces against which intertextuality fights for an audience, the real power that binds the intertext into an apparent unity is narrative itself. We tell stories about music. And following the logic of emplotment, we seek in those stories the causative links that will join the unruly musical surface into an economical unified action. This analysis of the Fourth Symphony has fared no better in binding a misfortune of allusions and citations into a narrative about suffering. Though the analysis has been alert to some of the voices in the symphony, it has embraced a narrative function that links the intertext into a unified reading. In telling a narrative about narrative, we discover that in its motivation to account for suffering narrative causes suffering by casting out the untold voices of an intertext in the service of a safe and rational order of things.

In telling the Fourth Symphony as a purposeful and all-too-human temporality, this analysis has necessarily cast its glance back to a tradition of musical narrative. Unlike other intertextual analyses that move forward and backward in time from the moment of a text's birth, this analysis can turn only to the past. Within its first horizon of meaning, the Fourth Symphony still lies open to a text unwritten, whose strange configuration of signs will ask its readers to search for an intertext. As those future readers look back to the Fourth Symphony, they may find the first signs of a code that we, who hear the symphony in its time of origin, have yet to dream. That unknown code will give the signs of this symphony a new pertinence, erasing the narrative I have sketched and telling a new one. The symphony will ride the surface of history, picking up new voices along the way and losing others to the erosion of time. Like any text, this symphony is more than an intertextuality: it is a life of intertextualities, asking its readers to tell the story of its becoming. And yet the Fourth Symphony will ever be peopled by the fragments of the past, murmuring stories that only the future can hope to understand in that moment when we see face to face.

Glossary

Abduction. An insight. A leap of interpretation. A hypothesis. Peirce coined the term *abduction* and set it within a trichotomy of logic that included deduction and induction. For Peirce, abduction—the first formation of a hypothesis in the face of striking phenomena—explained how science could move from the known to the unknown. Borrowing from Eco (1976, 129–33) and Hatten (1994, 257–68), the present study views abduction as part of the process of coding. See also Fann (1970). See *Overcoding* and *Undercoding*.

Anxiety of Influence. Bloom's well-known term for poetic belatedness. The later poet strives to write something new in the shadow of the thought that an earlier poet has already written everything worth saying. The anxiety of influence views poets as combatants in an agon whose prize is the immortality of their poetry in the western canon. See Bloom (1973). For extensions of Bloom's literary theory to the study of music, see Straus (1990) and Korsyn (1991).

Arrival Six-Four. Hatten's term for a six-four chord "serving as resolution of thematic or tonal instabilities, often with a Picardy-third effect" (Hatten 1994, 288). Though the chord usually resolves dissonances built up prior to its appearance, it need not move to a cadence. The expressive effect of the arrival six-four brings it in contact with codes for transcendence, salvation, or, when the chord is minor, tragic reversal. As such, *transcendent* or *tragic* six-four chords may signal moments of *peripeteia* in musical narratives.

Centralization. Straus's term for a syntactic trope in which "musical elements that are peripheral to the structure of the earlier work . . . move to the structural center of the new one" (Straus 1990, 17). Centralization is one of eight tropes that Straus develops to illustrate how twentieth-century composers distance their music from the tonal past in response to the anxiety of influence. See *Compression* and *Generalization*.

Code. A convention of communication that organizes signs into a system correlating signifiers to signifieds within a particular cultural domain. A code may be pictured as a constellation of signs acting as interpretants of a single sign. As a convention of communication, a code involves a notion of the competency necessary for a reader to recognize that code and use it in interpretation. Codes are provisional and open to change over time. See Eco (1976).

Compression. Straus's term for a syntactic trope in which "elements that occur diachronically in the earlier work . . . are compressed into something synchronous in the new one" (Straus 1990, 17). See *Centralization* and *Generalization*.

Death of the Author. An idea in postmodern thought that questions the extent to which an author can write herself into her own texts. Though associated with Barthes's essay "The Death of the Author" (1977), notions of the author's putative death run through the writings of Foucault, Derrida, Nietzsche, and the Russian Formalists, among others. Motivations for questioning the author function in texts include challenging the idea that a single meaning for a text resides in its author, wondering about the extent to which the author is also the narrator of a text, and reinvesting interpretive energy into the reader as the site where meaning takes place. See Burke (1992). See *Transcendental Signified.*

Dialogic. Bakhtin's term for the diversity of languages, voices, and social speech types that appear within the nineteenth-century novel (Bakhtin 1981). Dialogism influences Kristeva's term *intertextualité*, which views all writing as the site of crossing texts. See *Monologic.*

Emplotment. The creative act by which a writer brings together events, characters, motivations, etc., in a chain of causation called *plot.* Emplotment also has an esthesic level, in which the reader of a text searches for the logic of causation that brings together particular events, characters, temporalities, etc., in a narrative. Poietically, to emplot is to make a text as a narrative. Esthesically, to emplot is to hear/read a text as a narrative.

Esthesic. The esthesic level of semiotics concerns itself with the processes that the reader undergoes in making sense of a text. An important distinction must be made between the reader as a *receiver* of a text and as a *producer* of a text. Most current theories of semiotics reject the idea that a reader passively receives a text. Instead, the reader brings codes, strategies, and intertexts to a reading in order to structure and make sense of a text. The term *esthesic* (instead of *reader*) is associated with Nattiez (1990b). In the present study esthesic intertextuality concerns itself with those texts that a reader brings to her reading, often without regard to the historical relationships between those texts. See also Eco (1976), Jauss (1982), and Riffaterre (1983).

Extroversive and Introversive. For Jakobson (1971) *extroversive* and *introversive* semioses refer, respectively, to the ways in which signifiers point both outside and inside a text. Agawu (1991) borrows this distinction for his study of the interaction between topics and tonal processes.

Generalization. Straus's term for a syntactic trope in which "a motive from the earlier work is generalized into the unordered pitch-class set of which it is a member" (Straus 1990, 17). See *Centralization* and *Compression.*

Hermeneutic Reading. The formation of an intertext in order to interpret strange passages as meaningful. This narrow definition comes from Riffaterre (1983), who describes hermeneutic and heuristic reading as two strategies for making sense of poetry. In the first, heuristic reading, the reader moves through the poem with the assumption that its signs will make literal sense. In the second, hermeneutic reading, the reader returns to strange passages (*ungrammaticalities*) in the poem and forms intertexts that might render them meaningful. See *Ungrammaticality.*

Hermeneutics of Recovery. An archeology that seeks to recover how people once understood an artwork by reconstructing its original context and conventions of interpretation. See *Hermeneutics of Suspicion.*

Hermeneutics of Suspicion. An interpretive stance that wonders what ideologies of the text are lost to us if we unquestioningly adhere to a hermeneutics of recovery. A hermeneutics of suspicion views texts as historically bound to ideologies of economics, politics, power, and gender. Because texts are often blind to those ideologies, they can unknowingly serve a social function to affirm those ideologies. See Jameson (1981).

Heuristic Reading. A first reading in which the reader assumes that the signs of a text will make literal sense. See *Hermeneutic Reading* and *Ungrammaticality.*

Iconic Sign. A sign in which there is a likeness between the signifier and the signified. We might say, for example, that much of the music of Messiaen uses iconic signs for birdsong. Monelle (2000, 19) introduces the important distinction that, when music imitates the sounds of birds, those imitations are often indexical to the real signifieds of the text: nature, joy, spring. See *Indexical Sign*.

Immanent. In Nattiez's semiological tripartition, the immanent level concerns the text, or trace, as opposed to the reader (*esthesic* level) and the writer (*poietic* level) (Nattiez 1990b). Although Nattiez explains that the reader must reconstruct the immanent level, his use of the term *neutral* to describe this level has opened criticism that there is no neutral object of the text independent of our esthesic efforts to reconstruct it. See Hatten (1992).

Indexical Sign. A signifier that points to its signified by contiguity, cause and effect, association. Peirce's famous example is that the footprints that Robinson Crusoe saw in the sand were indexical signs of another human. See *Iconic Sign*.

Influence. In the present study, influence is a narrow form of intertextuality that implies agency: the later writer borrows from or alludes to a text by the earlier writer. Influence is a form of poietic intertextuality, and it may involve a perspective that seeks to fix texts in history in order to tell narratives of artistic greatness. See *Intertextuality*.

Intertextuality. Any crossing of texts. The term (*intertextualité*) comes from Kristeva (1980a) as a definition of the text. Broadly conceived, intertextuality may be transhistorical and unlimited, so that all texts branch out infinitely to other texts. Intertextual studies may limit the term to poietic, esthesic, historical, stylistic, or canonical concerns. See *Influence*.

Kenosis. Bloom's term for a rhetorical trope that is a "breaking-device similar to the defense mechanisms our psyches employ against repetition compulsions" (Bloom 1973, 14). The trope is one of six that Bloom develops in his theory of the anxiety of influence. Korsyn (1991) maps Bloom's tropes onto musical correlates. See *Anxiety of Influence* and *Tessera*.

Matrix. In Riffaterre (1978) the matrix is a simple and hypothetical sentence that a poem transforms. In search of the matrix (central meaning) of a poem, the reader often confronts *ungrammaticalities*—places where the poem fails to make sense— and must make intertexts in a hermeneutic reading that strives to make sense of the poem. See *Hermeneutic Reading, Heuristic Reading,* and *Ungrammaticality*.

Monologic. Bakhtin's term for any writing that is deaf to the voices of other texts or that aspires to keep those other voices outside the boundaries of the text (Bakhtin 1981). A monologic reading is one that views the text as self-contained and closed to other texts. See *Dialogic*.

Musical Persona. The narrating presence in music. Cone (1974) asks us to consider that the musical persona is a mask worn by the composer. We take the same care in separating the composer's voice from the musical persona as we do in separating the voice of an author from the narrator of a novel. Abbate (1991) argues that when we conflate the voice of the composer with the musical persona we run the risk of reading a musical text monologically, hiding the multiple voices that weave themselves in the text. See *Monologic* and *Dialogic*.

Overcoding. Eco's term to describe the filling out of a code: "on the basis of a pre-established rule, a new rule was proposed which governed a rarer application of the previous rule" (Eco 1976, 133). Overcoding adds detail to a previous code and involves abduction. See *Abduction* and *Undercoding*.

Peripeteia. A sudden reversal of circumstances. Ricoeur (1984) argues that narratives function to account for suffering. Moments of suffering often coincide with *peripeteia*, which may clue the listener to a musical narrative.

Plot. The chain of causation that links actions, temporality, characters, and their motivations in a narrative (Cobley 2001, 5). In Aristotelian poetics, plot is unified, economical action. With modern narrative theory, though, plot involves the logic that links events. See *Emplotment*.

Poietic. The poietic level of semiotics concerns itself with the processes that the writer undergoes in making a text. Poietic intertextuality examines the texts available to a writer/composer in her historical period. Poietic intertextuality may be narrowed to a study of influence. See *Esthesic, Immanent,* and *Semiological Tripartition*.

Precursor. Within Bloom's theory of the anxiety of influence, the precursor is the historically prior poem that casts itself upon the later poem. The present study replaces *poem* with *text* and frames it within the transhistorical vision of intertextuality, so that the precursor can be any other text, without regard to historical priority. See *Anxiety of Influence*.

Semiological Tripartition. In the work of Nattiez (1990b), a conception of communication that rests on three levels: poietic, immanent, and esthesic, representing the addresser, the message itself, and the addressee, respectively. Important to this theory is the claim that readers (esthesic) do not receive meaning, they make meaning. See *Poietic, Esthesic,* and *Immanent*.

Syncretism. A musical syntactic trope in which independent lines in the precursor are conceived newly as simultaneities (harmonies) in the later text. This trope is an addition to the eight syntactic ones that Straus (1990) discusses in relation to twentieth-century music. See *Centralization, Compression,* and *Generalization*.

Tessera. Bloom's term for a rhetorical trope in which a later text completes an earlier one. The implication of tessera is that the later poet hopes to show that the earlier poet "failed to go far enough" in her poetry (Bloom 1973, 14). See *Anxiety of Influence* and *Kenosis*.

Text and Work. The present study follows Barthes's distinction that the text is a methodological field open to a multiplicity of meaning, while the work is a document tied to its author and its cultural/historical point of origin (Barthes 1981).

Token. An instance of a type. Within Peircean semiotics, a token has a perceptible reality, while a type is a conceptual category. Symphony is a type, and Brahms's Symphony No. 1 is a token of that type. A token can be a representative from a type, but it cannot fully represent its type. In the present study tokens are also instances of an intertext. See *Type*.

Topic. A code that associates a conventional label with a constellation of musical signs. Topics of musical discourse are types (minuet, strict style, horse topic, etc.) that are instanced by tokens (Mozart's Minuet in G, Bach's Little Fugue in G Minor, Schumann's *Wilder Reiter*). In the present study a topic is an intertext that allows for connections between its tokens. See Ratner (1980), Agawu (1991), Monelle (2000).

Transcendental Signified. The illusion that an unequivocal meaning for a text rests in the presence and voice of its author. The hope to read a text as if we are face to face with its author can suffer from an overly optimistic view that the signifers of language can ever come to rest in unmoving signifieds. Derrida (1974) uses the term to question a metaphysics of presence in western philosophy that values the spoken word as more stable than the written one. See *Death of the Author*.

Trope. Any sign or configuration of signs in one text that is a transformation of such signs in another text. A trope can be syntactic or semantic. For a narrower definition of trope, see Hatten (1994, 166–72, 295).

Type. A conceptual category instanced by tokens. In the present study, types are developed by culling potential tokens that form an intertext. See *Token*.

Undercoding. Eco's term for a "rough" coding that takes place in the absence of a previous code (Eco 1976, 135). This provisional coding involves abduction. See *Abduction* and *Overcoding*.

Ungrammaticality. Strangeness, a sign that departs from previous syntactic or semantic codes. The term comes from Riffaterre (1978), where it is any part of the poem that resists interpretation. The reader facing an ungrammaticality forms intertexts in search of a meaning for the puzzling sign or configuration of signs. See *Hermeneutic Reading*, *Heuristic Reading*, and *Matrix*.

Notes

1. Eco, Chopin, and the Limits of Intertextuality

1. Richard Lanham defines *prosopopoeia* as an inanimate object represented and "addressed or made to speak as if it were human" (Lanham 1991, 123).

2. A reader attentive to the dates of publication for the quoted passages may well wonder how Bakhtin's work managed to influence Kristeva's. The publication history of Bakhtin's writings is too complex for a rehearsal here. It suffices to note that he completed his most important work decades before its publication. At the time that Kristeva was writing about intertextuality, she was one of few people familiar with Bakhtin's work, and her essays introduced his thought to French literary critics. See Allen (2000), Clark and Holquist (1984), and Todorov (1984).

3. I am aware that the texts being compared are all translations that might take on meanings, connotations, and allusions that would never occur to readers of the original versions. This problem, however, illustrates that texts are constantly taking on new intertexts because of the changing social, artistic, political, economic, and even historical contexts of their readers.

4. In a postscript added to later editions of *The Name of the Rose*, Eco admits to the place of allusion and quotation in this novel. He claims, for example, that while writing a love scene in *Rose*, he surrounded himself with file cards filled with quotations from religious texts (Eco 1984, 521).

5. Two early articles that outline criteria for establishing sources in literary studies are Craig (1931) and Dodge (1911).

6. Bloom writes, "The profundities of poetic influence cannot be reduced to source-study, to the history of ideas, to the patterning of images" (Bloom 1973, 7). In keeping with this vision of influence, Bloom rarely documents intertextual connections. Perhaps his most stunning argument in this regard is the contention that a precursor may be a "poem that never got written" (96).

7. For a more detailed exposition of Lutosławski's life and music, see Rae (1994) and Stucky (1981).

8. See Hyde (1996), which is an intertextual modification of Greene (1982). Hyde proposes four types of imitation (reverential, eclectic, heuristic, and dialectic) that describe the ways that modern composers respond to the music of the past. For example, according to Hyde, Ravel's *Tombeau de Couperin* is reverential in relationship to the music of Rameau, while Bartók's music is heuristic in relationship to the folk songs of eastern Europe, because he updates their musical language. Dialectic imitation represents the highest form of intertextual relationship, because both precursor and latecomer are on an equal footing within a text. Well known for her pioneering articles on the music of Schoenberg, Hyde, not surprisingly, places some music by Schoenberg in the dialectic category. Hyde's

theory is a welcome alternative to the agon that is central to Bloom's anxiety of influence.

9. The extent to which Bartók's music would have been recognized in the Poland of World War II is debatable. Polish musical culture groped only uncertainly toward modernism in the years prior to the war. Even Lutosławski's composition teacher, Witold Maliszewski, claimed not to comprehend Lutosławski's *Symphonic Variations* (1938), which is often compared to Stravinsky's *Petrushka*. However, by 1954, when the audiences of Warsaw heard the premier of Lutosławski's *Concerto for Orchestra*, few would have missed the connection to Bartók. The situation is complicated by Lutosławski's later claims that the only listener for whom he ever wrote was himself (Lutosławski 1968). For more detail about musical life in Poland in the mid–twentieth century, see Rappoport-Gelfand (1986), Dobrowolski (1975), and Jarocinski (1965).

10. Nearly every sensitive account of Chopin's music, especially of his etudes, remarks upon the influence of Bach. Particularly nuanced readings of this connection are found in Wason (2002) and Samson (1997, 65–69; 1985, 58–80). Also common to writings about Chopin is commentary about the near miracle that the Polish composer would happen to study with Adalbert Żywny, one of the few teachers in Warsaw who both knew and taught the music of Bach.

11. Samson (1992, 1–14) has sketched the two broad types of music featured in a piano concert in Paris of the mid-1830s. First, there were the display pieces, tailored to public demand for ever more dazzling virtuosic feats. Though these pieces were often of limited artistic value, they would eventually become important precursors for more avant-garde works of the later 1830s. Second, there were the pieces of the classical repertoire that were just beginning to make inroads to concert life. Some composers, like Hummel, divided their energies between composition in both styles. Chopin was one of the first, however, to find ways of integrating the two styles. For an account of the works in the virtuosic style that a Parisian audience might have associated with Chopin's etudes, see Finlow (1992).

12. For an exposition of syncopations in Joplin's music, see Wooldridge (1992). Important precursors to Wooldridge's work are articles by Pressing (1983) and Rahn (1987) that illustrate isomorphisms between the structure of the western diatonic scale and the attack-point patterns of rhythms prominent in some nonwestern musics. Thus one could extend the intertext I have discussed and include the rhythmic practices of these musics.

13. Two other texts that make plain the melody of Bach's prelude are the manuscript as it appears in the *Clavierbüchlein für Wilhelm Friedemann Bach* and Schenker's analysis of Bach's prelude in the *Five Graphic Analyses*. In the former Bach writes out the complete rhythmic texture in only the first few measures; following these opening measures, Bach writes only the five-voiced chords that underlie that texture. In the latter, one of Schenker's most well known sketches, the rhythmic reduction at the level of the foreground shows the upper-voice melody of the prelude.

14. Kristeva first uses the term *intertextualité* in "Le texte clos" (translated as "The Bounded Text" in Kristeva 1980a). An expansion of this early definition appears in "Bakhtine, le mot, le dialogue, et le roman" (translated as "Word, Dialogue, and Novel" in Kristeva 1980b). In the latter article Kristeva outlines the connection between intertextuality and Bakhtin's notion of dialogism.

15. For a historical account of the rise of intertextuality as a concept in literary theory and of the multiple practices that it has engendered, see Allen (2000).

16. The terms *poietic* and *esthesic* are borrowed from Nattiez (1990b).

17. It could be argued that Barthes's *S/Z* (1974) comes close to accounting for every word of a literary text (in this case the novella *Sarrasine* by Honoré Balzac). However, far from striving for a unified structural account of every word in Balzac's story, Barthes endeavors to trace five codes of reading throughout the work. He makes no attempt to relate these codes to a single unifying structure.

18. Kristeva's theory of the *phenotext* and the *genotext* appears in *Revolution in Poetic Language* (1984). She admits that elements of dispersion (genotext) exist to varying degrees in different types of writing; and, like others who study intertextuality, she focuses particularly on avant-garde literature of the late nineteenth and early twentieth centuries with the intent of pinpointing a moment in literary history when the genotext comes to the fore.

19. A short list of writings addressing the problem of unity, often from a postmodern standpoint, includes Littlefield (1996), Scherzinger (1996), Subotnik (1996), Krims (1998), Street (1989), and Snarrenberg (1987).

20. Rameau's appeal to science is known well enough to forgo further comment. A fine account of Fétis's desire to make music theory scientific is offered in Schelhous (1991). Finally, Babbitt's call for a scientific music theory appears in the canonical text "Past and Present Concepts of the Nature and Limits of Music" (Babbitt 1972a).

21. An essay that attempts to uncover the rhetoric of scientific writing is Gerald Holton's "Quanta, Relativity, and Rhetoric" (1993), which illustrates the ways that scientists make their discoveries look as if they were inevitable, even though it is the natural progression of science to encounter setbacks and reversals. Inquiries into the nature of scientific writing, which often claims to be above the problems of rhetoric, form a part of postmodern literary theory as well. Christopher Norris (1990), for example, details Jürgen Habermas's critique of an old argument by Jacques Derrida that scientific, aesthetic, and common languages are all varieties of rhetoric. Norris mediates on the side of Derrida, claiming that writers, regardless of their claims to rational thought, need to be aware of the destabilizing effects of rhetoric.

22. Blasius reminds us that Schenker's early works (*Harmony* and *Counterpoint I*) admitted a much broader canon than did his *Free Composition*. Particularly striking is the excision of music from the New German School in Schenker's later works. Though we might read this tightening of the canon as a political statement against modernism, Blasius posits a second argument, in which Schenker's metaphor of the "inner life of the tones" requires him "to define this inner life in terms of a loosely specified body of works—a canon; and to deepen his epistemology, he is required, by compensation, to tighten his own version of the canon" (Blasius 1996, 100). My argument parallels this one by claiming that Schenker's tightening of the canon is an attempt to defend against the threat that intertextuality presents to any theory of deep structure in music.

23. The original French reads *il n'y a pas de hors-texte*. The translation in this chapter comes from an anonymous reader, who in response to an early draft of this book

suggested it as a better alternative to Gayatri Spivak's translation: *There is nothing outside of the text* (Spivak offers the alternative "there is no outside-text": Derrida 1974, 158). Monelle translates the same passage as "there isn't any outside-of-the-text" (Monelle 2000, 151).

24. For Straus's response to Krims's critique, see his "Post-structuralism and Music Theory (A Response to Adam Krims)" (1995).

2. The Appeal to Structure

1. Kerman (1985, 60); Palisca (1980, 741). Palisca's definition is the launching point for Kerman's oft-cited polemic about the myopia of modern theorists and the "subversive" nature of "their dogged concentration on internal relationships" (Kerman 1985, 73).

2. Agawu borrows the terms *introversive* and *extroversive* semiosis from Roman Jakobson, for whom the former defines signifiers that point within a text and the latter defines signifiers that point outside a text (Agawu 1991, 23; Jakobson 1971, 704–705).

3. As Lawrence Zbikowski tells us, the ways that music theory has entangled itself with matters of performance, composition, aesthetics, etc., underscore the very nature of theorizing (Zbikowski 2002, 124–25, 130–34). Theories solve puzzles, and the theorist must proceed as if the theory at hand has the power to do the solving. See also Thomas Kuhn's remarks on science and puzzle solving (Kuhn 1996, 35–42).

4. Lewin's imaging of musical perception based on musical behaviors finds resonance in Boretz's description of what motivated his "Meta-Variations": "Listening reconstructed as do-it-yourself composing. Composing revitalized as speculative listening, inspired rather than repressed by subsisting in the environment of existing other music" (Boretz 1989, 113).

5. Kerman (1980, 315). Alan Street turns this disapproving critique of analysis and organicism back to Kerman by reminding us that Kerman insulates German instrumental music from other repertoires and reserves for it the use of structural analysis, thus failing to reject organicism outright (Street 1989, 90).

6. In their preface to *Understanding Rock,* for example, John Covach and Graeme Boone write, "Ultimately, we find no better justification for analyzing rock music than this: it is part of us, and we like it" (Covach and Boone 1997, ix). Without trying to ascribe any devious intent on their part, we might read those slippery pronouns closing this justification as signifiers for the act of analysis itself: analysis is part of us, and we like analysis. Misread in this way, analysis of rock music is analysis for its own sake.

7. Daniel Chua is careful to distinguish the beautiful from the sublime in nineteenth-century conceptions of absolute music (Chua 1999, 228–34). Schopenhauer, Wagner, and Nietzsche associate absolute music with the sublime: a primal, noumenal, boundless unity beyond human comprehension, with the power to destroy individual existence. Hanslick will have nothing to do with this conception of the sublime, preferring to align music with the beautiful: the self-enclosed unity of a form that is one with substance. See also Carl Dahlhaus's discussion of Nietzsche and absolute music (Dahlhaus 1989b, 30–34).

8. The German reads: "Der Inhalt der Musik sind tönend bewegte Formen" (Hanslick 1966, 59). In his translator's essay Geoffrey Payzant connects this thesis to a statement in Hanslick's Foreword that the beauty of music "is inherent in tonal relationships [*Tonverbindungen*]" (Hanslick 1986, 95). As such, Payzant reads the word *tönend* in Hanslick's thesis as a reference to musical tones rather than to the more general notion of sound.

9. Chua writes, "what is absolute about music is not ultimately music itself but a transcendental sign of absence that enabled German Idealists and the early Romantics to make instrumental music mean nothing in order that it might mean everything" (Chua 1999, 168). Chua's argument rests on the ambiguity of zero as both inside and outside the system of numbers, and as both totality and nothingness.

10. In a brief sketch of musical semiotics, Eco also acknowledges the relationship between music and structural anthropology, pointing particularly to the Preface of *The Raw and the Cooked* (Eco 1976, 10). See also Chase (1972).

11. The translation comes from Culler (1975, 50), who renders the passage more concisely than do John and Doreen Weightman: "I therefore claim to show, not how men think in myths, but how myths operate in men's minds without their being aware of the fact" (Lévi-Strauss 1969, 12). Culler's translation forms an intertext with a theme common to structuralism: the death of man as an object of study, and the reconstitution of man as a nexus of discourse. This antihumanist perspective finds a famous instance in *The Order of Things,* where Foucault matches Nietzsche's proclamation that God is dead with an affirmation of "the end of man" (Foucault 1970, 385). Common to this trope in structuralism is the idea that man does not think in language, but that language thinks in man. Bristling at such ideas, Bloom writes that deep reading "exorcises" the Death of the Author, the self as fiction, and the most "pernicious" phantom that "language does the thinking for us" (Bloom 2000, 28).

12. Zbikowski's *Conceptualizing Music* (2002), which draws on a wide range of recent work in cognitive psychology and linguistics, though different in methodology than Lévi-Strauss's work, takes a similar stance. We find the mind structuring phenomena through categorization, cross-domain mapping, and conceptual modeling regardless of that mind's positioning historically or culturally. See, for example, Zbikowski's comparison of analyses by Rameau and Schenker, illustrating that despite incommensurable differences in their theories of tonal music, the cognitive structure behind the formation of these theories is remarkably similar (Zbikowski 2002, 119–33). See also his comparison of the conceptions of pitch among Europeans, the Kaluli of Papua New Guinea, the Balinese, and the Suyá of the Amazon, where Zbikowski shows that in all cases cross-domain mapping (metaphor) accounts for how cultures describe pitch (65–68).

13. Eco trumps Lévi-Strauss and claims that "the whole music science since the Pythagoreans has been an attempt to describe the field of musical communication as a rigorously structured system" (Eco 1976, 10). Eco here engages a familiar tactic, claiming the intellectual territory of music theory for the discipline of semiotics. Though his sketch of a musical semiotics is brief, Eco perspicaciously pinpoints a problem in defining a semantic level for music.

14. Lévi-Strauss (1963). I am indebted to an anonymous reader of an early version of

this chapter for directing my attention to Lévi-Strauss's classic study. Lévi-Strauss derives these structural methodologies from the work of N. Troubetzkoy, a member of the Prague linguistic circle.

15.   The translation is Culler's (1975, 43–44) from a passage in Lévi-Strauss's *Du miel aux cendres* (From Honey to Ashes).

16.   Szymanowki's music has not faired as well as it should outside of Poland, where he is still revered as one of the great composers of the twentieth century. "La fontaine d'Arethuse" from *Mythes* is one of his few chamber pieces to enjoy a place in the standard repertoire outside Poland. Perhaps the best study in English of Szymanowski's music is Samson's *The Music of Szymanowski* (1980).

17.   In the recapitulation of the violin sonata, Bartók sets the entrance of the violin's first theme in the same register that marks the opening of "La fontaine."

18.   John Clough (1979) formalizes the diatonic collection via a mathematical set-class theory familiar to the study of atonal music. Thus the diatonic scale is a 7-pc universe that can be represented by integers $0, 1, 2, \ldots 6$, where, for example, $C = 0$, $D = 1$, etc. Under this representation, the interval from C to D is 1; from D to E is 1; and from E to F is 1. It may seem counterintuitive to call the interval from E to F equivalent to the interval from C to D, but this result models a metaphor that we use about the diatonic scale, in which we think of movement up from pitch to pitch as travel along steps. The steps in the diatonic scale come in two sizes, and we reckon those sizes with reference to the chromatic collection within which the diatonic collection is embedded. I am co-opting Clough's formalization for the pentatonic collection, which is a 5-pc universe that can be represented by integers $0, 1, 2, 3, 4$. In reference to the opening of "La fontaine," $D\flat = 0$, $E\flat = 1$, $G\flat = 2$, $A\flat = 3$, and $B\flat = 4$. Thus the interval from $E\flat$ to $G\flat$ is 1, and from $G\flat$ to $A\flat$ is 1. Like the steps of the diatonic scale, these pentatonic steps come in two sizes, and we can reckon those sizes either with reference to the diatonic collection within which the pentatonic is embedded or with reference to the chromatic collection. The observation about "La fontaine," then, amounts to describing how the melodic lines of both the right and left hands travel stepwise through their respective universes, and that within these universes both melodies cross their small (minor) and large (major) steps.

19.   What I am calling *syncretism* is similar to what Straus calls *compression,* a trope that he describes as happening whenever "elements that occur diachronically in the earlier work . . . are compressed into something synchronous in the new one" (Straus 1990, 17). Straus lists as an example two triads that were once in a functional relationship (tonic and dominant) that appear as a single vertical structure in a twentieth-century work.

20.   Forte (1994) considers the possibility that the octatonic collection structures Webern's *Six Bagatelles,* Op. 9. Publications that deal with the interaction of the octatonic and other collections are too numerous for a complete listing here. Among these are Bass (1994), Cohn (1991a; 1991b), Taruskin (1985), and van den Toorn (1983).

21.   Richard Parks (1980) discusses combinations of smaller sets in "Brouillards" and the ways that they sometimes result in octatonic collections, though the octatonic per se is not the focus of his analysis. While acknowledging that references to pentatonic, whole-tone, and other "exotic" scales have been a useful part of early

approaches to Debussy's music, Parks prefers to avoid discussion of these devices, because they imply that Debussy "poured forth a confusion of harmonic and tonal distortions, contradictions and exoticisms, which need only to be properly identified and labeled to be understood" (Parks 1980, 120). While I understand Parks's motivation to reveal through set theory the economy of means that organizes pitch in Debussy's music, the marginalization of pentatonic and other exoticisms results in closing off the radical intertextuality so crucial to these texts.

22. Among efforts to bring Derridian deconstruction to music analysis, perhaps the most closely argued is Rose Rosengard Subotnik's "How Could Chopin's A-Major Prelude Be Deconstructed?" in her *Deconstructive Variations* (1996). This essay includes an introduction to many of the issues that surround deconstruction, including problems of historicization, intention, and transcendental signification. Like the present chapter, Subotnik's essay brings together two readings of a musical text in an effort to illustrate contradictions within western musical thought. Although Subotnik makes reference to the tradition within which structural analysis makes sense of the musical text, her essay forms no overt intertext between two or more texts in deconstructing Chopin's prelude. For other deconstructive readings of music, see Snarrenberg (1987) and Scherzinger (1996). A critique of these essays may be found in Krims (1998). See also Samuels (1989).

23. Straus's definition of *centralization* reads: "Musical elements that are peripheral to the structure of the earlier work (such as remote key areas and unusual combinations of notes resulting from linear embellishments) move to the structural center of the new one" (Straus 1990, 17). His definition of *generalization* reads: "A motive from the earlier work is generalized into the unordered pitch-class set of which it is a member. That pitch-class set is then deployed in the new work in accordance with the norms of post-tonal usage" (ibid.).

24. Although Finlow discusses Hummel's etudes as precursors to those of Chopin, the etude in question was published in 1833, three years after Chopin completed the first etudes of his Op. 10. As such, the work in question is illustrative more of harmonic procedures common in Chopin's time and less of real influence.

25. Harrison (1995). Charles Smith's remarkable, though unpublished, harmony text (1990) treats many of the augmented-sixth chords detailed by Harrison as chromatic dominants. Among these, Smith cites examples that are spelled like the augmented sixth of the subdominant. Rather than view these chords as varieties of augmented sixth, Smith derives them from vii^{o7} chords in which $\hat{2}$ is lowered. He also points out that these altered dominants are the so-called *tritone substitute* chords of jazz harmony.

26. Harold Schonberg (1987, 343) describes the incredible popularity once enjoyed by Moszkowski's music. One of Moszkowski's Etudes, Op. 72, even appears as an encore in a recording of one of the most legendary piano recitals of the twentieth century, Vladimir Horowitz's return to Carnegie Hall in May 1965, following his twelve-year retirement. A peculiar detail of this recital, showing the vagaries of musical popularity, was that following Horowitz's hair-raising performance of this etude and the uproarious ovation that ensued, an audience member was heard shouting, "That's trash; it's garbage!"

27. Particularly in Schenkerian writings much attention has focused on ways of choosing between two conflicting yet equally well formed readings. The classic

contribution in this area is probably Carl Schachter's "Either/Or" (1990). For an approach that views such problems as the result of conflicts between harmony and design, see Beach (1993). For a claim that Schenkerians often privilege one of two well-formed readings in order to highlight motivic parallelism, see Cohn (1992).

28.   Brown, Dempster, and Headlam invoke Kerman's *Contemplating Music* as their only example of those who "attack the significance of formal music theories on the grounds that they somehow force the music into the service of the theory" (Brown, Dempster, and Headlam 1997, 183). Though Kerman does make such claims, his agenda is clearly far beyond a mere questioning of the relationship between theory and analysis.

29.   Agawu, Hatten, and Monelle all make clear their debt to Ratner's work. Even the subtitle of Agawu's book, *A Semiotic Interpretation of Classic Music*, makes intertextual connection to Ratner's title, so that we can read Agawu's subtitle to mean that the book to follow will be a semiotic interpretation of Ratner's theory of topics in *Classic Music*.

3. On Codes, Topics, and Leaps of Interpretation

1.   Concerning an inflexible theory of codes in Georges Mounin's *Introduction à la sémiologie* (1970), Jonathan Culler writes, it "is something like Morse code or traffic signs, where one can look up a signifier in a code book and discover its signified" (Culler 1975, 19). Following Jacques Derrida, Culler attributes this type of theory to a metaphysics of presence that longs for a univocal meaning within the sign.

2.   Characterizing Eco's conception of semantic space at larger levels, Robert Hatten writes that such space is "more like an encyclopedia than a dictionary—with rich entries and cross-references rather than narrow definitions for each concept—and thus more like a network than a strictly logical hierarchy" (Hatten 1995, 373).

3.   Responding to a critique of his work by David Lidov, Nattiez considers the possibility that a correspondence between the poietic and esthesic levels might be called a code. The problem with this construal, according to Nattiez, is "the fact that the esthesic process reconstructs the message: it encounters the poietic, it does not 'receive' it" (Nattiez 1990b, 29–30, n29). Valid as this argument is, it marginalizes core concepts in Eco's theory that are in accord with a view that the reader makes rather than receives the text.

4.   Eco mindfully reminds us of the provisional status of a code. Codes are "fuzzy concepts" (Eco 1976, 82); they are "not a natural condition of the Global Semantic Universe nor a stable structure underlying the complex of links and branches of every semiotic process" (126). Any picture of a code is thus "viewed as a purely temporary device posited in order to explain a certain message" (127).

5.   On the relationship between personal interpretation and community, see Jameson (1981, 68–74). Here Jameson confronts Northrop Frye's *The Anatomy of Criticism* and argues that individual interpretation ultimately must return itself to a social hermeneutic so that personal transfiguration through reading can become a figure for the transformation of the community.

6.   Eco's figure for the traffic light is not as richly coded as is Figure 3.1. In an earlier

picture of this code, Eco attempts to account for the first signifieds that would act as interpretants for *stop* versus *go* (Eco 1976, 127). These first-level associations are denotations in Eco's model, and as such they become a focus for Nattiez's critique of semiotic codes as a model for communication.

7.   Riffaterre (1983, 3–4). Jacobson's celebrated model of communication rests on six functions: the addresser who utters the message, the addressee, the contact that is the physical medium of the message, the message itself, the context of the message, and a code for its interpretation. It is a relatively simple affair to devise examples that fit Jacobson's model. I hand to a stranger on the street a blue letter *A* carved into a wood block, and she may well wonder at the meaning of this message. I hand to a student in my classroom a paper with a red letter *A* written on the top, and she apprehends that I am expressing the quality of her work. That sign, *A*, is empty without its context, contact, and code for its interpretation. Nattiez criticizes Jacobson's schema on the grounds that it defines codes too unproblematically as immanent and shared (Nattiez 1990b, 18). Riffaterre reduces Jacobson's schema, finding that contact is presupposed by the existence of the other five elements.

8.   Riffaterre (1983, 106). Compare Dahlhaus's opinion: "insisting that music ultimately resides in the 'communicative process' and not in the 'dead letter' will carry little or no weight when confronted with the disappointing discovery that the stereotyped evidence which historians of reception are forced to resort to from want of documents can hardly vie with the subtleties attainable by structural analysis of music" (Dahlhaus 1989a, 39). See also Dahlhaus's essay on reception theory, where the problem often is multiplicity of reception rather than want of documentation (150–65).

9.   The same problem adheres to music analysis. As Kofi Agawu aptly expresses it: "Music analysis can scarcely proceed without postulating a listener, yet the difficulty of specifying the relevant features of a listening subject has led writers to invoke a variety of constructs, some of them hypothetical, many of them designed to evade the challenge of providing an ethnographically secure characterization" (Agawu 1996 [1998], 10).

10. Monelle develops the horse topic in a discussion of nineteenth-century music (Monelle 2000, 45–65). Typical of the musical horse is that it gallops in $\frac{6}{8}$, $\frac{9}{8}$, or $\frac{12}{8}$, and that its rhythmic iconic-sign is a persistent triplet, dotted triplet, or iambic figure. Without overtly referencing topics, William Kinderman catches the two codes in this movement of Schubert's sonata, remarking on the "persistent tarantella rhythm" and the poetic evocation of a "ride on horseback" (Kinderman 1997, 161).

11. Agawu also addresses the extension of topics into the nineteenth century, finding that, though they abound in Romantic music, they tend to be subsumed into private codes within the styles of individual composers. As such, Agawu rightly questions the extent to which we can make straightforward transfer of eighteenth-century topics to the study of nineteenth-century music (see Agawu 1991, 135–43).

12. Peirce's thoughts on abduction are scattered in his collected papers (1931, 1960), and most commentators recognize that abduction became more closely tied to induction and deduction in his later work. For an account of this development in

Peirce's writings, see Fann (1970). Peircean abduction is still a topic of study in the philosophy of science, since it accounts for hypothesis as a stage in logic.

13. Archived messages for the SMT list may be found by following links from the web page of the Society for Music Theory, http://www.societymusictheory.org.

14. Hatten lists the canon approach along with one that focuses on private, subjective codes as "legitimate" strategies of interpretation that go beyond situating the artwork within its original historical, stylistic context (Hatten 1994, 270–71).

15. On the "emic/etic" ("insider/outsider") distinction, see Nettl (1983).

16. See Hatten (1994, 44–45), Sebeok (1994, 19), and Peirce (1955, 101–102). In Peirce's terminology, token and type are called *sinsign* and *legisign*, respectively.

17. See Williams (1990, 77). Berlioz's review of Liszt's performance appeared in the *Revue et gazette musicale* of 12 June 1836. In addition to praising Liszt's interpretive mastery, calling him a "new Oedipus" solving the riddles of Beethoven's Sphinxian late works, Berlioz commends Liszt for performing the *Hammerklavier* with "not a note omitted, not one added (I followed, score in hand)." Among other things, the review is evidence of a growing concern to invest authority into the score.

18. There is much dispute over the formal sections of Liszt's sonata. For an account of the most influential structural analyses of the work, see Hamilton (1996, 31–48). In addition, though Liszt's only known programmatic association for the sonata referred to a dramatic connection between one of its themes and the defiant mood of Beethoven's *Coriolan* overture, there is a tradition of interpreting the work within the Faust legend and seeing the various themes as Faustian characters (30, 36, 46).

19. This discussion of virtuosity and its significance is indebted to Samson's *Virtuosity and the Musical Work* (2003).

20. Liszt expresses this desire to break from the virtuoso compositions in a letter of 1846 to Duke Carl Alexander of Weimer, quoted in Hamilton (1996, 6).

21. On the problems with the formal marker *development* in descriptions of Chopin's music, see Berger (1996).

22. On the tendency in the nineteenth century to associate Chopin and his music with weakness, effeminacy, and the otherworldly, see Kallberg's finely nuanced "Small Fairy Voices," in Kallberg (1996, 62–86). In his "Harmony of the Tea Table," Kallberg offers a gendered account of Chopin's music, including analysis of a later trend to deflect tropes around Chopin's effeminacy by cultivating descriptions of manly vigor in his music (42–45).

23. For pastoral as a literary topic, see Gifford (1999). For pastoral as a musical topic, see Jung (1980). See also Hatten (1994, 92–104).

24. Narrative readings of nineteenth-century ballet must account for the tradition of composition that invested authority solely in the ballet master, who could ask the composer to delete or add scenes and dances, and who could even suggest motives, themes, and orchestration (see Wiley 1985, 1–23). The scenes in question here all come at critical narrative events in the ballet, with the possible exception of the fairy's retelling of the story to the prince.

25. The interview is quoted in Anderson (1993, 138). As for the scale, there is no critical agreement on its exact arrangement (211–14).

26. The review appears in *Evening Mail,* 2 November 1917; quoted in Anderson (1993, 139).

27. For a review of attempts to come to terms with the changing horizons of a text and how they affect interpretation, see Jauss (1989, 197–231).

28. Where Samson differs from the dialogic approach of hermeneutic analysis is in his opinion that historical and canonical methodologies must maintain a "certain disciplinary integrity . . . before seeking a project of interdisciplinary mediation" (Samson 1996, 43). These comments must be read, I believe, within a concern Samson later voices that historicist approaches in current musicology too readily deny the fruits of close structural analysis. See Samson (2003, 1–7).

4. Bloom, Freud, and Riffaterre

1. Hatten (2000, xi). Hatten argues for three stages in musical semiotics and lists representative scholars: formalist (Nattiez), hermeneutic (Hatten, Lidov, and Tarasti), and staging (Monelle). While definitions for formalist and hermeneutic semiotics are self-evident, staging semiotics is defined by Hatten as a confrontation between semiotic theory and postmodern thought. For further reading on the trend to turn musical semiotics toward hermeneutics, see Agawu (1996 [1998]), Gruber (1996 [1998]), and Hatten (1996 [1998]).

2. Possibly the most celebrated early attempt to wed semiotic and hermeneutic practices is Barthes's *S/Z* (1974), which systematically analyzes Balzac's novella *Sarrasine* with reference to five codes: hermeneutic, semantic, symbolic, proairetic (action), and cultural. For musical analogs to Barthes's narrative codes, see Abbate (1989) and McCreless (1988). Eco's forays into interpretation are well known and require no comment here.

3. Freud's essay appeared first in 1919, and the original German is reprinted in the collected works (Freud 1947). Passages quoted in this chapter are from Alix Strachey's translation (Freud 1958). For a broader cultural context within which to read Freud's essay, see Royle (2003, 1–74).

4. Lawrence Kramer calls Freud's comparative philology "*Wissenschaft* with a vengeance!" (Kramer 1990, 204). Kramer's characterization informs the argument here that Freud engages the uncanny in order to master it and its implications of death.

5. Freud (1958, 369), Kramer (1990, 203–209). Carl Jung writes of two occasions in which Freud fainted during conversations that dealt with death. During the first occasion, in 1909, Freud was dismayed at Jung's discussion of a natural mummification process that occurs in certain bogs of Northern Germany. Jung reports: "He [Freud] was inordinately vexed by the whole thing and during one such conversation, while we were having dinner together, he suddenly fainted. Afterward he said to me that he was convinced that all this chatter about corpses meant I had death-wishes toward him. I was more than surprised by this interpretation" (Jung 1965, 156). The second such occasion, Jung writes, occurred in 1912, when Freud fainted during a discussion of the practices of the pharaohs upon the

deaths of their fathers (157). If Jung is to be believed, then Freud's interest in *das Unheimliche,* especially its relationship to death, may have been more personal than he was willing to admit in the essay.

6.   Kerman (2001–02, 158). Kerman cites a conversation with Lawrence Kramer, who suggests that, in any analysis that follows Freud, one would expect the uncanny effect to be more pronounced at each recurrence within a musical text.

7.   Tovey uses the phrase "strangely new and yet familiar" to characterize the return of the Aria in Bach's *Goldberg* Variations (Tovey 1978, 72). Tovey makes no reference to the uncanny per se, but Kramer brings Tovey's phrase into play for a discussion of ghostly returns in music (Kramer 2002, 262–63).

8.   Chua (1999, 228–34). Like Kurth in his analysis of the Dionysian, Chua turns to Nietzsche, for whom absolute music engenders a force powerful enough to demolish the soul. Dahlhaus makes a similar argument concerning Nietzsche's descriptions of absolute music (Dahlhaus 1989b, 32–34).

9.   Schenker (1997, 51). The discussion on the status of G minor in the *Eroica* owes a debt to Barry's essay on that symphony. See also my review of her essay (Klein 2003).

10.   Wagner (1978, 1:378). Referring to this passage from Cosima Wagner's diary, in which Richard was reported to have said that the $C_\sharp$ from the *Eroica* was the very first note of modernity, Chua pushes that musical modernity backward from Beethoven's Third Symphony to the rise of instrumental music in the sixteenth and seventeenth centuries (Chua 1999, 9). The $C_\sharp$ in question, therefore, is no harbinger of modernity but a crisis in modernity.

11.   Hugh MacDonald (1988) writes that, in nineteenth-century music, $G_\flat$, and at times $D_\flat$, is associated with the otherworldly, the ecstatic, and the sublime. These signifieds rest on an opposition between the relative distance of a key to its home tonic, and the absolute distance of a key from C. $D_\flat$ is marked in opposition to C, and as such it is still a rare key for Beethoven's historical period. MacDonald singles out the second movement of the *Appassionata* as the only work that Beethoven sets in the key of $D_\flat$ major. It is in this sense that $D_\flat$ is considered distant, despite the fact that it is closely related to F minor, the home tonic of the sonata.

12.   Kramer (2002, 278). The idea of melody as sign for human consciousness goes back at least to Rousseau, for whom the voice and its melody are opposed to the alienation of the instrumental and its harmony (see Chua 1999, 98–104). Kramer argues that however real this musical subjectivity may seem in the moment, it is always a spectral voice, dislocated in time and space from the fullness of its origin. Framed within an essay on influence and our relation to the past, Kramer's thoughts are in accord with much of this chapter.

13.   Associations between the subdominant in nineteenth-century music and extra-musical meaning appear in the work of Charles Rosen, who writes that the subdominant represents "a diminishing tension and a less complex state of feeling, and not the greater tension and imperative need for resolution implied by all of Beethoven's secondary tonalities" (Rosen 1972, 383). Rosen's thoughts on the matter create an opposition, dominant/subdominant, which can be mapped onto multiple extra-musical ones: tension/relaxation, bright/dark, optimistic/pessimistic, forward/reverse, masculine/feminine, straight/gay, etc.

14. The characterization is Adorno's in reference to Beethoven's late-period music, where repeating phrases remind him of the short rhymes spoken in fairy tales (Adorno 1998, 135–36). Kerman references the same passage from Adorno in his analysis of the uncanny in Beethoven's Quartet, Op. 131 (Kerman 2001–02, 156).

15. Hermann Danuser hears the narrative of the first part of *Gurrelieder* within three temporal categories: *Ahnung* (premonition), *Vergegenwärtung* (presentation), and *Erinnerung* (memory). For Danuser, memory is narrated by the "Song of the Wood Dove" (Danuser 1994, 79–80).

16. Kerman (2001–02, 158; see note 6, this chapter). More generally, Agawu warns against any "quick marriages of convenience between structural patterns (emerging from theory-based analysis) and elements of expression (emerging from hermeneutics)" (Agawu 1996 [1998], 11). One must be wary when searching for musical structures in support of an interpretation and avoid the tendency to view these structures as proof of that interpretation.

17. Bailey (1977, 51). For a discussion of semitonal relations in nineteenth-century music, and a survey of theories that have tried to account for them, see McCreless (1996).

18. There is question regarding the point at which the performer should begin the repeated exposition. Most editions show a repeat sign just before m. 5, so that the first four measures are absent from the repeated exposition. Charles Rosen considers these editions to be in serious error, resulting from Chopin's practice of publishing works simultaneously in Paris, Leipzig, and London (Rosen 1995, 279–82). In Rosen's view the London and Paris editions of the sonata are correct, indicating that the exposition should be repeated at m. 1. The Leipzig edition is charged with the faulty placement of the repeat sign, though Rosen notes that in a later edition Brahms corrected the error. Though one could argue that the dominant of D♭, closing the exposition, could resolve deceptively to the B♭-minor chord in m. 5, Rosen considers this a perfunctory harmonic effect, "not even piquant enough to be interesting" (280). Edward T. Cone also questions the placement of the repeat sign in this sonata (Cone 1972, 65). Jeffrey Kallberg concludes as well that Chopin intended the first four measures to be included with the repeated exposition (Kallberg 1996, 285, n85). Anatole Leiken is not persuaded by these arguments and looks to historical, editorial, and structural evidence to support his view that Chopin intended the repeated exposition to begin at m. 5 (Leiken 2001).

19. Cone is the first to use the term *apotheosis* to describe such themes in Chopin's music. Cone defines apotheosis as "a special kind of recapitulation that reveals unexpected harmonic richness and textual excitement in a theme previously presented with a deliberately restricted harmonization and a relatively drab accompaniment" (Cone 1968, 84). See also Samson's discussion of apotheosis in Chopin's music (Samson 1992, 75–76, 84) and Kallberg's use of apotheosis to describe the expressive range in Chopin's Polonaise-fantasie (Kallberg 1996, 117).

20. Petty hears the second theme of this sonata as Chopin's way of asserting composerly identity in the face of an anxiety over the influence of Beethoven (Petty 1999, 286).

21. Petty hears the opening of the "Funeral March" as the melodic point of closure that was promised but interrupted at the end of the Grave section in the first

movement. Petty notes as well that the D♭–B♭ motive finds its double in the bass of the Funeral March, and that the same motive participates in a number of enlargements across the tonal structure of the march (Petty 1999, 286–89, 292–94).

22. Rosen deftly shows the simple harmonic plan behind this monophonic movement (Rosen 1995, 294–302). Still, he admits that what is so disturbing about the movement "is that certain of the elements of the art of music are reduced almost to zero" (285).

23. Musgrave (1983). Musgrave notes that Brahms's personal library included a copy of Schopenhauer's *Parerga und Paralipomena,* which Brahms had fully annotated. Kurt Hofmann also notes an annotated copy of *Die Welt als Wille und Vorstellung* in that library (Hofmann 1974, 104). Daniel Beller-McKenna uses Schopenhauer's writings in an interpretation of Brahms's *Vier ernste Gesänge,* though he concludes that Brahms could not accept the extreme pessimism of that philosophy (Beller-McKenna 1994).

24. Bailey (1990), Brodbeck (1990); see also Brown (1983). Brodbeck's reading of the Third Symphony suggests a Bloomian agon over canonical strength, wherein quotations in the symphony entail corrective swerves that reveal a determination to beat the New Germans at their own game.

25. Jan Swafford conjectures that the piano pieces of Opp. 116–19 were "love songs to women in Brahms's life" (1997, 587). These piano pieces certainly had a powerful effect on Clara Schumann. In her diary entry of 2 September 1893, referring to these late piano works, Clara writes how wonderful it is that Brahms can mix passion and tenderness in the smallest of spaces ("Wie er im kleinstem Raum Leiderschaft mit Zartheit vereint, das ist ganz wundervoll") (Litzmann 1910, 573). And in an entry for 19 October 1893, Clara reveals how important these pieces were in shoring up her failing physical and emotional strength. Though the physical and mental demands of learning them meant that she could only study the late pieces for a little time each day, Clara still saw them as a source of comfort ("Ich spiele jetzt täglich etwas von den Brahmsschen neuen Stücken. . . . Leider kann ich nur sehr wenig daran studiren, es gehört die größte Anspannung des Deistes dazu, Allem gerecht zu werden, zu einigen Stücken auch körperliche Kraft. Wie danke ich ihm wieder dieses Labsal, das er mir bereitet, inmitten meiner tiefen Traurigkeit! Wie erhoben fühle ich mich stets, wenn ich so ein halbes Stündchen mich ganz und gar vergessen konnte") (ibid.). Regarding any extramusical meaning that Brahms may have intended for these late pieces, Parmer has written about the poetic quote that appears as the epigraph to the Intermezzo in E♭, Op. 117, No. 1 (Parmer 1997, 367–79). In addition, Max Kalbeck, Brahms's friend and early biographer, associates the Intermezzo in E♭ Minor, Op. 118, No. 6, with a rather bleak poem that Brahms copied in one of his notebooks. Kalbeck reprints the poem in the appendix to volume 4 of his Brahms biography (Kalbeck 1914, 304, 552).

26. The word *supplement* has taken on Derridean overtones in postmodern texts, where its dual meaning as something necessary to fill a lack and as something optional to append a complete object invites deconstruction (see Derrida 1974, 141–64; Norris 1987, 63–70). I take the word *supplement* in this problematic sense to describe the coda of Brahms's intermezzo: it both shores up the har-

monic action and appends the thematic material. The coda is both necessary and an addition.

27. I am indebted to Janet Schmalfeldt for pointing out this motivic feature to me.

28. Cone (1977). Cone's conviction about the identity of the chord in mm. 1–2 is not shared by at least two theorists. Schenker sketches the chord as a C-major harmony (1979, Fig. 110/d3). And Robert Morgan writes of the intermezzo that it begins in F major (Morgan 1999, 193).

29. Schenker (1979, 88–89, and Fig. 110d/3). Schenker uses the term *auxiliary cadence* in reference to cadential structures that lack an opening tonic, and he reflects such a structure as an incomplete *Ursatz* or *Ursatz* transfer. In only two of Schenker's seventeen illustrations of the auxiliary cadence does he show it governing an entire piece: Chopin's Prelude in A minor, Op. 28, No. 2, and the Brahms intermezzo in question. In reference to the Chopin prelude, Schenker opines that the incomplete *Ursatz* makes the piece a true prelude, and accepting a similar view for the intermezzo, we might consider it a true prelude for the six pieces of Op. 118, making the set an example of what Jonathan Dunsby calls a *multi-piece* (Dunsby 1983). As such, we might view problems like those of mm. 1–2 as compositional issues to be worked out in the following pieces, though such a view does little to address the expressive impact of the strangeness in the opening intermezzo.

30. On the *Fantasie*, see Marston (1992). Schumann originally conceived the work as a tribute to Beethoven, and he hoped that profits from its publication would go toward the Beethoven monument in Bonn that was then being planned. Signs of this tribute are the quotes from Beethoven's *An die Ferne Geliebte* in the first movement of the *Fantasie*, and the likeness between the work's second movement and that of Beethoven's Piano Sonata in A Major, Op. 101. Still, Schumann dedicates the work to Liszt, while both the epigraph and his personal correspondence make clear a poetic inspiration from Clara.

31. Danuser (1994). Danuser discusses variants of this cadence in Wagner's operas from *Der fliegende Holländer* through *Der Ring des Niebelungen*, and he looks as well to two post-Wagnerian works: Mahler's *Das Lied von der Erde* and Schoenberg's *Gurrelieder*. The cadence becomes such a cliché that Danuser finds it described in Thomas Mann's *Buddenbrooks*, where it is a barely disguised symbol for orgasm. The worldview inscribed in the cadence is one owing to Schöpenhauer's resigned pessimism.

32. Bailey (1985b, 124). Bailey claims that in the most common strategy commentators view $G\sharp$ of the "Tristan" chord as a substitute for the A that follows. A thorough account of these views is well beyond the scope of the discussion here. See Bailey (1985a, 179–303) and Nattiez (1990b, 216–38).

33. Drawing on Eco (1976, 183), Monelle discusses the negative reaction accorded to instances of *ratio facilis* in music, where there is a belief that musical signification is one in which expression and content are perfectly motivated, perpetual instances of *ratio difficilis* with no need of the conventions of codes. This view grants to music the power of a perfect signifying system (Monelle 2000, 15–16).

34. Monelle explains that in the sixteenth century the semitone descent associated

with words like *pianto* and *lagrime* was generally consonant and "not strictly an *appoggiatura*" (Monelle 2000, 67). In addition, Monelle points out that the *sospiro* (sigh) was usually portrayed by a rest (Brahms too uses short rests after the appoggiatura figures). The descending semitones are more properly connected to weeping in sixteenth- and seventeenth-century repertoires.

5. Narrative and Intertext

1. Zbigniew Skowron draws this portion of Lutosławski's notebook from a catalog, *Lutosławski homagium*, which accompanied an exhibition in 1996 at the "Kordegarda" Gallery in Warsaw (Skowron 2001, 15). Lutosławski's Notebook of Ideas (*Zeszyt mysli*) is in the collection of the Paul Sacher Foundation in Basel, Switzerland.

2. Kaczyński calls such ascents in Lutosławski's music *in paradiso*, the musical signifier for Christian belief. Maja Trochimczyk cites private conversations to document this interpretation on the part of both Kaczyński and Rae. Trochimczyk concludes that because Lutosławski's music eschews codes for emphatic proclamation of the resurrection, these ascending gestures have more in common with images of prayer (Trochimczyk 2001, 118–19).

3. Concerning the effects of ideology in mapping signifiers onto signifieds, see Cook (2001).

4. In addition to Cone and Scruton, Monelle also warns against confusing the musical persona with the subjectivity of the composer. His remarks in this regard center on Barthes's essay about the death of the author. Monelle's exegesis of both that essay and the related notion of the "transcendental author" informs the present discussion (Monelle 2000, 165–69). Abbate reminds us that conflation of the musical persona with the composer, explicit in the title of Cone's *The Composer's Voice*, suggests a monovocal authority speaking to us while hiding the voices of others that might be present in the text. Abbate prefers to hear music as animated by multiple voices in contrast to "Cone's monologic and controlling 'composer's voice'" (Abbate 1991, 13). Mediating these two positions, Lawrence Kramer writes, "for our sense of a single originating speaker to become decentered, it must first have been at the center" (Kramer 1995, 121).

5. Barthes's essay is reprinted and translated as "The Death of the Author" in *Image—Music—Text* (1977). Foucault's essay is reprinted and translated as "What Is an Author?" in *Language, Counter-memory, Practice* (1977).

6. Wimsatt and Beardsley (1957). Wimsatt and Beardsley's stance was aesthetic, not hermeneutic. Their essay challenged the idea that one could compare a poem with the poet's intent in order to make an evaluation about its aesthetic achievement. Their argument grabbed the work from the hands of the author and placed it into the hands of the critic. See Patterson (1995).

7. The claim needs more unpacking than I have done here. First, there is a concern in modern philosophy with questioning the aporias of language. We see in Wittgenstein's *Philosophical Investigations,* for example, puzzlement over the conflicting uses of ordinary language, making strange our daily discourse (see also Perloff 1996 and Staten 1984). Second, in Derrida's work, a similar concern

focuses on how the aporias of language affect the logic of the canonical texts in western philosophy. Third, in Foucault's work particularly, we see an awareness of these problems of language coupled to a preoccupation with the power of institutions in forming our notions of reality. A reaction against such power relations is evident in the opening of Foucault's essay on the author, where he responds to critics who claimed he had misread texts cited in *Les mots et les choses* (published as *The Order of Things* in English). As a means of freeing interpretation around texts, Foucault, as historical figure, appears intent to question the authority we lend the author and to view that authority as a product of power and discourse.

8. For another account of Derrida's ideas and their implications for musical interpretation, see Subotnik (1996, 62-81). See also Alastair Williams (2001, 21-47).

9. Eco (1990, 6). Eco remarks upon the irony that his *The Limits of Interpretation* (1990) should appear closely upon the translation in English of his much earlier *The Open Work* (1989 [1965]). To the belief that the open work allows for the free association of signifier and signified, Eco opines that "to say that interpretation (as the basic feature of semiosis) is potentially unlimited does not mean that interpretation has no object and that it 'riverruns' for the mere sake of itself" (Eco 1990, 6). How to set the limits of interpretation within musicology is a topic worth further study. Concerning this problem, see Hatten (1996 [1998]) and Cook (2001).

10. Culler's pragmatic response to the problems of interpretation is that the very liveliness of our literary institutions depends on the dual facts that we can never settle matters of interpretation and that we must convince our peers of an interpretation (Culler 1997, 61-62).

11. John Casken makes a similar remark regarding his reading of Lutosławski's Cello Concerto (Casken 2001, 52). There is extensive documentation of Lutosławski's life, music, and creative processes. Among many published interviews of Lutosławski are Rust (1995a), Nikolska (1994), Michalski (1988), Kaczyński (1984), and Varga (1976); additional interviews are embedded in many of the major studies of Lutosławski's music, including Homma (1996), Klein (1995), Rae (1994), Rust (1995b), Couchoud (1981), Stucky (1981), and Nordwall (1968). The Paul Sacher Foundation holds Lutosławski's sketches and manuscripts with the exception of some fair copies (final manuscripts) that the composer gave to performers who premiered his works. Extant are sketches for nearly all of his music after 1960.

12. More precisely, Lutosławski describes his training as a Russian approach to the analysis of compositions primarily from the Viennese Classical period (Rae 1994, 7). This formal approach, taught by Witold Maliszewski, who studied with Rimsky-Korsakov, emphasized the psychological impact of musical structure. On Lutosławski's musical education, see Rae (1994, 6-11) and Stucky (1981, 3-14).

13. Regarding theorists' involvements in the fictional analytical worlds they create in their accounts of music, see Guck (1994).

14. Douglas Rust's theorizing of the term *akcja* takes Lutosławski at his word and develops accounts of musical action as the temporal succession of pitch and texture (Rust 1995b, 56-106). In my own work on Lutosławski I have argued for readings

of his music that attend to the registral/textural changes that take place over relatively long spans of time, though I have not referenced Lutosławski's *akcja* in these analyses (Klein 1995, 93–170; 1999b).

15. Nattiez (1990a) also uses the tripartition in his critique of narrativity in music. Basically, though, since Nattiez contends that music has no intrinsic ability to narrate, interpretive acts that narrativize music remain on the poietic and esthesic levels for him.

16. The word *attribute* in these descriptions refers to Cook's "Theorizing Musical Meaning" (2001). Cook contends that when drawing meaning from music, listeners attend to those attributes that will support that meaning. Because listeners naturally focus on only a few of music's potentially unlimited attributes, different listeners may arrive at wildly different meanings for the same music. Cook may be using the term *attribute* as opposed to *structure* in order to allow for listening strategies that focus on surface events in the music without excluding the possibility of focusing on deeper-level structures. I use the term here with the same motivation. Like the study of narrative, Cook's theory might be structured by Nattiez's tripartition, where the attributes are the immanent level and the listener is the esthesic level (Cook never discusses the composer, though it would be easy enough to include a poietic level in his theory). Troublesome in Cook's theory, Nattiez's tripartition, and my borrowing of this work for a study of narrative is the idea that attributes (and structures) are somehow in the music. It may just as well be the case that we project these attributes and structures on the music, so that the immanent level collapses into the esthesic and the poietic. On the problem of the immanent level in Nattiez's tripartition, see Hatten (1992).

17. In fairness, Lutosławski's comments about the dramatic content of music may refer to a simple formal rhetoric in which certain musical ideas are more appropriate for opening material, while other ideas are more appropriate for development material, etc. Clue to this conception is Lutosławski's discussion of four formal functions that his teacher, Maliszewski, applied to the analysis of the Beethoven sonatas (Rae 1994, 7–8). These four functions (Introductory, Narrative, Transitional, Concluding) appear to be similar in conception to Agawu's "Beginning-Middle-End Paradigm" and Hatten's "Locational Function," both of which describe the types of thematic material appropriate for different formal sections of late-eighteenth-century music, as applied recursively from the level of the phrase to the level of an entire movement (Agawu 1991, 51–79; Hatten 1994, 112–32). This type of formal analysis does consider how musical material mirrors a narrative without mapping a particular story onto the music.

18. Ricoeur (1998, 277). This essay first appeared as "La fonction narrative" in *Etudes théologiques et religieuses* 54 (1979). The essay is a concise version of an argument regarding the relationship between history and narrative that appears again in the first volume of Ricoeur's *Time and Narrative* (1984).

19. The terms *fabula* and *sjužet* are sometimes taken to mean story and plot, respectively. In Chapter 1 we saw that Bakhtin's dialogism describes the way that utterances mix different types of language. The novel, for example, mixes everyday language for its dialogues, poetic language for its descriptions, and so forth. Barthes's five codes, though directed at how readers make sense of texts, imply that different types of writing make up a literary work. Musical extensions of

Barthes's codes appear in Carolyn Abbate's "What the Sorcerer Said" (1989), Patrick McCreless's "Roland Barthes's *S/Z*" (1988), and Robert Samuels's *Mahler's Sixth Symphony* (1995).

20. Of the objection that music has no narrator, perhaps the most famous example is Abbate's claim that music has "no ability to posit a narrating survivor of the tale who speaks of it in the past tense" (Abbate 1989, 230; see also Abbate 1991, 30–61). Lacking a narrator, the mark of diegesis, music cannot properly be called narrative according to a tradition reaching back to Aristotle. Recent work on narrative, though, has shown the difficulty of maintaining the distinction between mimesis and diegesis. J. Hillis Miller, for example, argues that Sophocles' *Oedipus Rex* fails as an example of mimesis, because the action of the play is "made up exclusively of people standing around talking or chanting" (Miller 1998, 10). To be sure, the extent to which narrators are constructed in music is open to debate, along with correlates like whether or not music can lie. The point here is that recent narrative theory does not disqualify music, drama, dance, or painting as narrative solely on the question of diegesis.

21. Although these *battuta* sections are unmetered, coordination of the various parts is ensured by systematic cueing every three seconds.

22. Speech-act theory originates with *How to Do Things with Words* (1962), in which the philosopher John Austin recognizes that unlike *constatives,* which make a truth claim about the world, what he calls *performatives* do something to the world. Examples include christening a baby, naming a ship, and promising an action.

23. Ricoeur (1984, 42–45). Ricoeur's characterization of plot comes during a discussion of Aristotle's *Poetics*. Following Aristotle, Ricoeur describes as marvelous "those strokes of chance that seem to arrive by design" (43). Though Aristotle's *Poetics* sets forth a model for tragedy, Ricoeur takes up the themes of reversal, recognition, and suffering as parts of a more general model of narrative.

24. Nikolska (1994, 91, 106). For an account of Chopin's influence on Lutosławski's later works, see Harley (2001, 185–88).

25. Though there is variation in Lutosławski's treatment of harmonic aggregates, they are generally ordered pitch collections containing all twelve pitch-classes, where each pitch-class is fixed in a single octave. There is little consistency in the terminology used to describe these twelve-note chords. Stucky (1981) uses the term *harmonic aggregate.* Rae (1994) uses the terms *12-note chord* and *chord-aggregate.* Homma uses the term *Zwölfton-Harmonik* (twelve-tone harmony). Lutosławski, who spoke fluent English, was inconsistent with his use of terms as well.

26. In an interview regarding his Piano Concerto, Lutosławski claims that he resorted to large sound masses in the 1960s because techniques for working with a small number of simultaneous sounds were still a question for him (Michalski 1988, 13).

27. Trochimczyk (2001, 107–10). Trochimczyk hears the falling tritone as signifier for these topoi within an intertext of music by Liszt, Szymanowski, and Górecki.

28. Cone (1968, 84). Following Cone's lead, Kallberg describes the expressive sweep of Chopin's Polonaise-fantasie, Op. 61, in terms of apotheosis (Kallberg 1996, 117). Samson discusses Chopin's music in similar terms (Samson 1992, 75–76, 84). In an otherwise positive review of Samson's earlier *The Music of Chopin*

(1985), Schachter takes Samson to task for a failure to develop Cone's idea of apotheosis (Schachter 1989, 189–90). Schachter posits the overtures of Weber as the immediate ancestors to Chopin's apotheoses, though he admits that the concept gains potency in Chopin's music.

29. The narrative sweep of Chopin's ballades makes it easy to understand how his contemporaries associated them with stories of Poland's tragic history. Early in their reception history, these ballades were thought to be inspired by the poems of Adam Mickiewicz, with inconclusive evidence linking the Second Ballade, in particular, to the poem *Świteź*, in which a Polish pastoral setting suffers the invasion of Russian soldiers (Samson 1992, 16).

30. For one of many essays on the return of tradition in Lutosławski's late music, see Whittall (2001).

31. For a detailed reading of the narrative in Chopin's Fourth Ballade, see Klein (2004).

32. Beginning with his Quartet, Lutosławski began composing two-movement works, in which the first movement was short and episodic while the second was longer and more directed. The first movement in these larger works generally contains a brief refrain that structures the many short episodes. Well known is Lutosławski's claim that the first movement in this model has the single purpose of engaging the listener without weighing down the musical action with serious material (Kaczyński 1984, 20–21).

33. In particular, the contrapuntal procedure involves what Richard Cohn calls *transpositional combination,* an ordered operation that brings a set-class through transpositional levels that belong to another set-class. Cohn first describes this process as it relates specifically to the music of Bartók (Cohn 1988; see also Cohn 1991a). In the case of Bartók, the transpositional levels often form an interval cycle (Cohn 1991b). For another account of interval cycles in Bartók's music, see Antokoletz (1984, 271–311). For a detailed account of transpositional combination in the music of Lutosławski, see Klein (1995, 69–78).

Works Cited

Abbate, Carolyn. 1989. "What the Sorcerer Said." *19th-Century Music* 12, no. 3: 221–30.
———. 1991. *Unsung Voices: Opera and Musical Narrative in the Nineteenth Century.* Princeton, N.J.: Princeton University Press.
Adorno, Theodor W. 1992. *Mahler: A Musical Physiognomy* (1971). Trans. Edmund Jephcott. Chicago: University of Chicago Press.
———. 1998. *Beethoven, The Philosophy of Music: Fragments and Texts.* Trans. Edmund Jephcott. Stanford, Calif.: Stanford University Press.
Agawu, Kofi. 1991. *Playing with Signs: A Semiotic Interpretation of Classic Music.* Princeton, N.J.: Princeton University Press.
———. 1996 [1998]. "Music Analysis versus Musical Hermeneutics." *American Journal of Semiotics* 13, no. 1–4: 9–24.
Allen, Graham. 2000. *Intertextuality.* London: Routledge.
Anderson, Donna K. 1993. *Charles T. Griffes: A Life in Music.* Washington, D.C.: Smithsonian Institution Press.
Antokoletz, Elliott. 1984. *The Music of Béla Bartók: A Study of Tonality and Progression in Twentieth-Century Music.* Berkeley: University of California Press.
Austin, J. L. 1962. *How to Do Things with Words.* Cambridge, Mass.: Harvard University Press.
Babbitt, Milton. 1972a. "Past and Present Concepts of the Nature and Limits of Music." In *Perspectives on Contemporary Music Theory,* ed. Benjamin Boretz and Edward Cone, 3–9. New York: W. W. Norton.
———. 1972b. "The Structure and Function of Musical Theory." In *Perspectives on Contemporary Music Theory,* ed. Benjamin Boretz and Edward Cone, 10–21. New York: W. W. Norton.
Bailey, Robert. 1977. "The Structure of the Ring and Its Evolution." *19th-Century Music* 1, no. 1: 48–61.
———, ed. 1985a. Richard Wagner, *Prelude and Transfiguration from "Tristan and Isolde."* New York: W. W. Norton.
———. 1985b. "An Analytical Study of the Sketches and Drafts." In Richard Wagner, *Prelude and Transfiguration from "Tristan and Isolde,"* ed. Bailey, 113–46. New York: W. W. Norton.
———. 1990. "Musical Language and Structure in the Third Symphony." In *Brahms Studies: Analytical and Historical Perspectives,* ed. George S. Bozarth, 405–21. Oxford: Oxford University Press.
Bakhtin, Mikhail M. 1981. *The Dialogic Imagination* (1975). Trans. Caryl Emerson and Michael Holquist. Austin: University of Texas Press.
Barnett, Gregory. 2002. "Topic Theory and the Late-Seicento Sonata." Paper delivered at National Conference of AMS/SMT, Columbus, Ohio.
Barry, Barbara R. 2000. *The Philosopher's Stone: Essays in the Transformation of Musical Structure.* New York: Pendragon Press.
Barthes, Roland. 1974. *S/Z* (1970). Trans. Richard Miller. New York: Hill and Wang.

———. 1975. *The Pleasure of the Text*. Trans. Richard Miller. New York: Hill and Wang.

———. 1977. "The Death of the Author" (1968). In *Image—Music—Text*, trans. Stephen Heath, 142–48. London: Fontana.

———. 1981. "Theory of the Text." In *Untying the Text: A Post-structuralist Reader*, ed. Robert Young and trans. Ian McLeod, 31–47. London: Routledge.

Bass, Richard. 1994. "Models of Octatonic and Whole-Tone Interaction: George Crumb and His Predecessors." *Journal of Music Theory* 38, no. 2: 155–86.

Beach, David. 1993. "Schubert's Experiments with Sonata Form: Formal-Tonal Design versus Underlying Structure." *Music Theory Spectrum* 15, no. 1: 1–18.

Beller-McKenna, Daniel. 1994. "Brahms on Schopenhauer: The *Vier ernste Gesänge*, Op. 121, and Late Nineteenth-Century Pessimism." In *Brahms Studies* 1, ed. David Brodbeck, 170–88. Lincoln: University of Nebraska Press.

Berger, Karol. 1996. "The Form of Chopin's Ballade, Op. 23." *19th-Century Music* 20, no. 1: 46–71.

Berry, Wallace. 1989. *Musical Structure and Performance*. New Haven, Conn.: Yale University Press.

Blasius, Leslie David. 1996. *Schenker's Argument and the Claims of Music Theory*. Cambridge: Cambridge University Press.

Bloom, Harold. 1973. *The Anxiety of Influence: A Theory of Poetry*. New York: Oxford University Press.

———. 1994. *The Western Canon: The Books and School of the Ages*. New York: Harcourt Brace & Company.

———. 2000. *How to Read and Why*. New York: Scribner's.

Boretz, Benjamin. 1970. "Meta-Variations: Studies in the Foundations of Musical Thought." Ph.D. dissertation, Princeton University. Published in serial form, revised, in *Perspectives of New Music* 8, no. 1 (1969): 1–75; 8, no. 2 (1970): 49–112; 9, no. 1 (1970): 23–42; 9, no. 2, and 10, no. 1 (1971): 232–70; 11, no. 1 (1972): 146–223; 11, no. 2 (1973): 156–203.

———. 1989. "The Logic of What?" *Journal of Music Theory* 33, no. 1: 107–16.

Brodbeck, David. 1990. "Brahms and the New German School." In *Brahms and His World*, ed. Walter Frisch, 65–80. Princeton, N.J.: Princeton University Press.

Brown, A. Peter. 1983. "Brahms' Third Symphony and the New German School." *Journal of Musicology* 2, no. 4: 434–52.

Brown, Matthew, and Douglas J. Dempster. 1989. "The Scientific Image of Music Theory." *Journal of Music Theory* 33, no. 1: 65–106.

Brown, Matthew, Douglas Dempster, and Dave Headlam. 1997. "The ♯IV (♭V) Hypothesis: Testing the Limits of Schenker's Theory of Tonality." *Music Theory Spectrum* 19, no. 2: 155–83.

Burke, Seán. 1992. *The Death and Return of the Author: Criticism and Subjectivity in Barthes, Foucault and Derrida*. Edinburgh: Edinburgh University Press.

Burkholder, J. Peter. 1983. "Museum Pieces." *Journal of Musicology* 2, no. 2: 115–34.

———. 1984. "Brahms and Twentieth-Century Classical Music." *19th-Century Music* 8, no. 1: 76–77.

———. 1991. "Musical Time and Continuity as a Reflection of the Historical Situation of Modern Composers." *Journal of Musicology* 9, no. 4: 412–29.

Burnham, Scott. 1995. *Beethoven Hero*. Princeton, N.J.: Princeton University Press.

Casken, John. 2001. "The Visionary and the Dramatic in the Music of Lutosławski." In *Lutosławski Studies*, ed. Zbigniew Skowron, 36–56. Oxford: Oxford University Press.

Chase, Gilbert. 1972. "American Musicology and the Social Sciences." In *Perspectives in Musicology,* ed. Barry S. Brook, Edward D. E. Downes, and Sherman van Solkema, 202–26. New York: W. W. Norton.

Cherlin, Michael. 1993. "Schoenberg and *Das Unheimliche:* Spectres of Tonality." *Journal of Musicology* 11, no. 3: 357–73.

Chua, Daniel K. L. 1999. *Absolute Music and the Construction of Meaning.* Cambridge: Cambridge University Press.

Clark, Katerina, and Michael Holquist. 1984. *Mikhail Bakhtin.* Cambridge, Mass.: Belknap Press.

Clayton, Jay, and Eric Rothstein. 1991. "Figures in the Corpus: Theories of Influence and Intertextuality." In *Influence and Intertextuality in Literary History,* ed. Jay Clayton and Eric Rothstein, 3–36. Madison: University of Wisconsin Press.

Clough, John. 1979. "Aspects of Diatonic Sets." *Journal of Music Theory* 23, no. 1: 45–61.

Cobley, Paul. 2001. *Narrative.* New York: Routledge.

Cohn, Richard. 1988. "Transpositional Combination in Bartók." *Music Theory Spectrum* 10: 19–42.

———. 1991a. "Bartók's Octatonic Strategies: A Motivic Approach." *Journal of the American Musicological Society* 44, no. 2: 262–300.

———. 1991b. "Properties and Generability of Transpositionally Invariant Sets." *Journal of Music Theory* 35, no. 1: 1–32.

———. 1992. "The Autonomy of Motives in Schenkerian Accounts of Tonal Music." *Music Theory Spectrum* 14, no. 2: 150–70.

Cone, Edward T. 1968. *Musical Form and Musical Performance.* New York: W. W. Norton.

———. 1972. "Editorial Responsibility and Schoenberg's Troublesome 'Misprints.'" *Perspectives of New Music* 11, no. 1: 65–75.

———. 1974. *The Composer's Voice.* Berkeley: University of California Press.

———. 1977. "Three Ways of Reading a Detective Story—Or a Brahms Intermezzo." *Georgia Review* 31, no. 3: 554–74.

Cook, Nicholas. 1987. *A Guide to Musical Analysis.* London: W. W. Norton.

———. 1996. *Analysis through Composition: Principles of the Classical Style.* Oxford: Oxford University Press.

———. 2001. "Theorizing Musical Meaning." *Music Theory Spectrum* 23, no. 2: 170–95.

Couchoud, Jean-Paul. 1981. *La musique polonaise et Witold Lutosławski.* Paris: Stock.

Covach, John R., and Graeme M. Boone, eds. 1997. *Understanding Rock: Essays in Musical Analysis.* New York: Oxford University Press.

Craig, Hardin. 1931. "Shakespeare and Wilson's *Arte of Rhetorique,* An Inquiry into the Criteria for Determining Sources." *Studies in Philology* 28, no. 4: 618–30.

Culler, Jonathan. 1975. *Structuralist Poetics: Structuralism, Linguistics, and the Study of Literature.* Ithaca, N.Y.: Cornell University Press.

———. 1981. *The Pursuit of Signs: Semiotics, Literature, Deconstruction.* Ithaca, N.Y.: Cornell University Press.

———. 1997. *Literary Theory: A Very Short Introduction.* New York: Oxford University Press.

Dahlhaus, Carl. 1989a. *Foundations of Music History* (1977). Trans. J. B. Robinson. Cambridge: Cambridge University Press.

———. 1989b. *The Idea of Absolute Music* (1978). Trans. Roger Lustig. Chicago: University of Chicago Press.

Danuser, Hermann. 1994. "Musical Manifestations of the End in Wagner and in the Post-Wagnerian *Weltanschauungsmusik.*" *19th-Century Music* 28, no. 1: 64–82.

de Man, Paul. 1982. Introduction to *Toward an Aesthetic of Reception*, by Hans Robert Jauss, vii–xxv. Minneapolis: University of Minnesota Press.

Derrida, Jacques. 1974. *Of Grammatology* (1967). Trans. Gayatri Chakravorty Spivak. Baltimore: Johns Hopkins University Press.

Dobrowolski, Andrzej. 1975. "The Effect of 'Warsaw Autumn' on the Development of Music Life in Poland." *Polish Music* 10, no. 1: 5–8.

Dodge, R. E. Neil. 1911. "A Sermon on Source-Hunting." *Modern Philology* 9, no. 2: 211–23.

Dunsby, Jonathan. 1983. "The Multi-piece in Brahms: *Fantasien* Op. 116." In *Brahms: Biographical, Documentary and Analytical Studies*, ed. Robert Pascall, 167–89. Cambridge: Cambridge University Press.

Eagleton, Terry. 1983. *Literary Theory: An Introduction*. Minneapolis: University of Minnesota Press.

Eco, Umberto. 1976. *A Theory of Semiotics*. Bloomington: Indiana University Press.

———. 1984. *The Name of the Rose* (1980). Trans. William Weaver. New York: Harcourt Brace & Company.

———. 1989. *The Open Work* (1965). Trans. A Cancogni. Cambridge, Mass.: Harvard University Press.

———. 1990. *The Limits of Interpretation*. Bloomington: Indiana University Press.

———. 1992. *Interpretation and Overinterpretation*. Cambridge: Cambridge University Press.

Eliot, T. S. 1968. "What Is a Classic?" In *On Poetry and Poets*, 52–74. New York: Noonday Press.

Fann, K. T. 1970. *Peirce's Theory of Abduction*. The Hague: Martinus Nijhoff.

Fink, Robert. 1993. "Desire, Repression & Brahms's First Symphony." *Repercussions* 2, no. 1: 75–103.

Finlow, Simon. 1992. "The Twenty-seven Etudes and Their Antecedents." In *The Cambridge Companion to Chopin*, ed. Jim Samson, 50–77. Cambridge: Cambridge University Press.

Forster, E. M. 2002. "Story and Plot" (1927). In *Narrative Dynamics: Essays on Time, Plot, Closure, and Frames*, ed. Brian Richardson, 71–72. Columbus: Ohio State University Press.

Forte, Allen. 1959. "Schenker's Conception of Musical Structure." *Journal of Music Theory* 3, no. 1: 1–30.

———. 1973. *The Structure of Atonal Music*. New Haven, Conn.: Yale University Press.

———. 1994. "An Octatonic Essay by Webern: No. 1 of the *Six Bagatelles for String Quartet*, Op. 9." *Music Theory Spectrum* 16, no. 2: 171–95.

Forte, Allen, and Steven E. Gilbert. 1982. *Introduction to Schenkerian Analysis*. New York: W. W. Norton.

Foucault, Michel. 1970. *The Order of Things: An Archaeology of the Human Sciences* (1966). New York: Random House.

———. 1972. *The Archaeology of Knowledge* (1969). Trans. A. M. Sheridan Smith. New York: Pantheon Books.

———. 1977. "What Is an Author?" (1969). In *Language, Counter-memory, Practice: Selected Essays and Interviews*, trans. Donald F. Bouchard and Sherry Simon, 113–38. Ithaca, N.Y.: Cornell University Press.

Freud, Sigmund. 1947. "Das Unheimliche" (1919). In *Gesammelte Werke*, vol. 12, 227–68. London: Imago Publishing.

———. 1958. "The 'Uncanny.'" In *On Creativity and the Unconscious*, trans. Alix Strachey, 122–61. New York: Harper.

Frye, Northrop. 1957. *Anatomy of Criticism*. Princeton, N.J.: Princeton University Press.

Gifford, Terry. 1999. *Pastoral*. London: Routledge.

Gillies, Malcolm. 1992. "Stylistic Integrity and Influence in Bartók's Works: The Case of Szymanowski." *International Journal of Musicology* 1: 139–60.

Grass, Günter. 1990. *The Tin Drum* (1959). Trans. Ralph Manheim. New York: Random House.

Greene, Thomas. 1982. *The Light in Troy: Imitation and Discovery in Renaissance Poetry*. New Haven, Conn.: Yale University Press.

Gruber, Gerold. 1996 [1998]. "Musical Hermeneutics in the Past Two Decades: Some Reflections on German and Austrian Publications." *American Journal of Semiotics* 13, no. 1–4: 43–59.

Guck, Marion. 1994. "Analytical Fictions." *Music Theory Spectrum* 16, no. 2: 217–36.

Hamilton, Kenneth. 1996. *Liszt: Sonata in B Minor*. Cambridge: Cambridge University Press.

Hanslick, Eduard. 1966. *Vom musikalisch-Schönen: Ein Beitrag zur Revision der Ästhetik der Tonkunst* (1854). 16th ed. Wiesbaden: Breitkopf & Härtel.

———. 1986. *On the Musically Beautiful: A Contribution towards the Revision of the Aesthetics of Music* (1891 [1854]). Trans. Geoffrey Payzant. Indianapolis: Hackett.

Harley, James. 2001. "Considerations of Symphonic Form in the Music of Lutosławski." In *Lutosławski Studies*, ed. Zbigniew Skowron, 163–93. Oxford: Oxford University Press.

Harrison, Daniel. 1995. "Supplement to the Theory of Augmented-Sixth Chords." *Music Theory Spectrum* 17, no. 2: 170–95.

Hatten, Robert. 1985. "The Place of Intertextuality in Music Studies." *American Journal of Semiotics* 3, no. 4: 69–82.

———. 1991. "On Narrativity in Music: Expressive Genres and Levels of Discourse in Beethoven." *Indiana Theory Review* 12: 75–98.

———. 1992. Review of Kofi Agawu's *Playing with Signs* and Jean-Jacques Nattiez's *Music and Discourse*. *Music Theory Spectrum* 14, no. 1: 88–98.

———. 1994. *Musical Meaning in Beethoven: Markedness, Correlation, and Interpretation*. Bloomington: Indiana University Press.

———. 1995. "Metaphor *in* Music." In *Musical Signification: Essays in the Semiotic Theory and Analysis of Music*, ed. Eero Tarasti, 373–91. New York: Mouton de Gruyter.

———. 1996 [1998]. "Grounding Interpretation: A Semiotic Framework for Musical Hermeneutics." *American Journal of Semiotics* 13, no. 1–4: 25–42.

———. 2000. Foreword. In Raymond Monelle, *The Sense of Music: Semiotic Essays*, xi–xiii. Princeton, N.J.: Princeton University Press.

Hawthorne, Jeremy. 1994. *A Concise Glossary of Contemporary Literary Theory*. 2nd ed. London: Edward Arnold.

Hofmann, Kurt. 1974. *Die Bibliothek von Johannes Brahms*. Hamburg: Karl Dieter Wagner.

Holton, Gerald. 1993. "Quanta, Relativity, and Rhetoric." In Holton, *Science and Anti-Science*, 74–108. Cambridge, Mass.: Harvard University Press.

Homma, Martina. 1996. *Witold Lutosławski: Zwölfton-Harmonik, Formbildung, "aleatorischer Kontrapunkt." Studien zum Gesamtwerk unter Einbeziehung der Skizzen*. Cologne: Bela.

Hussey, William. 1996. "Compositional Modeling, Quotation, and Multiple Influence

Analyses in the Works of Johannes Brahms: An Application of Harold Bloom's Theory of Influence to Music." Ph.D. dissertation, University of Texas.

Hutcheon, Linda. 1988. *A Poetics of Postmodernism: History, Theory, Fiction.* New York: Routledge.

Hyde, Martha. 1996. "Neoclassic and Anachronistic Impulses in Twentieth-Century Music." *Music Theory Spectrum* 18, no. 2: 200–35.

Hyer, Brian. 1995. "Reimag(in)ing Riemann." *Journal of Music Theory* 39, no. 1: 101–38.

Jackson, Timothy. 1995. "Aspects of Sexuality and Structure in the Later Symphonies of Tchaikovsky." *Music Analysis* 14, no. 1: 3–26.

Jakobson, Roman. 1971. "Language in Relation to Other Communication Systems" (1968). In *Selected Writings,* vol. 2, 697–708. The Hague: Mouton.

Jameson, Fredric. 1981. *The Political Unconscious: Narrative as a Socially Symbolic Act.* Ithaca, N.Y.: Cornell University Press.

Jarocinski, Stefan. 1965. "Polish Music after World War II." *Musical Quarterly* 51: 244–58.

Jauss, Hans Robert. 1982. *Toward an Aesthetic of Reception.* Trans. Timothy Bahti. Minneapolis: University of Minnesota Press.

———. 1989. *Question and Answer: Forms of Dialogic Understanding* (1982). Trans. Michael Hays. Minneapolis: University of Minnesota Press.

Jung, Carl G. 1965. *Memories, Dreams, Reflections.* Recorded and ed. Aniela Jaffé, trans. Richard and Clara Winston. New York: Vintage Books.

Jung, Hermann. 1980. *Die Pastorale: Studien zur Geschichte eines musikalischen Topos.* Bern: Francke.

Kaczyński, Tadeusz. 1984. *Conversations with Witold Lutosławski.* Trans. Yolanta May. London: Chester.

Kalbeck, Max. 1914. *Johannes Brahms.* Vol. 4. Berlin: Deutsche Brahms-Gesellschaft.

Kallberg, Jeffrey. 1996. *Chopin at the Boundaries: Sex, History, and Musical Genre.* Cambridge, Mass.: Harvard University Press.

———. 2001. "Chopin's March, Chopin's Death." *19th-Century Music* 25, no. 1: 3–26.

Karl, Gregory. 1997. "Structuralism and Musical Plot." *Music Theory Spectrum* 19, no. 1: 13–34.

Kerman, Joseph. 1980. "How We Got into Analysis and How to Get Out." *Critical Inquiry* 7, no. 2: 311–31.

———. 1985. *Contemplating Music: Challenges to Musicology.* Cambridge, Mass.: Harvard University Press.

———. 2001–02. "Beethoven's Op. 131 and the Uncanny." *19th-Century Music* 25, no. 2–3: 155–64.

Kinderman, William. 1997. "Schubert's Piano Music: Probing the Human Condition." In *The Cambridge Companion to Schubert,* ed. Christopher H. Gibbs, 155–73. Cambridge: Cambridge University Press.

Klein, Michael. 1995. "A Theoretical Study of the Late Music of Witold Lutosławski: New Interactions of Pitch, Rhythm, and Form." Ph.D. dissertation. State University of New York at Buffalo.

———. 1999a. "Lutosławski and the Canon: An Intertextual Study." In *Witold Lutosławski: The Man and His Work in the Perspective of the Musical Culture of the 20th Century,* ed. Jan Astriab, Maciej Jabłoński, and Jan Stęszewski, 53–65. Poznan: Poznan Society for the Advancement of the Arts and Sciences.

———. 1999b. "Texture, Register, and Their Formal Roles in the Music of Witold Lutosławski." *Indiana Theory Review* 20, no. 1: 37–70.

———. 2003. Review of Barbara R. Barry's *The Philosopher's Stone. Music Theory Spectrum* 25, no. 1: 150–58.

———. 2004. "Chopin's Fourth Ballade as Musical Narrative." *Music Theory Spectrum* 26, no. 1: 23–55.

Korsyn, Kevin. 1991. "Towards a New Poetics of Musical Influence." *Music Analysis* 10, no. 1–2: 3–72.

———. 1996. "Directional Tonality and Intertextuality: Brahms's Quintet op. 88 and Chopin's Ballade op. 38." In *The Second Practice of Nineteenth-Century Tonality*, ed. William Kinderman and Harald Krebs, 45–83. Lincoln: University of Nebraska Press.

———. 2001. "Beyond Priveleged Contexts: Intertextuality, Influence, and Dialogue." In *Rethinking Music*, ed. Nicholas Cook and Mark Everist, 55–72. Oxford: Oxford University Press.

Kramer, Lawrence. 1990. *Music as Cultural Practice, 1800–1900*. Berkeley: University of California Press.

———. 1995. *Classical Music and Postmodern Knowledge*. Berkeley: University of California Press.

———. 2002. *Musical Meaning: Toward a Critical History*. Berkeley: University of California Press.

Krampen, Martin. 1994. "Codes." In *Encyclopedic Dictionary of Semiotics*, 2nd ed., ed. Thomas A. Sebeok, vol. 1, 123–32. New York: Mouton de Gruyter.

Krims, Adam. 1994. "Bloom, Post-structuralism(s), and Music Theory." *Music Theory Online* 0, no. 11: http://societymusictheory.org/mto/.

———. 1998. "Disciplining Deconstruction (for Music Analysis)." *19th-Century Music* 21, no. 3: 297–324.

Kristeva, Julia. 1980a. "The Bounded Text" (1969). In *Desire in Language: A Semiotic Approach to Literature and Art*, trans. Thomas Gora, Alice Jardine, and Leon S. Roudiez, 36–63. New York: Columbia University Press.

———. 1980b. "Word, Dialogue, and Novel" (1967). In *Desire in Language: A Semiotic Approach to Literature and Art*, trans. Thomas Gora, Alice Jardine, and Leon S. Roudiez, 64–91. New York: Columbia University Press.

———. 1984. *Revolution in Poetic Language*. Trans. Margaret Waller. New York: Columbia University Press.

Kuhn, Thomas S. 1996. *The Structure of Scientific Revolutions* (1962). 3rd ed. Chicago: University of Chicago Press.

Kurth, Richard. 1997. "Music and Poetry, A Wilderness of Doubles: Heine—Nietzsche—Schubert—Derrida." *19th-Century Music* 21, no. 1: 3–37.

Lanham, Richard. 1991. *A Handlist of Rhetorical Terms*. 2nd ed. Berkeley: University of California Press.

Leiken, Anatole. 2001. "Repeat with Caution: A Dilemma of the First Movement of Chopin's Sonata op. 35." *Musical Quarterly* 85, no. 3: 568–82.

Lerdahl, Fred, and Ray Jackendoff. 1983. *A Generative Theory of Tonal Music*. Cambridge, Mass.: MIT Press.

Lévi-Strauss, Claude. 1963. "Structural Analysis in Linguistics and in Anthropology." In *Structural Anthropology* (1958), trans. Claire Jacobson and Brooke Grundfest Schoepf, 31–54. New York: Basic Books.

———. 1969. *The Raw and the Cooked: Introduction to a Science of Mythology* (1964). Trans. John and Doreen Weightman. New York: Harper & Row.

———. 1997. *Look, Listen, Read* (1993). Trans. Brian C. J. Singer. New York: Basic Books.

Lewin, David. 1986. "Music Theory, Phenomenology, and Modes of Perception." *Music Perception* 3, no. 4: 327-92.

———. 1987. *Generalized Musical Intervals and Transformations.* New Haven, Conn.: Yale University Press.

Lidov, David. 1999. *Elements of Semiotics.* New York: St. Martin's Press.

Littlefield, Richard. 1996. "The Silence of the Frames." *Music Theory Online* 2, no. 1: http://societymusictheory.org/mto/.

Litzmann, Berthold. 1910. *Clara Schumann: Ein Künstlerleben nach Tagebüchern und Briefen.* Vol. III. Leipzig: Breitkopf und Härtel.

Lutosławski, Witold. 1968. "The Composer and the Listener." In *Lutosławski,* ed. Ove Nordwall, trans. Christopher Gibbs, 119-24. Stockholm: Edition Wilhelm Hansen.

MacDonald, Hugh. 1988. "G♭." *19th-Century Music* 11, no. 3: 221-37.

Marston, Nicholas. 1992. *Schumann: "Fantasie," Op. 17.* Cambridge: Cambridge University Press.

Maus, Fred Everett. 1988. "Music as Drama." *Music Theory Spectrum* 10: 56-73.

McClary, Susan. 1991. *Feminine Endings: Music, Gender, and Sexuality.* Minneapolis: University of Minnesota Press.

McCreless, Patrick. 1988. "Roland Barthes's *S/Z* from a Musical Point of View." *In Theory Only* 10, no. 7: 1-29.

———. 1991. "Syntagmatics and Paradigmatics: Some Implications for the Analysis of Chromaticism in Tonal Music." *Music Theory Spectrum* 13, no. 2: 147-78.

———. 1996. "An Evolutionary Perspective on Nineteenth-Century Tonality." In *The Second Practice of Nineteenth-Century Tonality,* ed. William Kinderman and Harald Krebs, 87-113. Lincoln: University of Nebraska Press.

———. 1997a. "A Candidate for the Canon? A New Look at Schubert's Fantasie in C Major for Violin and Piano." *19th-Century Music* 20, no. 3: 205-30.

———. 1997b. "Rethinking Contemporary Music Theory." In *Keeping Score: Music, Disciplinarity, Culture,* ed. David Schwartz, Anahid Kassabian, and Lawrence Siegel, 13-53. Charlottesville: University of Virginia Press.

Michalski, Grzegorz. 1988. "An Interview with Witold Lutosławski." *Polish Music* 23, no. 2-3: 3-22.

Miller, J. Hillis. 1995. "Narrative." In *Critical Terms for Literary Study,* 2nd ed., ed. Frank Lentricchia and Thomas McLaughlin, 66-79. Chicago: University of Chicago Press.

———. 1998. *Reading Narrative.* Norman: University of Oklahoma Press.

Monelle, Raymond. 2000. *The Sense of Music: Semiotic Essays.* Princeton, N.J.: Princeton University Press.

Morgan, Robert P. 1999. "6 Piano Pieces, Opus 118." In *The Compleat Brahms: A Guide to the Musical Works of Johannes Brahms,* ed. Leon Botstein, 193-95. New York: W. W. Norton.

Morris, Robert D. 1987. *Composition with Pitch-Classes.* New Haven, Conn.: Yale University Press.

Mounin, Georges. 1970. *Introduction à la sémiologie.* Paris: Minuit.

Musgrave, Michael. 1983. "The Cultural World of Brahms." In *Brahms: Biographical, Documentary, and Analytical Studies,* ed. Robert Pascall, 1-26. Cambridge: Cambridge University Press.

Nattiez, Jean-Jacques. 1990a. "Can One Speak of Narrativity in Music?" *Journal of the Royal Music Association* 115, no. 2: 240-57.

———. 1990b. *Music and Discourse: Toward a Semiology of Music.* Trans. Carolyn Abbate. Princeton, N.J.: Princeton University Press.

Nettl, Bruno. 1983. *The Study of Ethnomusicology: Twenty-nine Issues and Concepts.* Urbana: University of Illinois Press.

Newcomb, Anthony. 1987. "Schumann and Late Eighteenth-Century Narrative Strategies." *19th-Century Music* 11, no. 2: 164–74.

Nikolska, Irina. 1994. *Conversations with Witold Lutosławski (1987–92).* Trans. Valeri Yerokhin. Stockholm: Melos.

Nordwall, Ove, ed. 1968. *Lutosławski.* London: J. & W. Chester.

Norris, Christopher. 1987. *Derrida.* Cambridge, Mass.: Harvard University Press.

———. 1990. "Deconstruction, Postmodernism and Philosophy: Habermas on Derrida." In Norris, *What's Wrong with Postmodernism: Critical Theory and the Ends of Philosophy,* 49–76. Baltimore: Johns Hopkins University Press.

———. 1991. *Deconstruction: Theory and Practice.* Revised ed. Routledge: London.

Palisca, Claude V. 1980. "Theory, Theorists." In *The New Grove Dictionary of Music and Musicians,* ed. Stanley Sadie, vol. 18, 741–62. London: Macmillan.

Parks, Richard S. 1980. "Pitch Organization in Debussy: Unordered Sets in 'Brouillards.'" *Music Theory Spectrum* 2: 119–34.

Parmer, Dillon. 1995. "Brahms, Song Quotation, and Secret Programs." *19th-Century Music* 19, no. 2: 161–90.

———. 1997. "Brahms and the Poetic Motto: A Hermeneutic Aid?" *Journal of Musicology* 15, no. 3: 353–89.

Patterson, Annabel. 1995. "Intention." In *Critical Terms for Literary Study,* 2nd ed., ed. Frank Lentricchia and Thomas McLaughlin, 135–46. Chicago: University of Chicago Press.

Peirce, Charles S. 1931, 1960. *Collected Papers of Charles Sanders Peirce.* Vols. 1–6, ed. Charles Hartshorne and Paul Weiss; vols. 7–8, ed. Arthur W. Burks. Cambridge, Mass.: Harvard University Press.

———. 1955. *Philosophical Writings of Peirce.* Ed. Justus Buchler. New York: Dover.

Perloff, Marjorie. 1996. *Wittgenstein's Ladder: Poetic Language and the Strangeness of the Ordinary.* Chicago: University of Chicago Press.

Petty, Wayne C. 1999. "Chopin and the Ghost of Beethoven." *19th-Century Music* 22, no. 3: 281–99.

Piaget, Jean. 1970. *Structuralism* (1968). Trans. and ed. Chaninah Maschler. New York: Basic Books.

Pressing, Jeff. 1983. "Cognitive Isomorphisms between Pitch and Rhythm in World Musics: West Africa, the Balkans, and Western Tonality." *Studies in Music* 17: 38–61.

Rae, Charles Bodman. 1994. *The Music of Lutosławski.* London: Faber and Faber.

Rahn, Jay. 1987. "Asymmetrical Ostinatos in Sub-Saharan Music: Time, Pitch, and Cycles Reconsidered." *In Theory Only* 9, no. 7: 23–37.

Rappoport-Gelfand, Lidia. 1986. *Musical Life in Poland: The Postwar Years 1945–1977.* Trans. Irina Lasoff. New York: Gordon and Breach.

Ratner, Leonard G. 1980. *Classic Music: Expression, Form, and Style.* New York: Schirmer Books.

Rawsthorne, Alan. 1966. "Ballades, Fantasy and Scherzos." In *Frédéric Chopin: Profiles of the Man and the Musician,* ed. Alan Walker, 42–72. London: Barrie & Rockliff.

Ricoeur, Paul. 1984. *Time and Narrative.* Vol. I (1983). Trans. Kathleen McLaughlin and David Pellauer. Chicago: University of Chicago Press.

———. 1998. "The Narrative Function" (1979). In *Hermeneutics and the Human Sci-*

ences, trans. and ed. John B. Thompson, 274–96. Cambridge: Cambridge University Press.

Riffaterre, Michael. 1978. *Semiotics of Poetry.* Bloomington: Indiana University Press.

———. 1983. *Text Production.* Trans. Terese Lyons. New York: Columbia University Press.

Rosen, Charles. 1972. *The Classical Style: Haydn, Mozart, Beethoven.* New York: W. W. Norton.

———. 1995. *The Romantic Generation.* Cambridge, Mass.: Harvard University Press.

Royle, Nicholas. 2003. *The Uncanny.* New York: Routledge.

Rust, Douglas. 1995a. "Conversation with Witold Lutosławski." *Musical Quarterly* 79, no. 1: 207–23.

———. 1995b. "Lutosławski's Symphonic Forms." Ph.D. dissertation, Yale University.

Samson, Jim. 1980. *The Music of Szymanowski.* London: Kahn & Averill.

———. 1985. *The Music of Chopin.* Oxford: Clarendon Press.

———. 1989. "Chopin and Genre." *Music Analysis* 8, no. 3: 213–31.

———. 1992. *Chopin: The Four Ballades.* Cambridge: Cambridge University Press.

———. 1996. "Chopin's Alternatives to Monotonality: A Historical Perspective." In *The Second Practice of Nineteenth-Century Tonality,* ed. William Kinderman and Harald Krebs, 34–44. Lincoln: University of Nebraska Press.

———. 1997. *Chopin.* New York: Schirmer Books.

———. 2003. *Virtuosity and the Musical Work: The "Transcendental Studies" of Liszt.* Cambridge: Cambridge University Press.

Samuels, Robert. 1989. "Derrida and Snarrenberg." *In Theory Only* 11, no. 1–2: 45–58.

———. 1995. *Mahler's Sixth Symphony: A Study in Musical Semiotics.* Cambridge: Cambridge University Press.

Schachter, Carl. 1989. Review of *The Music of Chopin* by Jim Samson and *The Music of Brahms* by Michael Musgrave. *Music Analysis* 8, no. 1–2: 187–97.

———. 1990. "Either/Or." In *Schenker Studies,* ed. Hedi Siegel, 165–79. Cambridge: Cambridge University Press.

Schelhous, Rosalie. 1991. "Fétis's Tonality as a Metaphysical Principle: Hypothesis for a New Science." *Music Theory Spectrum* 13, no. 2: 219–40.

Schenker, Heinrich. 1969. *Five Graphic Analyses* (1932). Ed. Felix Salzer. New York: Dover.

———. 1979. *Free Composition* (1935). Trans. and ed. Ernst Oster. New York: Longman.

———. 1997. "Beethoven's Third Symphony: Its True Content Described for the First Time" (1930). Trans. Derrick Puffett and Alfred Clayton. In *The Masterwork in Music,* vol. 3, ed. William Drabkin, 10–68. Cambridge: Cambridge University Press.

Scherzinger, Martin. 1996. "The Finale of Mahler's Seventh Symphony: A Deconstructive Reading." *Music Analysis* 14, no. 1: 69–88.

Schmalfeldt, Janet. 1985. "On the Relation of Analysis to Performance: Beethoven's Bagatelles Op. 126, Nos. 2 and 5." *Journal of Music Theory* 29, no. 1: 1–31.

Schonberg, Harold C. 1987. *The Great Pianists from Mozart to the Present.* New York: Simon & Schuster.

Schwandt, Erich. 1980. "Tarantella." In *The New Grove Dictionary of Music and Musicians,* vol. 18, ed. Stanley Sadie, 575–76. London: Macmillan.

Scruton, Roger. 1983. *The Aesthetic Understanding: Essays in the Philosophy of Art and Culture.* Manchester: Carcanet Press.

———. 1997. *The Aesthetics of Music.* Oxford: Oxford University Press.

Sebeok, Thomas A. 1994. *Signs: An Introduction to Semiotics.* Toronto: University of Toronto Press.

Shklovsky, Victor. 1965. "Art as Technique" (1917). In *Russian Formalist Criticism: Four Essays,* ed. and trans. Lee T. Lemon and Marion J. Reis, 3–24. Lincoln: University of Nebraska Press.

Skowron, Zbigniew. 2001. "Lutosławski's Aesthetics: A Reconstruction of the Composer's Outlook." In *Lutosławski Studies,* ed. Zbigniew Skowron, 3–15. Oxford: Oxford University Press.

Smith, Charles. 1990. *Tonal Models of Music.* Unpublished textbook.

Smith, Peter H. 2002. "The Sorrows of Young Brahms? On the Intersection of Structure and Tragic Expression in the C-Minor Piano Quartet." Paper delivered at National Conference of AMS/SMT, Columbus, Ohio.

Snarrenberg, Robert. 1987. "The Play of *Différance:* Brahms's Intermezzo, Op. 118, No. 2." *In Theory Only* 10, no. 3: 1–25.

Staten, Henry. 1984. *Wittgenstein and Derrida.* Lincoln: University of Nebraska Press.

Straus, Joseph N. 1990. *Remaking the Past: Musical Modernism and the Influence of the Tonal Tradition.* Cambridge, Mass.: Harvard University Press.

———. 1995. "Post-structuralism and Music Theory (A Response to Adam Krims)." *Music Theory Online* 1, no. 11: http://societymusictheory.org/mto/.

Street, Alan. 1989. "Superior Myths, Dogmatic Allegories: The Resistance to Musical Unity." *Music Analysis* 8, nos. 1–2: 77–123.

Stucky, Steven. 1981. *Lutosławski and His Music.* New York: Cambridge University Press.

Subotnik, Rose Rosengard. 1996. *Deconstructive Variations: Music and Reason in Western Society.* Minneapolis: University of Minnesota Press.

Swafford, Jan. 1997. *Johannes Brahms: A Biography.* New York: Vintage Books.

Taruskin, Richard. 1985. "Chernomor to Kaschei: Harmonic Sorcery, or Stravinsky's 'Angle.'" *Journal of the American Musicological Society* 38, no. 1: 72–142.

———. 1989. "Reply to Brown and Dempster." *Journal of Music Theory* 33, no. 1: 155–64.

———. 1993. "Revising Revision." *Journal of the American Musicological Society* 46, no. 1: 114–38.

Todorov, Tzvetan. 1984. *Mikhail Bakhtin: The Dialogical Principle.* Trans. Wlad Godzich. Manchester: Manchester University Press.

Tovey, Donald Francis. 1978. *Essays in Musical Analysis: Chamber Music.* Oxford: Oxford University Press.

Trochimczyk, Maja. 2001. "'Dans la Nuit': The Themes of Death and Night in Lutosławski's Œuvre." In *Lutosławski Studies,* ed. Zbigniew Skowron, 96–124. Oxford: Oxford University Press.

Tuchowski, Andrzej. 2001. "The Integrative Role of Motion Patterns in Lutosławski's Mature Symphonic Works: A Comparison of *Livre pour orchestre* and the Symphony No. 4." In *Lutosławski Studies,* ed. Zbigniew Skowron, 287–304. Oxford: Oxford University Press.

van den Toorn, Pieter. 1983. *The Music of Igor Stravinsky.* New Haven, Conn.: Yale University Press.

Varga, Balint Andras. 1976. *Lutosławski Profile: Witold Lutosławski in Conversation with Balint Andras Varga.* Trans. Stephen Walsh. London: Chester.

Wagner, Cosima. 1978. *Cosima Wagner's Diaries.* Trans. G. Skelton. London: Collins.

Wason, Robert W. 2002. "Two Bach Preludes/Two Chopin Etudes, or *Toujours travailler Bach-ce sera votre meilleur moyen de progresser.*" *Music Theory Spectrum* 24, no. 1: 103–20.

Whittall, Arnold. 2001. "Between Polarity and Synthesis: The Modernist Paradigm in

Lutosławski's Concertos for Cello and Piano." In *Lutosławski Studies,* ed. Zbigniew Skowron, 244–68. Oxford: Oxford University Press.

Wiley, Roland John. 1985. *Tchaikovsky's Ballets: Swan Lake, Sleeping Beauty, Nutcracker.*
Oxford: Clarendon Press.

Williams, Adrian. 1990. *Portrait of Liszt by Himself and His Contemporaries.* Oxford:
Clarendon Press.

Williams, Alastair. 2001. *Constructing Musicology.* Aldershot: Ashgate.

Wimsatt, W. K., and Monroe C. Beardsley. 1957. "The Intentional Fallacy" (1946). In
Wimsatt and Beardsley, *The Verbal Icon: Studies in the Meaning of Poetry,* 3–18.
Lexington: University of Kentucky Press.

Wittgenstein, Ludwig. 1997. *Philosophical Investigations* (1953). Trans. G. E. M. An-
scombe. Oxford: Blackwell.

Wooldridge, Marc C. 1992. "Rhythmic Implications of Diatonic Theory: A Study of
Scott Joplin's Ragtime Piano Works." Ph.D. dissertation, SUNY at Buffalo.

Woolf, Virginia. 1955. *To the Lighthouse* (1927). New York: Harcourt Brace Jovanovich.

Zbikowski, Lawrence M. 2002. *Conceptualizing Music: Cognitive Structure, Theory, and
Analysis.* New York: Oxford University Press.

Index

Note: page numbers in **bold** indicate chapters. Page numbers in *italics* indicate illustrations.

"Die Krähe" (Schubert), 80
Die Schöpfung (Haydn), 62
Don Giovanni (Mozart), 80
doom chords, 122
"dramaturgy," 112

Eco, Umberto: allusion and quotation,
143n. 4; on codes, 150n. 4; on hermeneutics, 77; on hermetics, 75; on interpreting
texts, 111; intertextuality and, 1–2, 2–3, 4,
11; Levi-Strauss and, 147n. 13; *The Limits
of Interpretation,* 159n. 9; Monelle on,
157n. 33; musical semiotics, 147n. 10; *The
Open Work,* 159n. 9; on semantic space,
150n. 2; on semiotics, 51–52, 53–54, 77;
on topics, 58–59
ecology metaphors, 46
Écrits (Lacan), 22
Elgar, Edward, 62
Eliot, T. S., 25
emplotment. *See* plot and emplotment
Encyclopedic Dictionary of Semiotics, 51
"Erlkönig" (Schubert), 57–58, 62
Eroica (Beethoven), 82–83, 88, 154n. 10
esthesic, 12, 138
Etude in C Major (Chopin), *39,* 41
Etude in C Major (Hummel), 41–42, *42*
Etude in C Major (Moszkowski), *43*
Everett, Walter, 60
expressive tonality, 89
extra-musical content, 112–15
extroversive, 138, 146n. 2

Fantasie (Schumann), 19, 47, 102–103, 117,
157n. 30
fashion, 22
Faulkner, William, 13
feminization, 49
Fétis, François-Joseph, 15
Fifth Symphony (Beethoven), 27
Fifth Symphony (Tchaikovsky), 62
Fink, Robert, 98
Finlow, Simon, 41, 149n. 24
First Ballade (Chopin), 72, 126, 132
First Symphony (Brahms), 62, 98
First Symphony (Mahler), 66
Five Graphic Analyses (Schenker), 144n. 13
*Five Poems of Ancient China and Japan,
Komuri Uta,* 70
Five Readers Reading (Holland), 55
Fontenelle, Bernard le Bovier de, 55
formalism, 47
Forster, E. M., 116
Forte, Allen, 23, 26–27, 33, 36–37, 47

Foucault, Michel, 2–4, 16, 29, 109, 147n. 11,
159n. 7
Fourth Ballade (Chopin): apotheosis, 126–29,
134–35; arrival six-four, 67–68, 72–74; nocturnes, 92–93
Fourth Symphony (Lutosławski): apotheosis,
126–30, *128;* beginning, *133;* conclusions,
134–36; described, 121–34; first theme, *131;*
form, *125;* main movement, 130–32; narrative, 116–21, 134; outcry in, *122;* second
theme, *131;* tragic turn, *123*
Franz, Robert, 62
Free Composition (Schenker), 23
Freud, Sigmund: death themes, 153–54n. 5;
Fink on, 98; hermeneutic model, 88; Lacan
on, 22; psychic tropes, 30; Schenkerian
analysis and, 46; "strangeness" and, 106–
107; on uncanniness, 21, 77–82, 88, 89–90,
92, 95, 96
Frye, Northrop, 120, 150n. 5
"Fugue of the Five Senses" (Chabrier), 27
"Funeral March" Sonata (Chopin), 91–92, *92,
94,* 94–95, 106

gender issues in intertextuality, 49, 124–26
generalization, 37, 138, 149n. 23
*Generalized Musical Intervals and Transforma-
tions* (Lewin), 23
A Generative Theory of Tonal Music (Lerdahl
and Jackendoff), 24
genotext, 15, 145n. 18
George Lieder (Schoenberg), 27
Gillies, Malcolm, 31
Gluck, Christoph Willibald, 26
Götterdämerung (Wagner), 102–103
Gounod, Charles-François, 9, 35
Grass, Günter, 1–2, 11
Griffes, Charles T., 70–72, *73,* 75
Gurrelieder (Schoenberg), 85–87, *86*

Halton, Gerald, 145n. 21
Hammerklavier (Beethoven), 54, 62–64, *63,*
74–76, 152n. 17
Hanslick, Eduard, 26, 113
Harley, James, 124
harmonic aggregates, 121, 161n. 25
Harrison, Daniel, 41
Hatten, Robert: on *arrival,* 72; on Beethoven's
Hammerklavier, 62–64; on Brahms's Intermezzo, 102; on Chopin's "Funeral March"
sonata, 93–94; on hermeneutic-semiotics,
54; on intertextuality, 20; on markedness,
22–23; *Musical Meaning in Beethoven,* 47;
on musical semiotics, 77; on narrative analy-

sis, 115; on Ratner, 150n. 29; on semantic space, 150n. 2; on stages of musical semiotics, 153n. 1; on syntactic coding, 66; on topics, 57, 58–59, 62; on transhistorical codes, 74–75; on troping, 13

Haydn, Franz Joseph, 62

Headlam, Dave, 46, 48, 150n. 28

Hendrix, Jimi, 60

hermeneutics, 54–55, 66, 77, 97, 153nn. 2,28; hermeneutic reading, 138; of recovery, 138; of suspicion, 138

heuristic imitation, 5

heuristics, 5, 97, 102, 138

"Hey Jude" (Beatles), 59–61

historical context, 143n. 3

historical intertextuality, 12

Hoffmann, E. T. A., 78, 80

Holland, Norman, 55

Holton, Gerald, 145n. 21

horse topics, 56–57, 62, 151n. 10

"How Could Chopin's A-Major Prelude Be Deconstructed?" (Subotnik), 149n. 22

How to Do Things with Words (Austin), 161n. 22

Hughes, Tim, 60

Hummel, J. N., 5, 41–42, *42*, 44–45, 49, 144n. 11, 149n. 24

Hutcheon, Linda, 111

Hyde, Martha, 5, 25, 143n. 8

Hyer, Brian, 24

"I Can't Explain" (The Who), 60

iconic sign, 139

immanent level, 139

indexical sign, 139

Indy, Vincent d', 62

influence, 4, 7, 11–12, 16–17, 18, 139, 143n. 6, 144n. 10

intentional fallacy, 109

Intermezzo in A Major (Brahms), 98–101, *100*, 102, *103*, 104–105, 111

interpretation, **51–76**, 110–11

intertextuality: contrasted with influence, 4, 7, 11–12; culture and, 28–29; defined, 139; efforts to limit, 15–16; gender issues, 49; limits of, **1–21**; musical and literary, 11; in novels, 2–3; term coined, 11, 144n. 14; theories of, 1; types of, 12

Introduction à la sémiologie (Mounin), 150n. 1

introversive semiosis, 138, 146n. 2

Invitation to a Beheading (Nabokov), 4

Jackendoff, Ray, 24

Jacobsen, Jens Peter, 87, 151n. 7

Jakobsen, Roman, 54, 146n. 2

James, Henry, 120

Jameson, Fredric, 55, 61, 75, 150n. 5

Jeux vénitiens (Lutosławski), 117–20

Joplin, Scott, 8, *9*

Jung, Carl, 153n. 5

Kabbalah and Criticism (Bloom), 30

Kaczyński, Tadeusz, 108, 113, 158n. 2

Kafka, Franz, 4

Kallberg, Jeffrey, 16–17, 117, 155n. 18

Karl, Gregory, 115

"Keinen hat es noch gereut" (Brahms), 62

kenosis, 31–32, 35, 139

Kerman, Joseph: on analysis, 25; challenges to music theory, 29; on ecology metaphor, 46–48; Freud and, 79, 88; on music theory, 150n. 28; on "piano teacher's rabbit hutch," 21–22; on uncanniness, 91

Kessler, J. C., 5

Kinderman, William, 90

Kircher, Athanasius, 57

Klein, Michael, 38

Korsyn, Kevin: on analysis, 48; Bloomian theory and, 30; Bloom's work and, 17–18; on Brahms's Romanze, 19; on Chopin's sonatas, 15–16; on influence, 25

Kramer, Lawrence: on fear of death, 107, 153n. 5; on Freud, 153nn. 4,5; on melody, 85, 154n. 12; on narrative, 114, 117, 118–19; on uncanniness, 78–79

Krims, Adam, 46, 48

Kristeva, Julia, 2–3, 11, 14–18, 143n. 2, 144n. 14, 145n. 18

Kurth, Richard, 79

Lacan, Jacques, 22

"La mort de l'auteur" (Barthes), 109

Lasso, Orlando di, 60

Le cheval de bronze (Auber), 62

Leiken, Anatole, 155n. 18

Lerdahl, Fred, 24

"Let the Sunshine In," 60–61

Lévi-Strauss, Claude, 14, 27–29, 30–31, 36, 147n. 13

Lewin, David, 17, 23–24, 27–29, 114, 146n. 4

Lidov, David, 52, 58–59

The Limits of Interpretation (Eco), 159n. 9

linguistics, 13, 24

L'Isle joyeuse (Debussy), 126

Liszt, Franz, 63–65, 74–76, 98, 124, 152nn. 17,18

literary criticism, 3

Littlefield, Richard, 48

locational functions, 34
Lockhead, Judy, 48
Look, Listen, Read (Lévi-Strauss), 14
Lutosławski, Witold: on artistic creation,
108; as author, 110; Bartók and, 144n. 9;
Cello Concerto, 113; *Chain 1*, 134; Chopin
etudes and, 9, 37–38; *Concerto for Orchestra*,
144n. 9; dramatic content, 112, 160n. 17;
on extramusical content, 114; Fourth Symphony, 21, 116–21, 121–34, *122, 123, 125,
128, 131, 133*; harmonic aggregates, 161n. 25;
interpretations, 11, 112–15; *Jeux vénitiens*,
117–20; *Musique funèbre*, 121, 123–24, 134;
in paradiso ascents, 158n. 2; *Partita*, 122,
132; pattern repetitions, 8; Piano Concerto, 121, 134; Quartet, 129–30; sources
on, 159n. 11; Study No. 1, 4–7, 6, 36, 37;
Symphony No. 4, **108–36**; *Tarantella*,
122; Third Symphony, 126–28; training,
159n. 12; two-movement works, 162n. 32

McClary, Susan, 119
McCreless, Patrick, 25, 47–48, 99
MacDonald, Hugh, 154n. 11
Mahler, Gustav, 21, 66, 114–15, 122, 134
Maliszewski, Witold, 144n. 9
Man, Paul de, 75
"Manic Depression" (Hendrix), 60
Márquez, Gabriel García, 13
Marxism, 119
Mathers, Daniel E., 60
matrix, 139
Maus, Fred, 115
meaning, 26–28
melody, 9–11, 85, 154n. 12
Mendelssohn, Felix, 43–44, 45, 62
metaphors in music, 27, 57
"Meta-Variations" (Boretz), 24
Meyer, Leonard B., 23, 28
Miller, J. Hillis, 118, 120, 161n. 20
mimesis, 116–17, 161n. 20
Missa Solemnis (Beethoven), 63
modernism, 48–49, 72, 154n. 10
Monelle, Raymond: horse topics, 151n. 10;
intertextuality theory and, 16, 20–21; on
musical narrative, 117; on *ratio facilis*,
157n. 33; on Ratner, 150n. 29; on semitone
descent, 157–58n. 34; *The Sense of Music*,
47; on signifiers, 115; on subjectivity of the
composer, 158n. 4; "The Death of the Author," 109–10; on topics, 56, 58, 62
monologism, 14–15, 139
monumentality, 26
Morris, Robert D., 24

Moscheles, Ignaz, 5
Moszkowski, Moritz, 42–43, *43, 44*, 149n. 26
Mounin, Georges, 150n. 1
Mozart, Wolfgang Amadeus, 19, 20, 80, 83, 117
Musgrave, Michael, 98
Musical Meaning in Beethoven (Hatten),
22–23, 47
musical perception, 146n. 4
musical persona, 139
Music and Discourse (Nattiez), 22–23
musicology, 3, 25, 48–49
music theory, 25, 48–49, 146n. 3
"Music Theory, Phenomenology, and Modes
of Perception" (Lewin), 27
Musique funèbre (Lutosławski), 121, 123–
24, 134
Musorgsky, Modest Petrovich, 62
Mythes (Szymanowski), 31, 34
myths, 27, 30–31

Nabokov, Vladimir, 4
The Name of the Rose (Eco), 1, 4, 143n. 4
narrative: in ballet, 152n. 24; in Chopin's ballades, 162n. 29; extra-musical content, 112–
15; *mimesis* and *diegesis*, 161n. 20; plot and,
116–21; of suffering, 134
Nattiez, Jean-Jacques, 22–23, 52, 58–59, 114–
15, 150n. 3
network metaphor, 2
Newcomb, Anthony, 117
*New Music Review and Church Music Re-
view*, 70
Nietzsche, Friedrich, 79, 109, 146n. 7
nocturnes, 92–93
Noge no Yama, 70

Oedipus Rex (Sophocles), 161n. 20
Of Grammatology (Derrida), 110
open texts, 111
The Open Work (Eco), 159n. 9
The Order of Things (Foucault), 147n. 11
Orfeo (Gluck), 26
"Original Rag" (Joplin), *9*
overcoding, 59, 139
Owen, Harold, 60

Palestrina, Giovanni Periluigi, 20
Palisca, Claude, 22
paradigmatic roles, 99
Parks, Richard, 148n. 21
Parmer, Dillon, 98
Parsifal (Wagner), 60
Partita (Lutosławski), 122, 132
pastoral discourses, 68, 70–71

pathological semiotics, 52
Payzant, Geoffrey, 147n. 8
Peirce, Charles, 58, 151–52n. 12
Peircean semiotics, 51, 62
"The Penal Colony" (Kafka), 4
peripeteia, 140
Perspectives of New Music, 23
Petrushka (Stravinsky), 144n. 9
Petty, Wayne, 15–16, 16–17, 91
phenotext, 15, 145n. 18
Philosophical Investigations (Wittgenstein), 51, 158–59n. 7
Piaget, Jean, 29
Piano Concerto (Lutosławski), 121, 134
Piano Quartet in C Minor (Brahms), 82
Piano Sonata in A Major (Beethoven), 63–64
Piano Sonata in C Minor (Schubert), 56, *57*
plagal cadences, *104*
Plato, 49
Platonic forms, 13
Playing with Signs (Agawu), 22–23, 47
plot and emplotment, 116–17, 120, 135, 138, 140, 160–61n. 19, 161n. 23
poetic influence, 143n. 6
Poetics (Aristotle), 116
poetry, 96
poietic intertextuality, 12, 140
Poland, 114, 144n. 9, 162n. 29
The Political Unconscious (Jameson), 55
Polonaise-fantasie (Chopin), 92
Pomp and Circumstance (Elgar), 62
positivism, 47
postmodernism, 48–49
poststructuralism, 45–46
precursor, 140
Prelude in C Major (Shostakovich), *10*, 10–11
Preludes and Fugues (Shostakovich), *10*, 10–11
program music, 114
Prokofiev, Sergei, 122, 134
prosopopoeia, 1, 143n. 1
Proust, Marcel, 12

"Quanta, Relativity, and Rhetoric" (Holton), 145n. 21
"Qu'est-ce qu'un auteur?" (Foucault), 109

Rae, Charles Bodeman, 108, 123–24, 126, 132
ragtime music, 8
Rameau, Jean-Philippe, 15, 28
Ratner, Leonard, 47, 58, 80
Ravel, Maurice, 31
The Raw and the Cooked (Lévi-Strauss), 27–28
Rawsthorne, Alan, 124
Reichardt, Johann Friedrich, 62

Remaking the Past (Straus), 17, 25, 79
repetition compulsion, 79
Requiem (Mozart), 83
"Resignation" (Beethoven), 63
"Rethinking Contemporary Music Theory" (McCreless), 47–48
Revolution in Poetic Language (Kristeva), 145n. 18
Ricoeur, Paul, 108, 116–17, 120, 161n. 23
"The Ride of the Valkyries" (Wagner), 62
Riemann, Hugo, 24
Riffaterre, Michael: on Brahms, 99, 102; on communication schemes, 54; on semiotics and hermeneutics, 77; on strangeness, 61, 96; on ungrammaticalities, 21, 40–41, 97–98
Rinzler, Paul, 59, 60–61
Robert, Walter, 63
Romanze (Brahms), 19
Romeo and Juliet (Prokofiev), 122
"Rose Adagio" (Tchaikovsky), 69–70
Rosen, Charles, 95, 154n. 13, 155n. 18
Rothstein, Eric, 11, 12

St. Matthew's Passion (Bach), 5
"St. Veronica Wipes His Face" (Davies), 9, *10*
salvation chords, 63
Samson, Jim, 74, 117, 124, 144n. 11, 153n. 28
Samuels, Robert, 20, 52–53, 56, 62
Sarrasine (Balzac), 153n. 2
Saussure, Ferdinand de, 22, 28, 99
Schenker, Heinrich: on auxiliary cadence, 157n. 29; on Bach, 144n. 13; on Brahms's Intermezzo, 101; on canonical works, 145n. 22; on composition, 23; on metaphors, 27, 114; on plot, 116; Schenkerian analysis, 15, 37–38, 40, 46–47; Schenkerian graphs, 24; on uncanniness, 83
Schenker's Argument (Blasius), 47
"Schenker's Conception of Musical Structure" (Forte), 47
Schoenberg, Arnold: George *Lieder*, 27; monumentality and, 25; motivic forms, 24; "Song of the Wood Dove," 85–87, 102, 106; Straus on, 17; use of tonality, 79, 96
Schonberg, Harold, 149n. 26
Schopenhauer, Arthur, 98, 106, 111, 146n. 7
Schubert, Franz: "Die Krähe," 80; "Erlkönig," 57–58, 62, 91; *Fantasie*, 47; Piano Sonata in C Minor, 56, 88–89, *89, 90;* uncanniness and, 78
Schumann, Clara, 99, 156n. 25
Schumann, Robert: Brahms's Romanze and, 20; *Carnaval*, 117; on Chopin's "Funeral March" sonata, 95; *Fantasie*, 19, 102, 117,

157n. 30; plagal cadences, *104*; *Widmung*, 19; "Wilder Reiter," 57, 62

Schwandt, Erich, 57

scientific process, 58

Scruton, Roger, 55, 108, 114–15

Sechs Klavierstücke (Brahms), 99

Second Symphony (Mahler), 114–15

semiological tripartition, 140

semiotics: *abduction* and, 58; codes, 13, 21, 80; hermeneutics and, 77, 153n. 2; topics and, 56–61, 62–75; uncanniness and, 98

Semiotics of Poetry (Riffaterre), 77

The Sense of Music (Monelle), 47

sexuality, 119. *See also* gender issues in intertextuality

Shakespeare, William, 95

Shklovsky, Victor, 95

Shostakovich, Dmitry, *10*, 10–11

signs: arrival chords and, 72; codes and, 51, 52–54, 76; conventions, 55–56; of death, 85; Eco on, 75; iconic, 139; indexical, 139; networks, 63; signifiers, 95, 111, 135, 151n. 6; tarantellas and, 57; topics and, 56, 58–59, 61, 62; traffic light example, *53*, 150–51n. 6; *transcendental signified*, 110; uncanniness and, 77; *unheimliche*, 80; unpredictability, 74

Skryabin, Alexander, 31

Sleeping Beauty (Tchaikovsky), 68, *71*, 72–73, 76

Smith, Charles, 41, 149n. 25

Smith, Peter, 81

Society for Music Theory, 22, 59

Sonata (Griffes), *73*

Sonata in B Minor (Chopin), 93–94

Sonata in B Minor (Liszt), 63, *64*, 66

Sonata in C Minor (Schubert), 88–89, *89, 90*

Sonata in E Minor (Weber), 56

Sonata in F Major (Mozart), 117

"Song of the Wood Dove" (Schoenberg), 85–87, *86*, 102, 106

Songs without Words (Mendelssohn), 62

Sophocles, 161n. 20

Sousa, John Philip, 62

Spaeth, Sigmund, 70–71

speech-act theory, 161n. 22

speech types, 20

Spinnerlied, Op. 67, No. 3 (Mendelssohn), 43–45, *44*

strangeness, 21, 95–98

Straus, Joseph, 17–18, 25, 30, 79, 148n. 19

Stravinsky, Igor, 17, 31, 33, 70, 144n. 9

Street, Allan, 48, 146n. 5

"Structural Analysis in Linguistics and in Anthropology," 27

structure and structuralism, 22–50; Barthes on, 13–14; meaning and, 27–29; music theory and, 21, 47; relativity of, 30–31; structural analysis, 25, 40

The Structure of Atonal Music (Forte), 23, 26–27

Sturm und Drang, 20, 56, 85

Subotnik, Rose, 48, 149n. 22

Sullivan, Tim, 60

Swafford, Jan, 104–105, 156n. 25

symbols, 87

Symphonic Variations (Lutosławski), 144n. 9

syncretism, *32*, 140, 148n. 19

syntactic codes, 60

syntagmatic roles, 99

Système de la mode (Barthes), 22

S/Z (Barthes), 2, 116, 145n. 17, 153n. 2

Szymanowski, Karol, 31, 32–36, *33*, 148n. 16

Tarantella (Lutosławski), 122

tarantellas, 56, 57

Taruskin, Richard, 25

Tchaikovsky, Pyotr Ilyich: Beethoven's *Hammerklavier* and, 75–76; Fifth Symphony, 62; "Rose Adagio," 69–70; sexuality themes, 111; *Sleeping Beauty*, 68, 69, *71*, 72–73, 76

Tempest (Beethoven), 132

tessera, 37, 140

texts, 140

A Theory of Semiotics (Eco), 51

Third Symphony (Brahms), 62, 156n. 24

Third Symphony (Lutosławski), 126–28

Thorgrim (Cowen), 62

The Tin Drum (Grass), 1

tokens, 62, 64–65, 68, 140

topics, **51–76**, 140, 151n. 11

To the Lighthouse (Woolf), 51

Tovey, Donald Francis, 79

"Towards a New Poetics on Musical Influence" (Korsyn), 17

tragic six-four chords, 66, 68

transcendence, 70, 72, 75, 110

transcendental signified, 110, 140

transformation, 14

transpositional combination, 162n. 33

The Trial (Kafka), 4

"Tristan" chords, 104–106, 111, 157n. 32

Tristan und Isolde (Wagner), 104–106, *105*

Trochimczyk, Maja, 121–23

tropes, 13, 141

Tuchowski, Andrez, 124

types, 62, 75, 141

uncanniness, **77–107**

undercoding, 59, 141

MICHAEL KLEIN, Assistant Professor of Music Theory at Temple University, has published articles on the music of Lutosławski and Chopin. He received his Ph.D. in music theory from SUNY Buffalo in addition to degrees in piano from the Eastman School of Music.

www.ingramcontent.com/pod-product-compliance
Lightning Source LLC
Chambersburg PA
CBHW070445100426
42812CB00004B/1210